# Culture Wise
# FRANCE

## The Essential Guide to Culture, Customs & Business Etiquette

by

Joe Laredo

SURVIVAL BOOKS • LONDON • ENGLAND

First published 2007

Copyright © Survival Books 2007
Cover photo © Roger Moss
Maps and cartoons © Jim Watson
Other photographs – see page 270

Survival Books Limited
26 York Street, London W1U 6PZ, United Kingdom
☎ +44 (0)20-7788 7644, ▤ +44 (0)870-762 3212
✉ info@survivalbooks.net
💻 www.survivalbooks.net

British Library Cataloguing in Publication Data.
A CIP record for this book is available
from the British Library.
ISBN 10: 1-905303-07-6
ISBN 13: 978-1-905303-07-6

Printed and bound in India by Ajanta Offset

# ACKNOWLEDGEMENTS

I would like to thank the many people who provided insights into French customs and behaviour that were outside my experience, including Kathy and Xavier Bréham, Bruce Epstein, Denise Eudes, Annie and Roger Graf, Alain and Annie Kesler, Thierry and Vincent Noël, Chantal Sauvanet, and Chris and Giselle Toomey. I am grateful to Kevin Gale at France Magazine for his help in compiling the list of books in Appendix B, to Peter Read for editing, Lilac Johnston for proof-reading, Grania Rogers for photo selection and editing, Di Tolland for DTP, and Jim Watson for the book and cover design, maps and cartoons. Finally a special thank you to all the photographers – the unsung heroes – who provided the superb photos, without which this book would be dull indeed.

# THE AUTHOR

Joe Laredo was born to French-speaking parents in 1957 and specialised in French and German at school. After hitchhiking round France during the hot summer of 1976, he took a joint degree at Trinity College, Cambridge, and then spent 1981 and 1982 working as a holiday rep in the French Alps, on the Côte d'Azur and in Tunisia. After numerous French holidays he moved with his wife to Normandy in 2001, where they now live with their daughter and various animals.

Joe has translated several books from French, including Albert Camus' L'Etranger, and written two other books about France and two about Ireland. He is also responsible for regularly updating Survival Books' best-selling books, Buying a Home in France and Living and Working in France, as well as editing many other titles. Joe writes occasionally for magazines about France, squash and piano music.

'If you need to find out how France works, then this book is indispensable. Native French people probably have a less thorough understanding of how their country functions.'

Living France

'It's everything you always wanted to ask, but didn't for fear of the contemptuous put down. The best English-language guide. Its pages are stuffed with practical information on everyday subjects and are designed to compliment the traditional guidebook.'

Swiss News

'Rarely has a 'survival guide' contained such useful advice. This book dispels doubts for first-time travellers, yet is also useful for seasoned globetrotters. In a word, if you're planning to move to the US or go there for a long-term stay, then buy this book both for general reading and as a ready-reference.'

American Citizens Abroad

'Let's say it at once. David Hampshire's *Living and Working in France* is the best handbook ever produced for visitors and foreign residents in this country; indeed, my discussion with locals showed that it has much to teach even those born and bred in l'Hexagone. It is Hampshire's meticulous detail which lifts his work way beyond the range of other books with similar titles. Often you think of a supplementary question and search for the answer in vain. With Hampshire this is rarely the case. He writes with great clarity (and gives French equivalents of all key terms), a touch of humour and a ready eye for the odd (and often illuminating) fact. This book is absolutely indispensable.'

The Riviera Reporter

'A must for all future expats. I invested in several books but this is the only one you need. Every issue and concern is covered, every daft question you have but are frightened to ask is answered honestly without pulling any punches. Highly recommended.'

Reader

'In answer to the desert island question about the one how-to book on France, this book would be it.'

The Recorder

'The ultimate reference book. Every subject imaginable is exhaustively explained in simple terms. An excellent introduction to fully enjoy all that this fine country has to offer, and save time and money in the process.'

American Club of Zurich

# SAID ABOUT SURVIVAL BOOKS

'The amount of information covered is not short of incredible. I thought I knew enough about my birth country. This book has proved me wrong. Don't go to France without it. Big mistake if you do. Absolutely priceless!'

Reader

'When you buy a model plane for your child, a video recorder, or some new computer gizmo, you get with it a leaflet or booklet pleading 'Read Me First', or bearing large friendly letters or bold type saying 'IMPORTANT – follow the instructions carefully'. This book should be similarly supplied to all those entering France with anything more durable than a 5-day return ticket. It is worth reading even if you are just visiting briefly, or if you have lived here for years and feel totally knowledgeable and secure. But if you need to find out how France works then it is indispensable. Native French people probably have a less thorough understanding of how their country functions. Where it is most essential, the book is most up to the minute.

Living France

A comprehensive guide to all things French, written in a highly readable and amusing style, for anyone planning to live, work or retire in France.

The Times

Covers every conceivable question that might be asked concerning everyday life. I know of no other book that could take the place of this one.

France in Print

A concise, thorough account of the do's and don'ts for a foreigner in Switzerland. Crammed with useful information and lightened with humorous quips which make the facts more readable.

American Citizens Abroad

'I found this a wonderful book crammed with facts and figures, with a straightforward approach to the problems and pitfalls you are likely to encounter. The whole book is laced with humour and a thorough understanding of what's involved. Gets my vote!'

Reader

'A vital tool in the war against real estate sharks; don't even think of buying without reading this book first!'

Everything Spain

'We would like to congratulate you on this work: it is really super! We hand it out to our expatriates and they read it with great interest and pleasure.'

ICI (Switzerland) AG

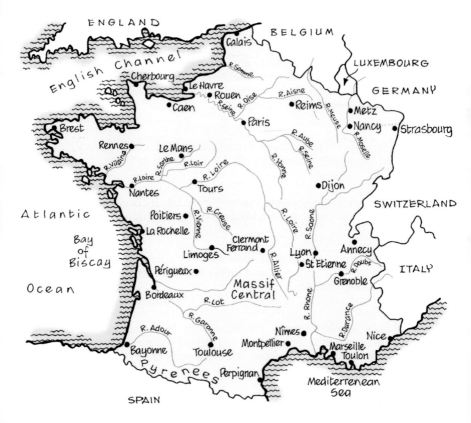

# CONTENTS

Notre Dame, Paris

# INTRODUCTION

If you're planning a trip to France or just want to learn more about the country, you'll find the information contained in Culture Wise France invaluable. Whether you're travelling on business or pleasure, visiting for a few days or planning to stay for a lifetime, Culture Wise guides enable you to quickly find your feet by removing the anxiety factor when dealing with a foreign culture.

*Culture Wise France* is essential reading for anyone planning to visit France, including tourists (particularly those planning to stay for a number of weeks or months), business people, migrants, retirees, holiday homeowners and transferees. It's designed to help newcomers avoid cultural and social gaffes; make friends and influence people; improve communications (both verbal and non-verbal); and enhance your understanding of France and the French people. It explains what to expect, how to behave in most situations, and how to get along with the locals and feel at home – rather than feeling like a fish out of water. It isn't, however, simply a monologue of dry facts and figures, but a practical and entertaining look at life in France – as it really is – and not necessarily as the tourist brochures would have you believe.

Adjusting to a different environment and culture in any foreign country can be a traumatic and stressful experience, and France is no exception. You need to adapt to new customs and traditions, and discover the French way of doing things; whether it's inviting the neighbours for *l'apéro*, understanding the local patois or doing *du business*. France is a country where many things are back to front: where not only do people drive on the right (which can be very disconcerting if you usually drive on the left), but books have their contents at the end, and computer keyboards have A and Z where you expect to find Q and W.

A period spent in France is a wonderful way to enrich your life, broaden your horizons, and hopefully expand your circle of friends. I trust this book will help you avoid the pitfalls of visiting or living in France, and smooth your way to a happy and rewarding stay.

*Bon courage !*

**Joe Laredo**
**July 2007**

Château de Chenonceau, Loire Valley

# 1.
# A CHANGE OF CULTURE

**W**ith almost daily advances in technology, ever-cheaper flights and knowledge about almost anywhere in the world at our fingertips, travelling, living, working and retiring abroad have never been more accessible, and current migration patterns suggest that it has never been more popular. But, although globalisation means the world has 'shrunk', every country is still a 'world' of its own with a unique culture.

Some people find it impossible to adapt to a new life in a different culture – for reasons which are many and varied. According to statistics, the most common cause of dissatisfaction is when non-working spouses find themselves without a role in the new country and sometimes with little to do other than think about what they would be doing if they were at home. Family concerns – which may include the children's education and worries about loved ones at home – can also deeply affect those living abroad.

> 'There are no foreign lands. It is the traveller only who is foreign.'
>
> Robert Louis Stevenson (Scottish writer)

Many factors contribute to how well you adapt to a new culture – for example your personality, education, foreign language skills, mental health, maturity, socio-economic situation, travel experience, and family and social support systems. How you handle the stress of change and bring balance and meaning to your life is the principal indicator of how well you'll adjust to a different country, culture and business environment.

## FRANCE IS DIFFERENT

Many people underestimate the cultural isolation that can be experienced in a foreign country, particularly one with a different language. Even in a country whose language you speak fluently you'll find that many aspects of the culture are surprisingly foreign – and France is no exception (despite the cosy familiarity engendered by cinema, television and books).

France is popularly perceived by the British as an easy expatriate option because it's only 'next door' and so cannot possibly be that different from the UK. The fact that tens of thousands of Britons have made France their home suggests that settling there must be a straightforward process. Americans often make similar assumptions – 'France is every man's second country,' declared Thomas Jefferson

process and one which can frustrate and exasperate foreigners.

Before you even encounter the local culture, however, you'll need to adapt to a totally new environment and new challenges, which may include a new job, a new home and a new physical environment, which can be overwhelming. Those who move to a new job in France may encounter a (very) steep learning curve. The chances are that you've left a job in your home country where you held a senior position, were extremely competent and knew all your colleagues. In France, you may be virtually a trainee (especially if your French isn't fluent) and not know any of your colleagues. The feeling that you're starting from scratch can be demoralising.

Even if you move to a part of France with a well-established expatriate community, such as Dordogne or certain Breton and Provencal villages, things that you're used to and took for granted in your home country may not be available, e.g. certain kinds of food, opportunities to engage in your favourite hobby or sport, and books and television programmes in your language. The lack of 'home comforts' can wear you down.

You'll also have to contend with the lack of a local support network. At home you had a circle of friends,

– and that was 200 years ago. They, and people from other countries, are often surprised and even shocked at how different France is from home – and from what they expected – and many survive only a few years before returning, disillusioned and disappointed.

Not only is France very different from any other country, but its values, beliefs, attitudes and customs – in short, its culture – are passed down through the generations by a process of osmosis, a process which is all but invisible to the foreigner.

Little is made obvious or explained; things are simply known, and the French are invariably astonished to discover that their knowledge is largely confined to their borders. 'You've never heard of so-and-so?' they will exclaim, citing some singer, actor or comedian whose name is familiar only to the French. Assimilating this obscure store of knowledge is a never-ending acquaintances, colleagues and possibly relatives you could rely on for help and support. In France, there's no such network, which can leave you feeling lost.

The degree of isolation you feel usually depends on how long you plan to spend in France and what you'll be doing there. If you're simply going on a short holiday you may not even be aware of many of the cultural differences, although if you are it will enhance your enjoyment and may save you a few embarrassing or confusing moments.

However, if you're planning a business trip or intend to spend an extended period in France – perhaps working, studying or even living there permanently – **it's essential to understand the culture, customs and etiquette at the earliest opportunity.**

## CULTURE SHOCK

Culture shock is the term used to describe the psychological and physical state felt by people when arriving in a foreign country, or even moving to a new environment in their home country (where the culture, and in some cases the language, may vary considerably by region or social class). Culture shock can be experienced when travelling, living, working or studying abroad, when in addition to adapting to new social rules and values, you may need to adjust to a different climate, food and dress. It manifests itself in a lack of direction and the feeling of not knowing what to do or how to do things, not knowing what's

appropriate or inappropriate. You literally feel like a fish out of water.

> 'When you travel, remember that a foreign country is not designed to make you comfortable. It is designed to make its own people comfortable.'
>
> Clifton Fadiman (American writer)

Culture shock is precipitated by the anxiety that results from losing all familiar rules of behaviour and cues to social intercourse – the thousand and one clues to behaviour in everyday situations: when to shake hands and what to say when we meet people; how to buy goods and services; when and how much to tip; how to use a cash machine or the telephone; when to accept or refuse invitations; and when to take statements seriously and when not to. These cues, which may be words, gestures or facial expressions, are acquired in the course of our life,

and are as much a part of our culture and customs as the language we speak and our beliefs. Our peace of mind and social efficiency depends on these cues, most of which are unconsciously recognised.

The symptoms of culture shock are essentially psychological, and are caused by the sense of alienation you feel when you're bombarded on a daily basis by cultural differences in an environment where there are few, if any, familiar references. However, there can also be physical symptoms, including an increased incidence of minor illnesses (e.g. colds and headaches) and more serious psychosomatic illnesses brought on by depression. You shouldn't underestimate the consequences of culture shock, although the effects can be lessened if you accept the condition rather than deny it.

## Stages of Culture Shock

Severe culture shock – often experienced when moving to a country with a different language – usually follows a number of stages.

The names of these may vary, as may the symptoms and effects, but a typical progression is as follows:

1. The first stage is commonly known as the 'honeymoon' stage and usually lasts from a few days to a few weeks after arrival (although it can last longer, particularly if you're insulated from the usual pressures of life). This stage is essentially a positive (even euphoric) one, when a newcomer finds everything an exciting and interesting novelty. The feeling is similar to being on holiday or a short trip abroad, when you generally experience only the positive effects of culture shock (although this depends very much on where you're from and the country you're visiting – see box).

---

### Paris Syndrome

Every year, a dozen or so Japanese tourists have to be repatriated from the French capital after falling prey to what has become known as 'Paris Syndrome'. This is what some polite Japanese tourists suffer when they discover that Parisians can be rude or that the city doesn't meet their expectations. The experience can be so stressful that they suffer a nervous breakdown and need to be hospitalised or repatriated under medical supervision.

**2.** The second (rejection or distress) stage is usually completely opposite to the first and is essentially negative and a period of crisis, as the initial excitement and holiday feeling wears off and you start to cope with the real conditions of daily life – except of course that life is nothing like anything you've previously experienced. This can happen after just a few weeks and is characterised by a general feeling of disorientation, confusion and loneliness. Physical exhaustion brought on by a change of time zone, extremes of hot or cold, and the strain of having hundreds of settling-in tasks to accomplish is an important symptom of this stage.

You may also experience regression, where you spend much of your time speaking your own language, watching foreign (non-French) television and reading foreign newspapers, eating food from home and socialising with expatriates who speak your language. You may also spend a lot of time complaining about the host country and its culture. Your home environment suddenly assumes a tremendous importance and is irrationally glorified. All difficulties and problems are forgotten and only the good things back home are remembered.

**3.** The third stage is often known as the 'flight' stage (because of the overwhelming desire to escape), and is usually the one that lasts the longest and is the most difficult to cope with. During this period you may feel depressed and angry, as well as resentful towards the new country and its people. You may experience difficulties such as not being understood, and feelings of discontent, impatience, frustration, sadness and incompetence. These feelings are inevitable when you're trying to adapt to a new culture that's very different from that of your home country, and they're exacerbated by the fact that you can see nothing positive or good about the new country and focus exclusively on the negative aspects, refusing to acknowledge any positive points. You may become hostile and develop an aggressive attitude towards the country. Other people will sense this and in many cases either respond in a confrontational manner or try to avoid you. There may be problems with the language, your house, job or children's school, transportation

... even simple tasks like shopping may be fraught with problems, and the fact that the local people are largely indifferent to all these problems only makes matter worse. They try to help but they just don't understand your concerns, and you conclude that they must be insensitive and unsympathetic to you and your problems.The transition between your old culture and customs, and those of your new country, is a difficult one and takes time to complete. During this process there can be strong feelings of dissatisfaction. The period of readjustment can last six months, although there are expatriates who adjust earlier and (although rare) those who never get over the 'flight' stage and are forced to return home.

> 'No matter how long I live among them, I don't think I will ever really understand these people.'
>
> George East (British writer)

4.  The fourth (recovery or autonomy) stage is where you begin to integrate and adjust to the new culture and accept the customs of the country as simply another way of living. **The environment doesn't change – what changes is your attitude towards it.** You become more competent with the language, and you also feel more comfortable with the customs of the host country and can move around without feeling anxiety. However, you still have problems with some

of the social cues and you don't understand everything people say (particularly colloquialisms and idioms). Nevertheless, you have largely adjusted to the new culture and start to feel more at home and familiar with the country and your place in it, and begin to realise that it has its good as well as bad points.

5.  The fifth stage is termed 'reverse culture shock' and occurs when you return to your home country. You may find that many things have changed (you will also have changed) and that you feel like a foreigner in your own country. If you've been away for a long time and have become comfortable with the habits and customs of a new lifestyle, you may find that you no longer feel at ease in your homeland.

    Reverse culture shock can be difficult to deal with and some

people find it impossible to re-adapt to their home country after living abroad for a number of years.

The above stages occur at different times depending on the individual and his circumstances, and everyone has his own way of reacting to them; the result is that some stages last longer and are more difficult to cope with than others, while other stages are shorter and easier to overcome.

> 'The whole object of travel is not to set foot on foreign land; it is at last to set foot on one's own country as a foreign land.'
>
> G. K. Chesterton (English writer)

Villefranche, C ôte d'Azur

## Reducing the Effects

Experts agree that almost everyone suffers from culture shock and there's no escaping the phenomenon; however, its negative effects can be reduced considerably and there are some things you can do even before leaving home:

- **Positive attitude** – The key to reducing the negative effects of culture shock is a positive attitude towards France (whether you're visiting or planning to live there) – if you don't look forward to a holiday or relocation, you should question why you're doing it. There's no greater guarantee for unhappiness in a foreign environment than taking your prejudices with you. It's important when trying to adapt to a new culture to be sensitive to the locals' feelings and try to put yourself in their shoes wherever possible, which will help you understand why they react as they do. Bear in mind that they have a strong, in-bred cultural code, just as you do, and react in certain ways because they're culturally 'trained' to do so. If you find yourself frustrated by an aspect of the local culture or behaviour, the chances are that they will be equally puzzled by yours.

- **Research** – Discover as much as possible about France before you go, so that your arrival and settling-in period doesn't spring as many surprises as it might otherwise do. Reading up on France and its culture before you leave home will help you familiarise yourself with the local customs and language, and make the country and its people seem less strange on arrival. You'll be aware of many of the differences in France and be better prepared to deal with them. This will help you avoid being upset by real or imaginary cultural slights, and also reduce the chance of your offending the locals by cultural misunderstandings.

Being prepared for a certain amount of disorientation and confusion (or worse) makes it easier to cope with it. There are literally hundreds of publications about France as well as dozens of websites for expatriates (see **Appendices B** and **C**). Many sites provide access to expatriates already living in France who can answer questions and provide useful advice. There are also 'notice boards' on many websites where you can post messages or questions.

> **'Travellers never think that THEY are the foreigners.'**
>
> Mason Cooley (American aphorist)

● **Visit France first** – If you're planning to live or work in France for a number of years or even permanently, it's important to visit the country to see whether you think you would enjoy living there and be able to cope with the culture before making the leap. Before you go, try to find someone who has visited France and talk to him about it. Some

Knot garden

companies organise briefings for families before departure. Rent a property before buying a home and don't burn your bridges until you're certain that you've made the right decision.

● **Learn French** – Along with adopting a positive attitude, overcoming the language barrier will probably be the most decisive factor in combating culture shock and enjoying your time in France. The ability to speak French isn't just a practical and useful tool (that will allow you to buy what you need, find your way around, etc.) but the key to understanding France and its culture. If you can speak the language, even at a basic level, your scope for making friends is immediately widened beyond the limited expatriate circle.

Obviously not everyone is a linguist, and learning a language can take time and requires motivation. However, with sufficient perseverance virtually anyone can learn enough of another language to participate in the local culture. Certainly the effort will pay off and expatriates who manage to overcome the language barrier find their experience in France much richer and more rewarding than those who don't. If you make an effort at communicating with the local people in their own language, you'll also find them far more receptive to you and your needs.

- **Be proactive** – Make an effort to get involved in your new culture and go out of your way to make friends. Join in the activities of the local people, which could be a carnival, a religious festival or a sporting activity. There are often plenty of local clubs where you can engage in sport or keep fit, draw and paint, learn to cook local dishes, taste wine, etc.

  Not only will this fill some of your spare time, giving you less time to miss home, but you'll also meet people and make new friends. If you feel you cannot join a local club, perhaps because the language barrier is too great, then you can always participate in activities for expatriates, of which there are many in the most popular destinations. Look upon a period spent abroad as an opportunity to redefine your life objectives and acquire new perspectives. Culture shock can help you develop a better understanding of yourself and stimulate your creativity.

- **Talk to other expatriates** – Although they may deny it, many other expatriates have been through exactly what you're experiencing and faced the same feelings of disorientation. Even if they cannot provide you with advice, it helps to know that you aren't alone and that it gets better over time. However, don't make the mistake of mixing only with expatriates, as this will alienate you from the local culture and make it much harder to integrate.

Pont de Normandie

Don't rely on social contact with your compatriots to carry you through, because it won't.

● **Keep in touch with home** – Keeping in touch with your family and friends at home and around the world by telephone, email and letters will help reduce and overcome the effects of culture shock.

Culture shock is an unavoidable part of travelling, living and working abroad, but if you're aware of it and take steps to lessen its effects before you go and while you're abroad, the period of adjustment will be shortened and its negative and depressing consequences reduced.

● **Be happy** – Don't rely on others to make you happy; otherwise you won't find true and lasting happiness. There are things in life which you can change – and if you need them to change you must do it yourself. Every day we encounter circumstances over which we have little or no control, and to moan about them only makes us unhappier. So be your own best friend and nurture your own capacity for happiness.

## FAMILIES IN FRANCE

Family life may be completely different in France and relationships can become strained under the stress of adapting to culture shock.

Your family may find itself in a completely new and possibly alien environment, your new home may

'And that's the wonderful thing about family travel: it provides you with experiences that will remain locked forever in the scar tissue of your mind.'

Dave Barry (American writer & humorist)

scarcely resemble your previous one (it may be much more luxurious or significantly smaller) and the climate may be dramatically different from that of your home country.

If possible, you should prepare yourself for as many aspects of the new situation as you can, and explain to your children the differences they're likely to encounter, while at the same time dispelling their fears.

In a situation where one spouse is working (usually the husband) and the other not, it's usually the latter (and any children) who's more affected by culture shock. The husband has his work to occupy him, and his activities may not differ much from what he'd been accustomed to at home. On the other hand, the wife has to operate in a totally new environment, which differs considerably from what she's used to. She will find herself alone more often, as there will be no close relatives or friends on hand.

However, if you're aware that this situation may arise, you can take action to reduce its effects. Working spouses should pay special attention to the needs and feelings of their non-working partners and children, as the success of a family relocation depends on the ability of the wife and children to adapt to the new culture.

Good communication between family members is vital, and you should make time to discuss your experiences and feelings, both as a couple and as a family. Questions should always be raised, and, if possible answered, particularly when asked by children. However difficult your situation may appear in the beginning, it will help to bear in mind that it's by no means unique, and that most expatriate families experience exactly the same problems, and manage to triumph over them and thoroughly enjoy their stay abroad.

## A NEW LIFE

Although you may find some of the information in this chapter a bit daunting, don't be discouraged by the foregoing catalogue of depression and despair; the negative aspects of travelling and living abroad have been highlighted only in order to help you prepare and adjust to a new life. The vast majority of people who travel and live abroad naturally experience occasional feelings of discomfort

and disorientation, **but most never suffer the most debilitating effects of culture shock.**

As with settling in and making friends anywhere, even in your home country, the most important thing is to be considerate, kind, open, humble and genuine – qualities that are valued the world over. Selfishness, brashness and arrogance will get you nowhere – in France or in any other country. Treat France and its people with respect and they will reciprocate.

The majority of people living in France would agree that, all things considered, they love living there – and are in no hurry to return home. A period spent in France is a wonderful way to enrich your life, broaden your horizons, make new friends, and just maybe, even please your bank manager.

'Twenty years from now you will be more disappointed by the things you didn't do than by the ones you did do. So throw off the bowlines. Sail away from the safe harbour. Catch the trade winds in your sails. Explore. Dream. Discover.'

Mark Twain (American author)

Provence

# 2.

# WHO ARE THE FRENCH?

**F**or years, Western Europe's largest country has tempted foreigners to its shores, and nowadays France is more popular than ever: with some 75m visitors annually, it's the world's favourite tourist destination. It's also a popular retirement and relocation destination, not only for those from less-developed countries looking for better opportunities in the buoyant job market, but also for thousands of European Union (EU) citizens attracted by the unique combination of sparsely populated countryside, superb food and wine, and relaxed lifestyle.

But France isn't just a pretty country where you can eat out cheaply: it's an extremely diverse country populated by an even more diverse people, whose character and culture are deeply embedded in everyday life. The regional variety found in France is extensive and few countries can rival it for contrast – geographically, climatically or culturally.

To help you become more familiar with France and the French, this chapter provides information about France's history, its people and the country's icons.

> 'When God created France he found it so perfect that, to comfort those who couldn't live there, he created the French.'
>
> Daily Mail, 4th July 2000

## TIMELINE

Like many other European countries, France has a rich and chequered history. The main events that have shaped modern France are as follows:

### Early Settlers

**40,000-10,000 years ago** – The first known human inhabitants are cave dwellers (see box).

**4500-2000BC** – Neolithic man erects megaliths in Brittany that stand today.

**1000BC** – Settlement by the Gauls (related to the Celts), as well as by Iberians and Basques from what is now Spain, and Ligurians, who brought grape vines from Italy; the first Iron Age civilisation.

**800BC** – The Greeks put in an appearance on the Mediterranean coast; place names such as Antibes and Nice derive from Greek.

**59-52BC** – Conquest of Gaul by Julius Caesar and the beginning of Gallo-Roman civilisation; the Romans call the 'province' Gallia Narbonensis, build spectacular monuments, including the amphitheatre in Nîmes and the nearby Pont du Gard, and introduce

The French claim that Cro-Magnon man, one of the earliest known examples of Homo sapiens, is named after the owner of the land under which his remains were discovered in 1868 (in a cave in Les-Eyzies, Dordogne). The cave also contains some of the world's finest prehistoric paintings.

their language, Latin, which was to become French.

**300-600AD** – The Roman legacy is largely destroyed by invasions of 'barbarians' (so called because they were often bearded – *barbu* in French), including the Alemanni, Burgundians, Huns, Visigoths and the Germanic tribe called Franks, who established some political stability. Clovis, King of the Franks, converts to Christianity and marries the Burgundian princess Clotilda, basing his government in Paris and calling his land Francia.

## From States to Nation

**750** – The start of the Carolingian dynasty, one of whose leaders, Charlemagne, establishes a 'Holy Roman Empire', including France, in 768AD; his death signals the start of a break-up of the territory into independent 'states' such as Aquitaine, Burgundy, Provence and Toulouse.

**900** – Invading Vikings are bought off with an area of northern France roughly equivalent to modern Normandy (the Vikings were originally known as 'north men' – *normands*).

**987** – Hugues Capet founds the Capetian dynasty, which will last until 1328, but his kingdom covers only the area now called Ile-de-France, including Paris.

**1066** – The Duke of Normandy, *Guillaume* (William), conquers England.

### Demographics

Population: 63m
Population density: 100 inhabitants per km$^2$ (260 per square mile). Paris is Europe's most crowded capital, with 20,000 inhabitants per km$^2$ (over 50,000 per square mile)
Largest cities: Paris (11m including suburbs), Lyon (1.6m), Marseille (1.4m), Lille (1.1m)
Foreign population: 4.3m
Largest expatriate groups: Algerians (575,000), Portuguese (570,000), Moroccans (525,000)
State religion: France is officially a secular state
Most followed religion: Catholicism

The Middle Ages, from the 11th to 13th centuries, witness the appearance of France's great gothic cathedrals, including Notre-Dame de Paris, the city becoming the largest in Europe.

**1095** – French knights participate enthusiastically in the Crusades, whose aim is to wrest Palestine from Muslim rule.

**1214** – The English are driven out of most of France after their defeat at Bouvines by Philippe Auguste, who becomes the first true King of France, though his power is still confined largely to the northern half of the country; the southern half – known as Occitan, like its language (see box) – remains fragmented.

**1337-1453** – The so-called Hundred Years' War between France and England continues, on and off, for 116 years, during which the Black Death kills around a third of the population; the war is effectively ended by Joan of Arc, whose leadership inspires the French to overcome the English and eject them definitively from the whole of France – except Calais.

**14th-16th centuries** – Even after the Hundred Years' War, France is still far from united; the Duchy of Burgundy is integrated in 1477, Brittany in 1491 and it isn't until the early 17th century that France becomes a unified country.

## Renaissance & Revolutions

**1643** – Louis XIV (the 'Sun King') comes to the throne at the age of five and inaugurates a period of intellectual flowering, culminating

Louis XIV

in the Age of Enlightenment, which produced great thinkers and artists such as Descartes and Pascal, Corneille, Molière and Racine, Couperin, Lully and Rameau – a period, however, in which international trade, technological development and administrative systems stagnate and the peasants are neglected – with increasing resentment.

The population of France in 1700 was some 17m – three times that of England and Wales.

**1789** – 150 years of famine and misery are brought to a sudden and violent end amid chants of '*Liberté, égalité, fraternité*' – the French Revolution is sparked by the storming of the Bastille, a prison at the time containing only seven inmates, on 14th July; but idealism

soon gives way to anarchy as rival factions compete for power, and tens of thousands are guillotined.

**1799** – A young Corsican artillery officer, born Napoleone di Buonaparte, leads a coup d'état on 9th November, and crowns himself Emperor of France five years later.

**1815** – After Napoleon's defeat at Waterloo, and exile to Saint Helena, the monarchy is restored in the shape of Louis XVIII, but is little more successful than the pre-Revolutionary system.

> 'Eighteenth-century scientists, the French in particular, seldom did things simply if an absurdly demanding alternative was available'
>
> Bill Bryson, *A Short History of Nearly*

**1848** – Further revolutions, in 1830 and 1848, lead to the establishment of the Second Republic under Napoleon's nephew, Louis-Napoleon, who emulates his uncle in proclaiming himself Emperor Napoleon III in 1852; he nevertheless presides over France's belated industrialisation and economic resurgence.

**1870** – Napoleon III's disastrous war against Prussia leads to famine in the capital and the loss of Alsace and Lorraine; Napoleon's capture signals the end of the French monarchy.

**1871** – After yet another uprising and a failed experiment in radical socialism, known as the Paris Commune, the Third Republic is established, initially under Adolphe Thiers; this lasts until 1940.

## 20th Century

**1904** – The French and British finally settle their differences by signing the *Entente cordiale*.

**1905** – Church and state are officially separated; France begins to indulge in colonialism (see box).

**1914-18** – 1.3m Frenchmen are killed (and twice as many wounded) in futile trench warfare in north-east France, at the end of which Alsace and Lorraine are returned by the defeated Germans.

**1918-39** – A period of political and economic crisis, leading to the rise of the Popular Front, a left-wing alliance that introduces such social advances as paid holidays.

**1939-45** – 700,000 French people are killed in World War II, although

> 'There is a really anti-American sentiment over here. Perhaps the French resent the fact that this 200-year-old child of a country liberated them.'
>
> Ann Koepke (American expatriate)

most of France is occupied by the Germans from 24th June 1940 until 8th May 1945 (the latter date now a public holiday); the country is split between collaborators and resisters, though everyone subsequently claims to have taken part in the resistance.

**1944-46** – Leader of the 'Free French', De Gaulle is provisional President before giving way to the Socialist Félix Gouin.

**1946-58** – The Fourth Republic is marked by post-war reconstruction and a baby boom amid renewed political instability.

**1951** – France joins West Germany and other European nations in the European Coal and Steel Community (ECSC), leading to the formation in 1957 of the European Economic Community (EEC).

**1958** – De Gaulle returns to power and founds the Fifth Republic.

**May 1968** – A student revolt against government policies and lack of social reform escalates into a national strike; those who took part in the revolt are referred to as *soixante-huitards*.

**1969** – De Gaulle leaves office (he died a year later) and is succeeded as President by Georges Pompidou.

**1974** – Pompidou dies, succeeded by Valéry Giscard d'Estaing, who must weather the oil crisis and recession.

**1981** – Socialist François Mitterrand is elected President, and embarks on a programme of decentralisation and nationalisation.

**1992** – The French ratify the Maastricht Treaty on European Union by referendum.

**1995** – Former Prime Minister and neo-Gaullist Jacques Chirac is elected President, ending 14 years of Socialist leadership; France attracts international condemnation by conducting a series of nuclear tests in the Pacific.

> 'The French may no longer own much of the world, but French law, language and culture persist in every continent.'
>
> Nick Yapp & Michel Syrett, *Xenophobes Guide to the French*

American war grave, Normandy

## 21st Century

**2000** – Chirac is embroiled in a corruption scandal, which is to haunt him throughout his presidency.

**2001** – Compulsory military service is abolished.

**2002** – The euro replaces the franc, first minted in 1360; government privatisation plans prompt widespread public sector strikes which bring the country to a standstill.

**2003** – Over 11,000 people, mostly elderly, are estimated to have died as a result of an August heat-wave during which temperatures in Paris topped 40C (104F).

**2005** – A referendum rejects the proposed EU constitution and prompts a political shake-up, including the resignation of Prime Minister Jean-Pierre Raffarin; urban violence erupts in October after two youths of North African origin

are electrocuted in an electricity substation, allegedly after being pursued by police.

**2007** – Presidential elections bring to the fore France's first female candidate, unmarried socialist mother-of-four Ségolène Royal. She loses the May election to Nicolas Sarkozy.

## THE PEOPLE

France's widespread territory and varied geography, coupled with a history of invasion, emigration and immigration, have resulted in great diversity among its population; it's therefore impossible to list the characteristics of a 'typical French person'.

Apart from the differences in character between the inhabitants of different regions, such as those of Nord-Pas-de-Calais (reputed to be France's friendliest people), Normans (reputed to be the opposite) and Parisians (who make Normans seem gushing) – not to mention those of France's various overseas territories – there are the influences of a potpourri of foreigners from all

> '... it would be difficult to point to a "typical" Frenchman. If you first meet the French in the North of France, you may easily jump to the conclusion that all Frenchmen are surprisingly silent and dour. If you are in the South of France, you are more likely to think of all Frenchmen as very lively and talkative.'
>
> Instructions for British Servicemen in France 1944

over the globe to take into account. Even in appearance, the French vary enormously – from blonde northerners to swarthy southerners, from diminutive *dames* to monstrous *messieurs*.

But in spite of their many differences, most French people share some characteristics, including the following:

## Traditionalism

The French have a deep sense of being part of history, part of the fabric and progression of their country. One in three of them live in houses built before 1914 – in rural (and some urban) areas, not only are many homes centuries old, but they've been in the same family since they were built, passed down from generation to generation.

A striking manifestation of French traditionalism is the make-up of its thousands of small villages, where it's common for several members of the same family to live within a few hundred metres of each other, just as they have done for centuries.

The French therefore take great pride (see below) in doing things the traditional way, the way they've always been done – whether it's a question of cooking, making wine and spirits, shopping or doing business. This gives them a reassuring sense of permanence in a fast-changing world, and it's one of France's big attractions to foreigners, who often feel that life is as it was in their own country half a century ago. Change isn't something the French welcome – and certainly not change for change's sake. Their way of life has 'worked' for centuries, so why change it?

French traditionalism also manifests itself in their attachment to the land. To the French, the word *pays* doesn't mean 'country' but 'land' (France is their *patrie*, not *pays*). Look on a French map and you will see mysterious names that bear no relation to administrative *régions* or *départements*: these are France's *pays* – traditionally recognised lands that have 'always' existed. If you ask a French person

> 'I like the way people honour the traditional métiers, crafts and culinary traditions so that they aren't lost for ever.'
>
> Larry Davis (American businessman)

where he or she comes from, you will often be given the name of a *pays*. All French people are *paysans*, which doesn't translate as 'peasants', with its pejorative overtones, but as 'land people' – even if they live in the middle of a city. And city dwellers often have second homes in their *pays* (or at least in the country) to which they retreat at weekends and for holidays – in order to re-establish contact with the land.

Foreigners can also find French traditionalism intensely frustrating, as new ideas or different ways of doing things are regarded with suspicion if not hostility. '*C'est comme ça*' ('That's the way it is' – with the implication 'That's the way it always has been') is a common response to questions as to why something is done the way it is. But this attitude isn't mere obstinacy or laziness. It takes courage to assert one's values in the face of

opposition, and the French should be admired and respected for their refusal to bow to pressure to change a way of life that's the envy of many.

If you want to adopt the French way, you must accept their traditionalism and remember that being 'behind the times' has advantages as well as disadvantages.

## Pride

Closely linked to their traditionalism is the French sense of pride. The French are inordinately proud of their country, their language and their culture – especially French food and drink (particularly red wine). For this reason, they generally travel little, except to other French-speaking countries; fewer than 20 per cent holiday abroad, many of those in Club Méditerranée resorts, where most holidaymakers are French; a surprising number have never crossed the Channel to England – even those who live close to the Channel ports. This reinforces their belief that everything French is the best in the world, and to attempt to persuade them otherwise is one of the greatest challenges a foreigner can face – to tell them they're mistaken is one of the biggest *faux pas*.

Of course, the French have much to be proud of, and they rightly defend traditional practices, values and beliefs against outside influences. The French farmer José Bové has become a national hero (he regulars appears on prime time television) for his 'anti-globalisation' protests, which have included the dismantling of a McDonald's restaurant. But their primary concern is not with what is best for the world, but what is best for France.

It doesn't pay to underestimate French pride. The French take criticism badly and will rarely if ever apologise, even when clearly in the wrong. Their pride can also be somewhat hypocritical – especially when it comes to the French language. While most French people believe French to be the subtlest and most expressive language in the world (which, when used properly, it can be), they won't hesitate to pepper their speech, and even writing, with all the latest borrowings from English, which show them to be '*cool*'. Perhaps, to paraphrase Voltaire, the French want the best of all possible worlds.

## Intellectualism

French people are generally happier expressing ideas rather than emotions and can seem cold as a result. To the French, the mind rules the heart and not the other way round. Knowledge is everything. '*Je pense, donc je suis*' (I think, therefore I am), as the French philosopher Descartes famously wrote – or, as one wit put it, '*Je pense, donc je sais*' (I think, therefore I know). French population surveys don't mention people's ethnic origin but include a detailed analysis of the educational qualifications of people in each region.

The training of the mind begins at an early age – as soon as children can speak – and never stops.

Pompidou Centre, Paris

Education is largely a matter of learning (often by rote) rather than 'discovering'. At school, marks are deducted from a maximum of 20 for each mistake, rather than awarded up to a maximum for creativity or ingenuity; it's a survival-of-the-fittest approach where little provision is made for 'under-achievers' (other than ignominiously obliging them to repeat a year, and spend the rest of their schooldays with children a year or more younger than them).

Nevertheless, despite their rigorous education system, most French people have poor spelling (millions of them cannot even spell the word 'very' – which is 'très') and worse grammar.

It's common in France to meet people of 30 who have yet to finish their education, as one diploma leads to another. Even once they've obtained jobs, the French continue to train and amass qualifications; in fact, it's virtually impossible to obtain a job or change jobs without **precisely** the required qualification.

Experience counts for little or nothing. (Which is why the French are increasingly going abroad to work, particularly to England.)

A person's intellect is betrayed by the way he speaks and writes. Anyone who uses the wrong word – or a general word instead of a specific one – will invariably be corrected by someone else, in front of others. This includes children, wives/husbands, senior citizens and foreigners – so woe betide you if you describe a *brioche* as a *pain*.

> At Christmas, an Englishman commented to a French boy how beautiful his tree was: 'Quel bel arbre !'– to which the four-year-old replied: *'Ce n'est pas un arbre, c'est un sapin.'*

In order to prove their intellectual credentials, French politicians write books while in office and not afterwards.

The French will discriminate endlessly, finding infinitesimal differences between things that, to anyone else, are identical. This can (and often does) lead to snobbery, as everyone thinks he knows better than the next person where to shop, where to go on holiday, where to eat, etc. It can also lead to insensitivity, as a French person will often say what he thinks without pausing to consider the effect of this on others, and will gleefully discuss unpleasant or upsetting subjects on the most inappropriate occasions.

Nevertheless – and despite their reputation as a passionate people – the French value 'correctness' in behaviour and frown on impulsiveness or hot-headedness. Their sense of what is *correct* goes beyond manners and governs all aspects of relationships.

Their obsession with knowledge and exactitude also means that they are chronically insecure: not knowing something sends them into a silent panic and instigates a frantic 'cover-up' operation – because, of course, they know everything (see **Arrogance** below). When it comes to speaking foreign languages in particular (at which the French don't excel – largely owing to appallingly anachronistic teaching methods), French people will clam up rather than attempt to communicate in less than faultless English (or whatever language). Not that this makes them any more tolerant of foreigners' failure to use perfect French, *bien évidemment.*

The French reputation for intellectual rigour and logic is, however, largely undeserved – they can be as illogical as any other people, and indeed regard irrationality as an essential freedom, just like the flouting of rules and regulations. As France's most famous thinker, Blaise Pascal, wrote in his *Pensées* (Thoughts): '*Il n'y a rien de si conforme à la raison que ce désaveu de la raison*' (Nothing is more logical than the rejection of logic).

> When asked why she had never been to England, a French factory worker replied: 'Because France is marvellous.'

## Arrogance

Their 'superiority complex' (see above) can make the French appear arrogant. In fact, in the strict sense of the word, they **are** arrogant – but to the French this isn't an undesirable characteristic. It's an inevitable consequence of their obsession with knowledge (see above).

Everyone knows everything about everything – and even if he doesn't, he won't admit it. Not only that, but French people always know better than you. If you tell them something, don't expect them to reply: 'That's interesting.' They're far more likely to contradict or qualify what you've said with some arcane piece of knowledge of their own – which may or may not be reliable (see **Individualism** below).

French arrogance is nowhere more evident – or infuriating – than in their refusal to have anything translated into English by a native speaker; even major companies that export worldwide produce brochures and websites in incomprehensible 'Franglais', believing it to be perfect English.

The French have an opinion on everything and like nothing better than to be asked it. Even if you don't ask, they will often give their opinion and tell you what to do – even in your home; they cannot help themselves. Whether it's how to renovate your house, how to grow your vegetables or how to bring up your children, they know better and must give you instructions. It's inevitable, so there's no point in objecting or being offended – you might as well tell the grass not to grow or the wind not to blow. Accept it as part of life in France. Their

eagerness to impart knowledge is usually well meant and not merely a way of showing off. In fact, the French rarely brag – to do so is considered distasteful. They're particularly keen to 'educate' foreigners in the finer points of French life (and food) – and you would do well to take this instruction in good part.

> When it was discovered that the winning wine in a 19th century French competition was made in Australia, the 'offending' substance was promptly disqualified.

## Rudeness

The French reputation for rudeness is, by any standards other than those of the French, generally well deserved. To the French themselves, however, only Parisians are rude; all others are merely honest. Why should one automatically smile and

be 'friendly' to strangers? First find out what they want and whether they're worth being friendly to.

It isn't unusual to phone a business – whether a small shop or a large company – and hear simply: '*Allô*', '*Oui?*' or even '*Je vous écoute*' ('I'm listening'). And it's usually pointless to leave a message with anyone, whether in a business or a personal context, as you'll rarely be called back – if the message is listened to at all. You must ring again ... and again ...

> 'To the French, indiscriminate smiling at people they don't know is ... a display of the worst sort of hypocrisy. You smile at someone who has amused you, or pleased you, or made you happy; if they haven't, you don't. It's as simple as that.'
>
> Donald Carroll, *Surprised by France*

The French generally have few qualms about speaking their mind, and it isn't unusual to have a 'frank exchange of views' with someone and yet remain on friendly terms. As a foreigner, it's sometimes difficult to accept such frankness without being upset or offended, but in the long run it makes for more secure and genuine friendships than the tendency among some people (notably the British) to always be 'diplomatic' – i.e. beat about the bush and lace their speech with euphemisms, so that their true thoughts and feelings are disguised.

French 'rudeness' is also something of a rhetorical game. To

Arc de Triomphe, Paris

demonstrate their individuality (see below) French shop assistants and other 'service providers' will automatically refuse an initial request. This shouldn't be taken to mean that the request won't ultimately be satisfied, and you shouldn't take '*Non*' for an answer but explain the reasons behind your request, taking the opportunity to flatter the person dealing with you (e.g. 'I came to you because I know you do a good job'). This may elicit a 'let me see', or at least a sucking of air through teeth, which indicates that you're making progress ... and eventually, if you're polite and patient, you should get more or less – if not exactly – what you originally asked for (see box).

## Impatience

The French are also renowned for their impatience, but, as with most other aspects of their character, there are two sides to the story. On the one hand, they have no patience with anyone – French or foreign – who ums and ahs, especially on

the telephone. Pause in what you're saying for more than a second and you're likely to be interrupted by a peremptory '*Oui*' or '*Allô*' or even told in no uncertain terms that 'I haven't got all day' (especially by Parisians), if not simply cut off.

Similarly, in conversation – even with friends – few French people will wait while you find your words; if you're lucky they will find them for you or, more usually, merely cut in and take the conversation in another direction. To save even more time, everyone will often talk at once, on different subjects; meetings (e.g. AGMs) usually degenerate quickly into an incomprehensible babble, so that nothing is agreed or decided. The French love nothing more than to talk (with the possible exception of eating) – whether or not anyone is listening or can hear what they're saying.

French impatience is most evident on the roads, where even women in their 80s and 90s will put their feet to the floor and drive within an inch of the car in front with blissful disregard for speed limits, blind bends, other road users, fog, ice, and anything else that might restrict their ability to get from A to B in the shortest possible time. If you hold them up (e.g. by driving at only 10kph above the speed limit), they may not flash or toot you, but you can see them fuming in your rear-view mirror and craning their necks to the left to spy an opportunity to overtake – even if they're turning off at the next junction.

On the other hand, in certain situations the French can

demonstrate remarkable patience and staying power. Most notable among these is when they're eating – and even before eating. An ordinary French meal can last over two hours; when a celebration is in order, four, five and even six hours isn't unusual (the French take their eating **very** seriously), but it can be an hour or more after guests arrive before the first course is served – and **everyone** must be present (even if one guest is an hour late) before a single *apéritif* is served. When it comes to entertainment, the French capacity for endurance knows almost no bounds: not only can they sit in rapt concentration through two hours of classical music or literary monologues without an interval (or a drink), but they expect children as young as three to do likewise.

But even when merely waiting, the French are rarely in a hurry. Whether in a shop queue, at the doctor's or dentist's or – amazing as it may seem – in a traffic jam, most French are happy to while away a quarter of an hour or more until their turn arrives. The exception, of course, is Parisians.

Whatever the situation, beware of displaying impatience, as this will be greeted with indifference, resistance or outright hostility.

> 'We non-French people often think that the French are trying to insult us because we're foreign, but it's not true. They're like that with each other too.'
>
> Stephen Clarke, *Talk to the Snail*

## Individualism

It's never wise to believe everything you're told by a French person, as all knowledge is 'relative' and the French rarely agree on anything – as a matter of principle. Ask ten French people the difference between *un potiron* (pumpkin) and *une citrouille* (pumpkin), between *une chouette* (owl) and *un hibou* (owl) or between *une biche* (deer) and *un chevreuil* (deer), and you'll get ten different answers.

*Liberté, égalité, fraternité* may be the three guiding principles of French society, but most definitely in that order of importance. Everyone is free to think and (to a lesser extent) do what he wishes; everyone is equal, at least in so far as everyone is equally free; as for being fraternal, everyone is happy to fraternise with his equals but not with just anyone.

From this essential sense of freedom stems the anarchic streak in the French character, the propensity for doing whatever he (or she) likes – speaking his mind and 'interpreting' regulations (particularly those applying to driving and the payment of taxes), for example. Rules are only for other people (those who complain about drivers speeding through their village often do so themselves) and anyone is free to do anything – except 'under my windows' (*sous mes fenêtres*). This is the infamous *exception française*.

> 'To the French, there is a world of difference between rules and formalities. The former are to be ignored, the latter strictly observed. This is why they rely so heavily on a highly structured system of social etiquette: without it they would be at each other's throats.'
>
> Nick Yapp & Michel Syrett, *The Xenophobe's Guide to the French*

Individualism extends to married (and unmarried) couples, who don't become a 'unit' when they choose to live together but remain independent – of thought and action. It's therefore common for one partner not to know what the other is doing (or not to know what either of them is doing if the other is the 'keeper of the diary'), and for them to disagree openly – sometimes even acrimoniously – in public (e.g. over dinner). This usually doesn't mean that separation or divorce is just around the corner, but simply that the couple are eager to assert their individuality and show that they haven't become bored by each

other's company, boredom being anathema to the French (Coco Chanel is reported to have said that boredom is fattening).

> 'Of the original slogan of the French Revolution, "liberty" and "equality" have never ceased to preoccupy Frenchmen, often at the expense of national "fraternity".'
>
> *Instructions for British Servicemen in France 1944*

Closely related to individualism is the French antipathy to authority – and customers. Being told what to do is an infringement of freedom and individualism. The French therefore have a 'healthy' disrespect for authority and will try to find a way round every official system, an alternative system known as *système D* (which stands for *débrouillard* – someone who does things himself according to his own 'rules');

indeed, doing so is a point of honour. Since customers 'order' and 'demand', they're regarded with the same disdain, and it generally isn't until you humble yourself before the person you wish to provide you with a service or goods that you begin to get what you want (see **Rudeness** above).

## Bof

The 'word' *bof* (it's more of a noise, really) is often invoked by people attempting to sum up the French character, and the utterance – usually accompanied by a puffing-out of the cheeks and a shrugging of the shoulders – epitomises the people pretty well. It doesn't, of course, mean 'I don't know' (see **Intellectualism** above – it will be seen that the various traits of the French character are interconnected) but rather something like 'That may be true in theory but in practice it isn't necessarily so and, in any case, nothing is certain and we'll have to

> Although the French don't have an equivalent of the Spanish word mañana, meaning 'at some time in the future but almost certainly not tomorrow', they have a similar mental concept. Nothing is urgent, deadlines are merely guidelines and things will get done when the person doing them is good and ready.

see how things turn out' – or simply 'I couldn't care less'.

This laid-back, couldn't-care-less attitude – the famous French *laissez-faire* approach – is something of a sham, however, as the Frenchman's most prized quality – whether in a personal or a business context – is *le sérieux*. This doesn't translate as seriousness in the sense of dedication or a lack of humour, but seriousness in the sense of taking oneself and others seriously; showing and therefore earning respect, and doing what is expected – though not necessarily how or when it's expected.

What's extraordinary is that when there really **is** a deadline (e.g. the opening of an exhibition or event), everything 'appears' and 'happens' without any fuss or stress or apparent effort – perhaps not precisely on time, but not far off. In fact, perhaps the word that best sums up the French is not *bof* but 'effortlessness'. Whether cultivating an immaculate garden without seeming to do any gardening or managing to mingle calmly with guests while serving an entirely home-made four-course meal for 12,

the French have an inimitable art of making things look easy.

## HUMOUR

Humour is one of the most telling cultural indicators and, as every expat knows, there are few more uncomfortable situations than being the only one not roaring with laughter at a joke, and few more alienating than not understanding a pun or being unable to join in witty repartee. However, not 'getting' the humour is part and parcel of culture shock and something you'll have to

learn to accept until your language skills have advanced sufficiently for you to appreciate its subtleties – though not all French humour is strong on subtlety.

In stark contrast is the French penchant for slapstick. Its mildest incarnations are perhaps the mime shows of Marcel Marceau (b. 1923) and the almost wordless (but noisy) films of Jacques Tati (1908-82) – both of which are something of an acquired taste (even among the French). At the opposite extreme, French farce can degenerate into startling crudity, with recitations of obscene 'poems' accompanied by the exposure of bottoms (and worse) at family celebrations where young children are present.

The French are fond of stand-up comedy, but this is generally incomprehensible to all but the most linguistically accomplished foreigner. Regional stereotypes feature in French joke-telling, e.g. Normans are reckoned to be dour and mean, *Auvergnats* dim, *Provençaux* clannish and Parisians ... No one makes jokes about Parisians; they're beneath contempt. The most common butt of French jokes are the Belgians (*les Belges*), on account of their supposed stupidity and addiction to chips. 'Blonde' jokes are also common, but, as with French visual humour, jokes and witticisms often involve crude language and sexual innuendo.

Surprisingly, no one seems to be offended by crude 'humour'. Even people who appear rather staid will smile indulgently and no one ushers their children from the room or

French humour broadly takes two contrasting – even contradictory – forms: linguistic and farcical. The French language, with its silent endings and similar pronunciations of dissimilar words, lends itself admirably to word play, in which the French love to indulge.

> 'The French may claim to live in a classless republic, but they are very keen on keeping everyone in their place.'
>
> Stephen Clarke, *Talk to the Snail*

raises objections – and you would be wise to do likewise.

## THE CLASS SYSTEM

Ostensibly, France has no class system. After all, the Revolution killed off the monarchy and most of the aristocracy (though there are still plenty of dukes, barons, countesses, etc.) and made everyone else equal. In theory. In reality, the aristocracy is alive and well: it comprises 63m French people. Everyone isn't as important as everyone else; everyone is **more** important than everyone else, and deference is an attitude unknown to French people.

Much has been written about the supposed distinctions between the *grande bourgeoisie*, the *bonne bourgeoisie* and the *petite bourgeoisie* but in fact no one wants to be labelled '*bourgeois*', which has negative connotations of complacency and conservatism.

Although there's no caste system in French society, there's a clear social pecking order. This isn't determined by birth or 'accent' (no accent is any more 'posh' than any other, although everyone will happily make fun of those who speak with a different accent from their own) but largely by intellect. At the top are graduates of the *grandes écoles*, whose intellectual prowess has been honed to razor sharpness by a ruthless series of competitive exams (*concours*) – known unrepublicanly as *la voie royale* (the royal way). Then there are those with a *doctorat* (PhD), followed by those with an 'ordinary' university degree, known as a *bac plus*, i.e. the *baccalauréat* plus a number of years' third level study: *Master* (*bac +5*), *Maîtrise* (*bac +4*), *Licence* (*bac +3*) and *DEUG* (*bac +2*). Although passing the *baccalauréat* used to indicate a reasonable level of educational attainment, it's now virtually guaranteed provided you remain at school until 18; those who leave earlier may have only a *brevet*.

On the last rung are those with no educational qualifications, who are destined to fill the lowest-paid jobs. Not for the French the American model of 'anyone can become President'; if you don't have the

Carcassonne Castle, Aude

qualifications, you don't get the job and you remain stuck on the 'class' ladder.

But even the unqualified aren't quite at the bottom of the heap. There's still room for gypsies and assorted immigrants – mostly those from Africa – who are treated as third-class citizens by many French people (see below).

## CHILDREN

France has the third-highest birth rate among EU countries (12 births per 1,000 population per year – including rates of up to 40 in its overseas territories), after Ireland and Cyprus, and families with four or five children are common. This is partly because the French government encourages *familles nombreuses* (families with at least three children), who enjoy lower taxes and numerous benefits, but mainly for traditional reasons.

> 'Above and beyond the basic parental responsibility for the protection, care and feeding of one's offspring, there is in France the added duty to civilise them.'
>
> Donald Carroll, *Surprised by France*

Nevertheless, unlike Spanish children, French children are to be seen and not heard – a belief that is manifest in the number of infants as old as four or five who spend the majority of their lives with dummies (pacifiers) in their mouths.

Traditionally, children were taught to be quiet (*se taire*) and weren't allowed to speak at the dinner

table, for example – although this restriction is dying out, it's common to meet French people in their 30s and 40s who were brought up this way. As a result they were virtually unable to communicate – a disability often misinterpreted by foreigners as arrogance or haughtiness. Even if they're now permitted to speak, French children are trained to remain still and silent for long periods – during meals, concerts, etc. – and to sit with adults rather than go off and play on their own.

Children's behaviour is a reflection of the success or failure of their parents in educating them. A well-behaved child is *sage* (wise) and *bien élevé* (well brought up) and makes his parents proud of him – rather than being entitled to be proud of himself.

To the French, childhood isn't a period of precious innocence but a period of painful ignorance. Children must be taught to be adults, and training begins at a young age. They aren't expected to have opinions of their own but rather to absorb and regurgitate the ideas and opinions of their parents – and this is reinforced by a strict instructional education system. Until they've assimilated a certain amount of information and can join in an adult conversation, children are of little interest to most French adults, who – when they aren't telling them what to do or say – often ignore them completely. Neither are they expected to be autonomous and 'make their own way'; young children are rarely given pocket money, for example.

On the other hand, children are almost always involved in social occasions and rarely left with babysitters. (When they are, it's usually with family or friends – paid babysitters are a rarity in France.) If there are several children, they may be given a table to themselves but will be expected to behave as adults. This has the spin-off benefit that they're allowed to stay up much later than many of their northern

European counterparts – often until 1 or 2 in the morning. Children are welcome in the vast majority of bars, cafés and restaurants (only the most exclusive refuse entry to under 18s), and many eateries provide children's menus and high chairs – though not toys or play areas, of course.

This approach to upbringing is surprisingly 'successful'. French children still look up to their elders and are generally far less rebellious than British or American children, for example. They also seem to grow up much more slowly, or enjoy a longer childhood, depending on which way you look at it. Many 17- and 18-year-olds are tongue-tied and lacking in confidence, as if still suffering the pangs of puberty – and would be mistaken for children two years younger by most Anglo-Saxons.

French children are generally polite and considerate, and there's little 'yob' culture in French society. Teenagers go out with their parents at weekends and join in family holidays, and most value the family unit highly. Leaving home isn't a priority for most children, and many continue to live with their parents while at university, often until they're 30 or older. High property prices are partly the reason for this, but even young adults who can afford to often don't leave their parents' home until they get married.

## ATTITUDES TO FOREIGNERS

Because the French aren't generally well travelled (except to French-

speaking countries) and have little interest in other peoples, they're often surprisingly ignorant about foreign cultures. What they 'know' is often based on popular stereotypes or out-dated clichés gleaned from old books or films. A recent book entitled *Les Nouveaux Anglais* by Agnès Catherine Poirier, sets out to dispel many of the prevailing myths about the British (typically, she confuses 'English' with 'British'), but succeeds only in perpetuating most of them. These include the 'facts' that the English/British are obsessed with the aristocracy, behave like characters in Oscar Wilde's plays or P. G. Wodehouse's novels, that James Bond is a cultural icon and Benny Hill the acme of British humour.

> The French refer to most English-speaking people and even the Germans and Dutch as *les Anglo-Saxons*, which isn't a derogatory term but has overtones of a lack of cultivation and *savoir-vivre*.

Such beliefs are partly due to ignorance and partly to a subconscious desire to assert the superiority of all things French, but are seldom meant to be insulting;

therefore it's best to take them with a pinch of salt, remarking perhaps that they're equivalent to the myth that all French people wear striped shirts and berets, ride bicycles and eat raw onions.

There is, however, a darker side to French attitudes to foreigners. Just as the French claim to be considerate drivers, so they will tell you that they aren't racist or xenophobic. The truth isn't so clear cut and, although confined to a minority of the population, racism is sadly alive and well in France. The far-right 'politician' Jean-Marie Le Pen, who is also an MEP, makes no secret of his own views on race; when he has lunch at the European Parliament building, the three black waiters are instructed not to go near his table. Far from being dismissed as a dangerous extremist, Le Pen garnered almost 20 per cent of the vote in both the 1995 and 2002 presidential elections.

Like the inhabitants of most developed countries, the French are concerned about the impact on their culture of increasing numbers of immigrants (previously from Africa, following decolonisation, and lately from eastern Europe), but it seems that white-skinned people are less 'worrying' than dark-skinned people – which is worrying. The British and other northern Europeans, for example, who are flooding into the country and causing property prices to rise at an unprecedented rate, are generally welcomed (despite moans about the rise in property prices), even if they contribute nothing to the economy; whereas

Africans and Asians are often the subject of mockery or outright racist comments.

Unwanted minorities are 'herded' into faceless suburbs, especially around Paris, where the word *banlieue* has come to mean a particular kind of undesirable suburb. The 2005 Paris riots (the country's worst since 1968), were ostensibly sparked by police and administrative discrimination against non-white immigrants in just such a place; at that time Nicolas Sarkozy added insult to injury when he referred to the rioters as 'rabble' and promised to clean out the area with a 'pressure hose'.

## NATIONAL ICONS

Every country has its icons – people, places, structures, food (and drink) and symbols – which are revered or unique to that country, and have special significance to its inhabitants. The following is a list of some of France's principal icons to which you can expect to see or hear frequent references. (The author apologises for the many 'icons' missing from this list due to lack of space.)

### Icons – People

**Joan of Arc** (1412-31) – Jeanne or Jehanne d'Arc or Darc, known as *la Pucelle* (the Maid), was born in Domrémy – now called Domrémy-la-Pucelle in her honour – in Meuse. At the age of 13, she had a vision prompting her to lead the kingdom of France against the invading English, but just six years later fell foul of political intrigue and was martyred in Rouen, where a modern church named after her now stands. A standard French gibe at English visitors is '*Vous avez brûlé Jeanne d'Arc*' (You burned Joan of Arc), although the historical accuracy of this statement is open to debate.

**Astérix** (b. 1959) – France's most popular cartoon character (and the French love their *bandes dessinées*, commonly abbreviated to *BD*), created visually by Albert Uderzo and textually by René Goscinny. The subject of over 30 books, several films and France's second-most visited theme park; Astérix is 'leader' of the Gauls, who successfully defend the last corner of France against the heathen Romans.

**Charles Aznavour** (b. 1924) & **Maurice Chevalier** (1888-1972) – Two of France's most famous crooners, the former having written over 1,000 songs (including 150 in English) and sold over 100m records, and was still drawing full houses in his eighties; the latter, with his trademark straw hat and '*onh-onh-onh*' laugh, also performed into his ninth decade. Among their indelible songs are *La Bohème*, *For Me Formidable* and *Thank Heaven for Little Girls*.

**Brigitte Bardot** (b. 1934) – The original 'sex kitten', Bardot was seduced by film director Roger Vadim when only 15, and made a star by him four years later in the then shocking *Et Dieu créa la femme* (And God Created Woman); many films and almost as many lovers later she achieved equal notoriety for her animal rights foundation, created in 1986, and recently for her espousal of radical right-wing views.

**Napoléon Bonaparte** (1769-1821) – Remembered – and revered – in France, not for his military exploits or imperialist excesses, but for his administrative innovations encompassing education, banking, taxation, local government and even sewerage. These culminated in the *Code Napoléon*, on which French civil law is still based.

**Candide** (b. 1759) – Anti-hero of the satirical novel *Candide ou l'Optimisme* (Candide or Optimism) by philosopher François-Marie Arouet (pseudonym Voltaire), who naively believes that 'all is for the best in the best of all possible worlds' – a belief still held by the majority of French people.

**Gabrielle Bonheur 'Coco' Chanel** (1883-1971) – Widely regarded as the mother of French fashion design, influencing successors such as Christian Dior (1905-57), Pierre Cardin (b. 1922), Yves Saint-Laurent (b. 1936) and Jean-Paul Gaultier (b. 1952). Her most famous creation, Chanel no.5 perfume, launched in 1921, was so called because it was the fifth sample to be tested – appropriately this was Gabrielle's lucky number.

> 'If you wish to be a success in the world, promise everything, deliver nothing.'
>
> Napoleon Bonaparte

**Jacques Chirac** (b. 1932) – After 18 years as Mayor of Paris, two terms as Prime Minister and 12 years as President, 'Jacques the lad' announced his retirement from politics in March 2007. His claim that he 'always attempted to act in the best interests of France' is disputed by many, who believe he failed to solve the country's principal problems.

**Coluche** (1944-86) – Real name Michel Colucci, he became France's best known comedian, many of his one-liners passing into the language; he is also renowned for founding, the year before his death in a motorcycle accident, *Les Restos du Coeur*, a charity dedicated to raising money and collecting food and clothing for the homeless and needy.

**Claude Debussy** (1862-1918) & **Maurice Ravel** (1875-1937) – France's most celebrated composers, now considered 'central' but radical in their day. Debussy's *Prélude à l'après-midi d'un faune* (Prelude to the Faun's Afternoon) is regarded as one of the seminal works of the 20th century; ironically, Ravel's 'anti-composition' *Boléro* has become not only his, but one of the best known pieces of classical music of all time.

Eiffel Tower, Paris

**Alfred Dreyfus** (1859-1935) – A Jewish army officer who became the focus of one of France's biggest-ever scandals, *l'affaire Dreyfus*, when he was accused of treason (in 1894), stripped of his rank and sentenced to life imprisonment. He was pardoned five years later and readmitted to the army in 1906; the trumped-up charges and subsequent cover-up polarised the nation, and the affair has been the subject of half a dozen films and is still talked about today.

**Jean Gabin** (1904-76) – Real name Jean-Alexis Moncorgé, is generally regarded by the French as their finest actor, and his best known film, *La Grande Illusion* (1937), set during the First World War, one of the greatest films ever made. Despite (or perhaps because of) his international renown, Gérard Depardieu is generally derided by his countrymen as a ham.

**Charles André Joseph Marie de Gaulle** (1890-1970) – Self-appointed leader of the 'Free French' movement during the Second World War – though he spent much of the time in smart London accommodation. He became head of the provisional government between 1944 and 1946, and was President from 1958 to 1969, and is unequivocally revered by the French. Part of the text of his *Appel* to the French people, broadcast from London on 18th June 1940, can be found on many public buildings.

**Johnny Hallyday** (b. 1943) – Born Jean-Philippe Smet and dubbed 'the greatest rock star no one has ever heard of' in the English-speaking world, Hallyday is a living legend in France and, well into his sixties, still tours to sell-out houses as well as appearing in numerous advertisements. He recently emigrated to Switzerland to avoid French taxes.

**Victor-Marie Hugo** (1802-85) – Generally regarded as France's greatest Romantic writer – though some rate more highly Charles Baudelaire (1821-67), Guy de Maupassant (1850-93), Marcel Proust (1871-1922) or Emile Zola (1840-1902) – but principally for his poetry (especially *Les Contemplations*) and plays rather than his novels, which include *Les Misérables* and *Notre-Dame de Paris*.

**Molière** (1622-73) – Real name Jean-Baptiste Poquelin, France's most famous writer – though dismissed by many French people as second-rate – and sometimes referred to as the French Shakespeare, although he wrote almost exclusively comedies. His most famous plays include *L'Avare* (The Miser), *Le Malade imaginaire* (The Hypochondriac), *Le Misanthrope* (The Misanthropist) and *Tartuffe*, all of which are regularly performed at Paris' Comédie Française.

**Claude Monet** (1840-1926) – Unwitting founder of the Impressionist 'movement', thanks to his 1873 painting *Impression, soleil levant* (Impression, Sunrise), and France's most internationally famous artist. His house and water lily pond (at Giverny, near Vernon in Eure) can be visited, and the Musée Marmottan in Paris is devoted to his works. His most impressive creation – eight vast water lily canvases – is housed in the capital's recently refurbished Musée de l'Orangerie.

**Yannick Noah** (b. 1960) – Of half-Cameroonian descent, Noah caused a sensation when he won Roland Garros (the French Open) in 1983 – the last time a Frenchman won a Grand Slam tennis tournament – and went on to coach the French men's team to victory in the Davis Cup. He's regularly voted the most popular Frenchman, and is now a pop music star and charity worker. However, like his compatriot Johnny

Hallyday, he avoids French taxes by living abroad.

**Louis Pasteur** (1822-95) – Perhaps France's greatest scientist – though Marie and Pierre Curie are also in contention – best known for discovering a process for preventing milk from going sour, called pasteurisation in his honour. He was one of the founders of bacteriology, created the first rabies vaccine, and confirmed that certain diseases were caused by germs.

**Edith Piaf** (1915-63) – Born Edith Giovanna Gassion, reputedly under a gas light on Paris' Rue de Belleville, and nicknamed *Piaf* (sparrow) on account of her diminutive stature, she became and remains France's best known singer, her many hits including *Je ne regrette rien* and *La Vie en rose*.

> 'Women get more unhappy the more they try to liberate themselves.'
>
> Brigitte Bardot (French actress)

**Michel Platini** (b. 1955) & **Zinedine Yazid Zidane** (b. 1972) – Two of France's greatest footballers and national team captains. In 2006 both made headlines for very different reasons – Platini on his election as President of UEFA, 'Zizou', as Zidane is known, for felling an opponent with a head butt (now referred to as *le coup de boule*) in the 2006 World Cup final, which France lost on penalties.

**Alain Prost** (b. 1955) – France's most successful racing driver, who retired in 1993 after becoming World Formula One Champion for the fourth time. His record of 51 Grand Prix victories stood until 1991, when Michael Schumacher surpassed it, but his reputation was tarnished when his ill-fated racing team went bust in 2002 owing some €30m.

## Icons – Places

**Alps** – Western Europe's largest and highest mountain range, and the annual destination of millions of French ski fanatics, who generally overlook the fact that the Alps are 'shared' with several other countries. Their loftiest peak, Mont Blanc (4,808m/15,774ft), is disappointingly rounded and easy to climb.

**Côte d'Azur** – Sometimes referred to as the French Riviera, the 'Azure Coast' is one of the world's most famous holiday areas, comprising such legendary resorts as Antibes, Cannes, Nice and Saint-Tropez (and Monte Carlo, which isn't in France). It's hopelessly crowded in summer, when it's almost impossible to drive along the coast or find a square metre of sand to lie on.

**Lourdes** – One of the world's premier shrines, this town in south-west France owes its renown to Saint Bernadette, a local girl who in 1858, at the age of 14, had 18 visions of a 'beautiful lady in white' in a grotto then being used as a shepherds' shelter. It is here that she discovered a spring from which over 200m people have now drunk in the hope of a miraculous cure.

**Mont Saint Michel** – France's third-most visited monument after the Eiffel Tower and the Palace of Versailles (see below), this tiny island – which, much to Breton displeasure, is just in Normandy – consists of a granite rock 300m across and 90m high, on which perches a monastery dating back to the eighth century. In 2006, Prime Minister Dominique de Villepin announced a six-year, €150m project to remove accumulated silt and build a bridge to replace the current causeway linking it to the mainland.

**Oradour-sur-Glane** – This village, near Limoges in Limousin, was where German soldiers massacred 642 men, women and children on Saturday 10th June 1944, in a reprisal against the killing of German soldiers by the resistance. Known as *le village marty*, it has been left untouched since, and is a memorial to those who died in the Second World War – and all other wars.

**Versailles Palace** – The most ostentatious of France's numerous chateaux, designed for Louis XIV by Louis Le Vau (house) and André Le Nôtre (gardens) and built over a period of 46 years, between 1664 and 1710. The 10,000-room *Palais de Versailles* represents everything that the Revolution sought to do away with, and is visited largely by foreign tourists (especially Japanese).

## Icons – Symbols

**Accordion** – The archetypal French musical instrument – sometimes unkindly referred to as a 'squeezebox' or the 'poor man's piano' – takes several forms, from simple wooden boxes with a few buttons that can play in only one key, to shiny chrome monsters with piano keys on one side and a bewildering array of buttons on the other. All *accordéons* produce an instantly recognisable and indelibly 'French' sound, although no more than a few hundred are made in France each year.

**Beret & striped shirt** – The quintessential Frenchman of popular mythology is virtually extinct and, although berets and striped shirts are still worn, they're seldom seen on the same person at the same time. Worn mainly in the south-west until the mid-'20s, *le béret* enjoyed 30 years of national popularity before production dwindled to around 1m a year, a third of which are supplied to the army.

**Champs-Elysées** – One of the world's most famous streets – and its third-most expensive real estate – the Avenue des Champs-Elysées (Avenue of the Elysian Fields) is a curious mixture of cinemas, cafes, car showrooms, souvenir stalls and specialist shops. It stretches 2km from the Place de la Concorde to the Arc de Triomphe, the slightly convex slope creating a uniquely impressive vista. The Champs-Elysées were originally market gardens outside the city, linked by a road with the Palais des Tuileries in 1616.

**Citroën 2CV** – Of France's many iconic cars, including the Renault 4

('*quatrelle*') and Citroën DS (from *déesse*, meaning 'goddess'), the Deux-chevaux is probably the best loved. Named after its official horsepower rating but nicknamed *la deuche* or *deudeuche* – as well as *quatre roues sous un parapluie* (an umbrella on wheels) – it was launched at the 1948 Paris Motor Show, and continued to be manufactured in various incarnations until 1990; thousands are still seen on (and off) French roads, in various stages of decay.

**Cock** – Appeared on church towers after the Revolution, signifying a 'new dawn' and was used as France's emblem during the Second Republic (1848-52) and more recently as a sporting mascot and brand name, *Le Coq sportif.* It's believed to have been adopted because of the similarity between the bird's Latin name (*Gallus gallus*) and the ancient name for France, Gaul, but perfectly represents the French male: proud, preening, strutting, pointlessly vociferous and extravagantly promiscuous but unable to fly – in a word, cocky.

**Fête nationale** – Known in the

---

### Paris

One of the world's great capital cities and widely considered to be the most beautiful and the most romantic, its iconic monuments include the Arc de Triomphe, Eiffel Tower (see below), Louvre museum, Notre-Dame cathedral and Sacré-Coeur church. Its inhabitants, on the other hand, are regarded as France's most unwelcoming – especially by other French people.

> **Eiffel Tower**
>
> Built for the 1889 World Fair and intended to last only 20 years, France's most famous building, la Tour Eiffel (pronounced 'aifell'), is named after its designer, Gustave Eiffel (1832-1923), Chief Engineer of the French Western Railway. Eiffel also designed many of the locks on the Panama Canal and the iron skeleton of the Statue of Liberty, given to the US in 1881.

Anglo-Saxon world as 'Bastille Day', the 14th July is a national holiday commemorating the event that sparked the French Revolution in 1789, the storming of the Bastille in Paris – one of the seminal events not just in French but in world history. Today its historic references are all but forgotten and it's merely another excuse for French people to eat, drink and be merry.

**Gauloises** – Another French icon in the process of disappearing, the short, strong, unfiltered cigarettes generally known to foreigners as Gauloises, though this is one of several brand names. They began to lose their romantic image with the realisation that smoking causes disease as well as 'atmosphere'; production was moved to Spain in 2005.

**Guillotine** – Symbol of the French Revolution, the hideously simple machine, named after its designer, Joseph-Ignace Guillotin, a doctor and member of the Revolutionary Assembly. It was adopted as the official means of execution in 1792, superseding several less efficient – and less egalitarian – methods, and *Madame la Guillotine* is reckoned to

have been used up to 60,000 times during the Reign of Terror between June 1793 and July 1794. The last public guillotining in France was in 1939, the last execution in 1977, the death penalty being abolished four years later. (Dr Guillotin made amends for his murderous invention by devoting his final years to the development of a smallpox vaccine and the abolition of slavery.)

**Marianne** – The symbol of the French Republic, appearing on stamps and coins, her image dates back to antiquity and was adopted by the Revolutionaries to represent *la mère-patrie* (the mother country), in contrast to the male images that had previously symbolised France. Her name wasn't chosen until 1797, when it was simply France's most popular female name and therefore ideal as a representation of the common people.

**Michelin man** – Conceived in 1894 at the Universal and Colonial Exhibition in Lyon and born four years later, thanks to illustrator Marius Rossillon (known as O'Galop). He became known in France as *Bibendum* thanks to his Latin motto, '*Nunc est bibendum*' (Now is the time to drink) – referring not to any alcoholic beverage but to rain on the road.

**Moulin rouge** – Built in 1889 as a 'temple to music and dance', the Red Mill began by offering belly-dancing shows but soon became famous for the cancan (which the French bizarrely call *le French cancan*). Throughout the first half of the 20th century it enjoyed mixed fortunes as an operetta theatre, nightclub and cinema, before being restored to its former 'glory'.

**TGV** – *Le train à grande vitesse* (high-speed train) came off the drawing board in 1972 and set a world rail speed record of 318kph (200mph) the same year. The first high-speed line, between Paris and Lyon, opened in 1981 and the *TGV* recorded its billionth passenger in 2003; the network now extends to most parts of the country and links with high-speed lines in Belgium, Germany, Spain and the UK.

**Tour de France** – The world's most famous and prestigious cycle race, covering between 3,000 and 4,000km and following a different route each year (sometimes including stages in other countries), *le Tour* was started as a publicity event for the newspaper *l'Auto* in 1903, when it was won by a Frenchman, Maurice Garin. The last

French winner was Bernard Hinault in 1985, but the most famous is Jacques Anquetil, who, like Hinault, won it five times, between 1957 and 1964.

## Icons – Food & Drink

**Baguette** – The quintessentially French 'loaf', which, happily, can still be seen being walked or cycled home daily from the *boulangerie*. However, there's a lot more to French bread than the *baguette* and its big brother, the *pain*, and recent years have seen an explosion in the variety of loaves on offer.

**Bordeaux** – Of the great variety of French wines, those produced in the Bordeaux area are the most highly regarded – in France as well as worldwide – though greatness can be claimed only by a few reds (with the exception of the sweet Sauternes), much of the 'ordinary' Bordeaux lining supermarket shelves being little better than some *vin de table*.

**Champagne** – Indubitably the best sparkling wine in the world, and drunk freely at social occasions by most French people, who aren't attracted by the 'big name' (and big price) brands but seek out small producers, of whom there are literally hundreds and whose champagne is no less delicious

> The French have never heard of 'claret'; clairet (from which the English word for Bordeaux red wine derives) is a rarely seen rosé from the Bordeaux wine region.

**Cheese** – The exact number of French cheeses is probably unknown, but it's generally accepted that you could eat a different variety every day of the year, each corner of the country having its peculiar method of treating cow's, goat's or sheep's milk.

**Croissant** – Taking its name from its crescent shape, the croissant is France's unique contribution to breakfast food, croissants vary greatly in texture and taste from *boulangerie* to *boulangerie*, some being dry and flaky, while others are moist and stringy. If you like yours dark or pale, ask for one that's *bien cuit* or *moins cuit*.

**Foie gras** – Literally 'fatty liver', the result of force-feeding caged geese, this expensive 'delicacy' is soon to be outlawed by the European Commission – to the outrage of the French. It's traditionally served with *brioche* and washed down with sweet white wine (preferably Sauternes).

**Frogs' legs** – Surprisingly rarely eaten in France, where they're called 'frogs' thighs' (*cuisses de grenouille* – one of the trickiest dishes to get your tongue round when ordering) and mostly imported; often likened to chicken and normally served laden with garlic (see below).

**Garlic** – Although purchased in considerable quantities (globes are sold only in strings and not singly), *l'ail* is generally used unobtrusively in French cooking, and it's rare to be overwhelmed by a smell of garlic when encountering French people – unless they've just eaten a plate of frogs' legs or snails.

**Marrons glacés** – Despite the name (sugared horse chestnuts), this delicacy is made with sweet chestnuts (*châtaignes*) and, like all French delicacies, is expensive, a single *marron* costing up to €2; in any case, they're so rich that it's impossible to eat more than two at a time.

**Oysters** – Another of France's delicacies and another subject of gastronomic snobbery, some preferring them fleshy (*bien en chair*) and some watery (*bien en eau*), others insisting on *fines de claire*, *spéciales de claire* or *pousse en clair* and eating them only at certain times of the year; the relative merits of *huîtres de Mont Saint-Michel* and *huîtres de Marenne-Oléron* can be a topic of almost endless discussion. Whichever type are served (commonly on special occasions), they're eaten raw and taste mostly of seawater – try cooking them in cream and garlic for an altogether more enjoyable, if less authentic, experience.

**Snails** – Like many of France's culinary specialities, *escargots* are an acquired taste – or rather, taste of very little, other than the garlic butter they're normally swimming in when served as a starter. French people carrying plastic bags and bending double by the side of the road in wet weather are probably collecting snails, which must then be starved for a week to get rid of the slime ... *bon appétit*.

**Truffles** – The ultimate delicacy, *truffes* are rare, difficult to find (pigs are good at it) and **very** expensive, white truffles costing even more than the black variety – the world record price is currently €125,000 for a white Alba truffle weighing just 1.5kg.

> 'Yet, who can help loving the land that has taught us six hundred and eighty-five ways to dress eggs?'
>
> Thomas Moore (Irish poet, singer & songwriter)

Provence

Rodin, The Thinker (*Le Penseur*)

# 3.

# GETTING STARTED

One of the most difficult stages of adjustment to a new country is those first few days when you have a million and one things to do. This is stressful enough without the addition of cultural differences. This chapter will help you overcome the challenges of arriving and settling in France, including those posed by obtaining a residence permit, finding accommodation, renting or buying a car, opening a bank account, registering for taxes, obtaining healthcare, council services and utilities, finding schools for your children, getting online and staying informed – and French bureaucracy.

> 'In France, things are done on a "don't need to know" basis. Unless forced to do so, no one will tell you anything.'
>
> Stephen Clarke, Talk to the Snail

## IMMIGRATION

Immigration is an inflammatory issue in France – literally. The 2005 Paris riots, which were ostensibly sparked by police and administrative discrimination against non-white immigrants, resulted in the burning of some 10,000 cars, as well as dozens of factories, schools, sports centres and religious buildings. The government has recently introduced new laws to curb non-EU immigration and is cracking down on illegal immigrants, who can be forcibly repatriated, although a controversial plan to send immigrant children 'home' was quickly abandoned. This makes it more difficult for non-EU citizens to enter the country, while most EU nationals barely need to wave their passport at immigration officials as they cross the border.

Immigration officials (*police national*) and customs officers (*douaniers*) are generally polite, but the onus is on you to prove your *bona fides* and you should remain calm and civil, however long the entry procedure takes.

Technically, any foreigner wishing to stay in France for more than 90 days must obtain a residence permit (*titre de séjour*) – either temporary (*carte de séjour*), valid for up to ten years depending on your nationality circumstances, or permanent (*carte de résident*), usually issued to those who have lived in France for three consecutive years and speak fluent French. Curiously, even a 'permanent' residence permit is valid for only ten years and must be renewed; the only way to become permanently 'accepted' is to adopt French citizenship.

While in France, you should carry your passport or residence permit (if you have one), which you can be asked to produce at any time by police or other officials; if you don't have them, you can be taken to a police station and interrogated. You can carry copies, but some police and *gendarmes* won't accept these and you'll have a hard time arguing your rights with them.

EU citizens, however, are no longer obliged to have a *carte de séjour*, although this doesn't mean that they can get away without registering their presence (e.g. to the taxman) in France.

A residence permit must be obtained from your departmental *préfecture*, where you must present proof of identity and status in France (e.g. a salary slip, student card or social security documentation). Permits are issued fairly quickly – within a few days in some cases.

'Purchase a photocopier when you come to France – it will save you time and money.'

William Jaques (British expatriate)

## BUREAUCRACY

French bureaucracy (euphemistically called *l'administration*) is legendary

– and most foreigners have an 'epic' tale to tell of their dealings with it. You should be prepared for frustration caused by time-wasting and blatant obstruction on the part of officials. Often you may wonder whether the right hand knows what any other part of the body is up to (it usually doesn't), and you should expect to receive conflicting information from consulates, government departments, *préfectures* and town halls.

Red tape (*paperasse*) is a way of life in France, where every third person is a civil servant (see below). In order to obtain any sort of permit, you must complete numerous forms, answer dozens of irrelevant questions and provide mountains of documents with official translations to produce an impressive-looking *dossier*.

When dealing with officialdom, you must persevere, as the first answer is always '*Non.*'. You can sometimes speed up proceedings by employing a lawyer, although this is unusual in France and may be counterproductive.

Top tips for dealing with French red tape:

- Always find out from an official source **exactly** what you need before making an application.

- Double-check the opening hours of the office and ensure it isn't a public holiday.

- Always take a duplicate of everything.

- Expect not to have the right paperwork the first time.

- Allow plenty of time to make an application (and take a good book).

Accept bureaucratic hurdles as part of life in France and remember that the French have to go through the same process. If French bureaucracy ever threatens to get the better of you, treat yourself to a leisurely French meal and a bottle of wine and your trials and tribulations will pale into insignificance.

'The less important an official, the more officious he is likely to be.'

Donald Carroll, *Surprised by France*

> When filling in French forms – which you'll often have to do – put a cross and not a tick in boxes.

## Civil Servants

France has the world's highest civil servant/population ratio – estimates range from 28 per cent to an incredible 35 per cent of its working population, or some 5m civil servants (*fonctionnaires*) – also known, less complimentarily, as *cravattés* ('tie-wearers') and *chieurs d'encre* ('ink-shitters').

The civil service has traditionally been seen as a cushy number in France, where government workers are more or less guaranteed a job for life and enjoy privileged employment conditions and early retirement (sometimes at 50). As a result, civil servants have a reputation for being complacent and having no interest in their jobs – let alone in the lives of the people they deal with.

Nevertheless, not all civil servants are aloof and unhelpful, and pleasant surprises are in store for those used to faceless functionaries in other countries. It's possible, for example, not only to know the name of the person dealing with your tax affairs but also to dial his number directly and discuss it with him. Even better, you can make an appointment to see him and sort things out face to face (always the best way in France).

When dealing with civil servants (and indeed any French person), be as polite and calm as possible – you'll achieve nothing by getting angry or frustrated. He may remember your politeness and treat you well the next time – but don't bank on it.

> 'Before you embark on anything to do with officialdom, get a good night's sleep.'
>
> Janet McNicol (British expatriate)

## ACCOMMODATION

Finding suitable accommodation is one of your first and most important tasks on arrival in France – but it isn't always plain sailing.

### Rented Property

Property for rent isn't hard to find in France, but your success in securing it depends on a number of factors. Some landlords refuse to let their property to tenants of certain nationalities and/or skin colours. It isn't unheard of for a prospective tenant to arrange a meeting with a landlord by phone but to have the door shut in his face once the landlord sees that the tenant isn't white.

Some landlords are reluctant to let to **any** foreigners – stories of foreign tenants who disappear owing many months' rent are common – so don't be surprised if a landlord asks you to provide a guarantor (a third party who commits himself to

paying your rent if you don't) or a bank guarantee – whereby, in the case of non-payment by the tenant, the bank takes over payment on the tenant's behalf. (Some landlords insure against non-payment but the premiums are added to your rent.)

### Contracts & Payment

It's worth signing a rental contract, not only for your peace of mind but also because French rental law is more than generous to tenants. Don't be tempted to rent a property without a contract because, although it seems an easy option with no strings attached, you'll have no rights and the landlord no obligations. There are also potential problems with insurance. The landlord might claim that his 'word' is as good as a contract (under French law, oral agreements are considered legal), but in a court case it would be your word against the landlord's.

Furnished properties (other than holiday accommodation) are sometimes available for as little as three months, but the usual minimum period is a year. Furnished property is difficult to find, however, and obviously more expensive than unfurnished property. Some furnished properties have no crockery (*vaisselle*) or linen (*draps*).

You'll be asked to give your date and place of birth, to provide your passport or *carte de séjour* and to pay one month's rent plus a deposit equal to two months' rent in advance. A contract for a furnished property is called a *contrat de location de locaux meublés* and requires you to insure the furnishings against damage. The minimum rental period for unfurnished property (*locaux non-meublés*) is three years. A rental contract must be signed by all parties involved, including the agent handling the contract, if there is one. Next to their signature each party must also write the words *lu et approuvé* (read and approved). For a furnished rental you must give one month's notice (*préavis*); for unfurnished rental it's three months.

> When renting, you should ensure that there's a detailed inventory (état des lieux); otherwise you could be charged at the end of your tenancy for 'damage' that you haven't caused.

## Buying a Home

Property purchase in France is generally a straightforward process, but you may be surprised by the following aspects of the procedure:

- All property purchases must be carried out by a *notaire* (not exactly equivalent to a notary public in the UK), whose fees are fixed by the government and who 'represents' neither the seller nor the buyer but merely ensures that the law is observed. You're therefore advised to engage a lawyer to ensure that your interests are served.

- Fees associated with a purchase can add up to 15 per cent to the cost (estate agents' fees are especially high, although in theory these are paid by the vendor), which means that in spite of high price rises and the apparent potential for making money from buying and selling property, you need to own a house for at least three years simply to recover the associated fees.

> You should never be tempted to under-declare the price in order to pay lower fees as it can have serious consequences if it's discovered.

● The first step in buying a property is to sign a contract (*un compromis de vente*) and pay a deposit (generally 10 per cent of the price). If you don't complete the purchase (unless this is because you're unable to obtain a mortgage) you will lose the deposit.

● Once you've signed a contract, you're tied to a purchase date, irrespective of whether you manage to sell an existing property or not by that time; if you don't, you must take out a bridging loan (*un prêt relais*), which is common practice in France. There's no 'chain' of buyers and sellers which can be broken if anyone is unable to sell or pulls out of a purchase for any other reason (as in the UK), which means that gazumping is practically unknown in France.

● You will be told that a survey 'isn't necessary' or simply 'isn't done' in France. The latter may be true, but not the former and you should always have a property (particularly an old one) surveyed or at least inspected by a good builder who you trust.

● Completion usually takes place 10 to 12 weeks after the signing of the initial contract.

● There are no title deeds as such in France and proof of ownership is provided and guaranteed by registration of the property (*titre de propriétaire*) at the land registry (*cadastre*).

● A bank transfer can take a week or more to 'arrive' in the *notaire*'s account.

● It's common for vendors to abscond with appliances, cupboards, curtain rails, lampshades, light bulbs and even plants from the garden (although some leave all these things), so make sure everything you think you're buying is listed in your contract.

● All new properties carry guarantees of between one and ten years.

## BUYING OR HIRING A CAR

If you live anywhere except the middle of a city, you'll almost certainly want a car. Here are a few

It's possible to buy a car without having a driving licence. These miniature, lawnmower-engined vehicles, known as sans permis ('without licences'), have all mod cons and can reach 90kph (60mph) downhill with a following wind. The only catch is the price: they start at around €7,000.

tips on hiring (renting) and buying vehicles.

## Car Hire

Hiring a car in France is expensive – at least when compared to hiring in Spain or the US – particularly for short periods, although prices have come down recently. To hire a car you must be at least 18 years old, although most companies have increased this to 21 or even 25, and most also have an upper age limit of 60 or 65. You must have held a full licence for at least a year and present your original licence (not a photocopy) – non-EU licence holders require an international driving permit – and usually personal identification as well. Payment must usually be made by credit card.

When choosing a hire car, bear in mind the summer heat (air-conditioning is a must in the south) and the high accident rate on French roads due to often appalling driving standards – try to protect yourself by hiring a robust car rather than one of the cheaper models.

## Buying a Car

You must own or rent property in France to buy a car. The process is generally straightforward, although (not surprisingly) it involves a certain amount of paperwork. There are incentives for buying environmentally-friendly cars – or converting a petrol or diesel car to run on gas (LPG).

Whether you buy from a dealer or privately, however, used car prices are high (particularly compared with those in the UK) and you're often better off buying new.

France has several police forces with separate and clearly defined functions, most of whom carry guns. The infamous *gendarmes* are part of the army and not renowned for their intelligence or sense of humour – nor even for their knowledge of the law.

## EMERGENCY SERVICES

France has extremely efficient emergency services (*services d'urgence et d'assistance*) and, except in remote rural areas, the time between an emergency call and arrival is usually brief. However, telephone operators rarely speak English, so be prepared to explain briefly in French the type of emergency and your exact location – try to give a landmark, if possible (see **Emergency Phrases** below).

## Emergency Numbers

The main national emergency numbers are as follows:

| Emergency Numbers | |
|---|---|
| **Number** | **Service** |
| 112 | **All-purpose emergency number** |
| 15 | **Ambulance service (Service d'Aide Médicale d'Urgence/ SAMU)** |
| 17 | **Police (police-secours)** |
| 18 | **Fire service (sapeurs-pompiers – often referred to simply as pompiers)** |

# HEALTH SERVICES

The French health service is internationally renowned and regularly rated the best in the world, although like health services in most other Western countries, it's under financial strain and suffering increasing budget and staff cuts.

## State Healthcare

State and private health services coexist and overlap, state healthcare often being identical to private treatment. Those who qualify for state healthcare include employees, the self-employed contributing to French social security, and EU

pensioners who have reached retirement age in their home country, as well as the dependants of all these. If you qualify for state healthcare, you must register at your nearest social security office (*caisse d'assurance maladie* – listed on 💻 www.ameli.fr and in the information pages of phone books). You must present proof of employment or self-employment in France or form E-106 or E-121, proof of residence (e.g. a property deed, rental contract or proof of registration in your commune) and your passport. After registration, you'll receive a social security card (*Carte Vitale* – soon to be superseded by the *Carte Vitale 2*), the size of a credit card, with your social security number on it. This should be presented whenever you require medical treatment, although if you forget it, you can complete a form instead.

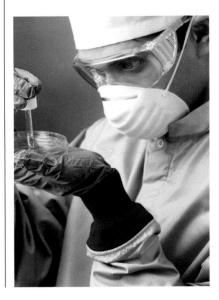

In some cases (e.g. consulting a doctor or dentist), you must pay and claim a refund afterwards; in others (e.g. when obtaining prescription medicines from a chemist) the refund is made 'on the spot'.

> As the state healthcare system rarely reimburses 100 per cent of the cost of treatment, many people take out complementary insurance (usually referred to as a *mutuelle*).

## Doctors

You're required to appoint a regular doctor (*médecin traitant*), who can be any registered doctor. If you need specialist care or (non-urgent) hospital treatment, you must first consult your regular doctor, who will refer you as appropriate.

It's usually possible to get an appointment the same day, and doctors allocate around 15 minutes per patient, so you're rarely kept waiting long. Most doctors have an 'open surgery' (*consultations libres*) for around two hours per day, when you can go along without an appointment and wait your turn. Out of hours, there's a number you can call to be put through to the nearest duty doctor. French doctors are reluctant to make house calls.

## Emergency Treatment

Not all hospitals offer emergency treatment – you should check where the nearest Accident & Emergency/ Casualty department (*Urgences*) is and how to get there from your home. In an emergency you can dial 15 for an ambulance (provided

by the *Service d'Aide Médicale d'Urgence/SAMU*) but, if you aren't admitted to hospital, you may be charged for the service; alternatively, you can call the fire brigade (on 18), who often provide a better service and won't normally charge a fee.

## Medicines

The French are pill poppers (hypochondriacs) and a visit to the doctor usually produces two or three prescriptions for potions, tablets and ointments, even for a minor ailment – not for nothing is the government increasingly 'encouraging' doctors and chemists to offer generic alternatives to branded medicines, and removing hundreds of medicines from the approved reimbursement list.

> The widespread belief that French doctors commonly prescribe suppositories is mistaken, although these are sometimes prescribed for infants, who cannot swallow pills.

Unlike in the UK, for example, medicines aren't 'made up' by a chemist while you wait, but are all pre-packaged and simply retrieved from a shelf by pharmacy staff – which doesn't mean that they aren't highly trained and unable to give detailed advice on when and how to take medicines; they even offer 'prescriptions' of their own for minor ailments without your needing to see a doctor. This system has the disadvantage that you often end up with 'spare' medicines – if, for example, you need only eight tablets but the packet contains 10 or 20.

It isn't possible to buy strong medicines such as antibiotics over the counter, however, and chemists' shops offer few non-medical products – they may stretch to babies' dummies and hot water bottles but no further.

Prescriptions issued by doctors are subsidised and you pay between nothing (e.g. for babies' medicines) and 100 per cent of the price (e.g. for most contraceptive pills), not a fixed amount per prescription. Some or all of the cost may be reimbursed if you have complementary insurance. There's no discount for medicinal products purchased without a prescription.

## Hospitals

If you have to go to hospital, France is one of the best countries to be in, as hospital facilities and services are generally second to none and waiting lists virtually non-existent for most procedures. In fact, during holiday periods – espcially the summer – many hospitals are half empty, as the French make sure **nothing** spoils their *vacances* (the only problem is all the doctors are also on holiday).

Public hospitals provide two- or four-bedroom wards with ensuite bathrooms and possibly a TV. In private hospitals (or private rooms in a public hospital), patients usually have individual rooms. Visiting times are usually flexible. The only possible criticism of French hospitals is that hospital food is rarely *haute cuisine*.

## Medical Procedures

If you have a scan or an X-ray, the results are given to you and it's up to you to take them to your doctor. Many people have an impressive *dossier* of medical records, which

> 'The French healthcare system can best be described as severely pigeonholed, as much of French administrative life and culture seems to be.'
>
> Beverly Laflamme (American expatriate)

should be kept in a safe place, as copies are impossible to obtain.

### Childbirth

France has one of the lowest infant mortality rates in the EU, but having a baby is a highly clinical experience. Ante-natal care is good – mothers are required to have at least two scans, monthly blood tests and check-ups, and may attend ante-natal classes. Don't, however, expect to be asked to provide a 'birth plan': home births are practically unheard of, as are water births, birthing balls, etc. Even giving birth on your side or sitting up is usually frowned upon, although hospitals are beginning to be more 'progressive' in this respect. Pain relief, however, starts and ends with an epidural (*péridurale*) – gas and air aren't available. Partners are allowed to be present at the birth, but not if there's a complication or a caesarean must be performed (which is more common than in many other countries).

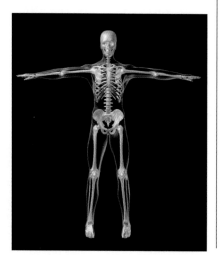

### Post-treatment Care

Mothers and babies normally stay in hospital for five days after the birth, although it's sometimes possible to leave earlier. However, in most cases subsequent post-natal care is carried out by doctors or baby-care centres (*centre de protection maternelle et infantile/PMI*). Don't expect home visits from doctors or midwives to check on you or your baby's health – the onus is on you to go for regular check-ups.

## INSURANCE

Compulsory insurance policies for individuals in France are as follows:

- third-party insurance for car owners;
- third-party property liability insurance for homeowners and tenants;
- third-party property liability insurance for schoolchildren;
- building insurance for mortgage holders;
- life insurance for mortgage holders.

Optional (but highly recommended) insurance policies include health (see below), comprehensive car and car breakdown, life (unless required as above), travel and household contents.

### Health Insurance

Even if you and your dependants qualify for state healthcare, you should ensure that you have full health insurance during the interval between leaving your last country of residence and obtaining health insurance (state or private) in France.

If you're staying for up to a year in France and aren't covered by a reciprocal health agreement (e.g. within the EU, using a European Health Insurance Card), you can take out a health insurance contract for *impatriés temporaires en France*, but this may not cover repatriation in the case of serious illness, for example.

## Car Insurance

All motor vehicles must be insured (third-party minimum) when entering France. If your car is insured in an EU country, it's automatically covered for third-party liability in France, but if you become resident in France and keep a foreign-registered car, you must import it and take out a new insurance policy with a company registered in France, which may be valid for only a year.

You must not only display a *vignette* behind the windscreen confirming that you have valid insurance (you will be sent a new one every six months), but must also carry a signed *attestation d'assurance* when driving.

> Car insurance policies usually cover anyone driving the vehicle, although the insured person must be the regular user. Rental car insurance, however, only covers named drivers.

## Household Insurance

Insuring your home and its contents is highly advisable and if you buy a property; in fact, if you take out a mortgage, your lender will probably insist that you have at least basic building insurance covering fire damage. Note that building insurance doesn't cover defects in a building or its design (e.g. an overweight roof that collapses), many policies don't include flood damage insurance, and the building must be secure against intrusion, e.g. iron bars (*grilles*) on windows and mortise-locks on external doors.

Contents insurance doesn't generally include objects in the garden, and for high-value objects such as antiques and jewellery, a separate policy is usually required. If you wish to insure your contents for more than a certain amount, e.g. €60,000, you may need to install an alarm system.

Nine out of ten homeowners have combined building and contents insurance (*assurance multirisques habitation*), and most household policies include third-party insurance (*responsabilité civile*).

## School Insurance

All schoolchildren should be insured against damage to school property and injury to themselves or others while at school, and while travelling to and from school, although strictly it isn't obligatory (except for school trips). In any case, most household policies include school insurance, although this is likely to be the bare minimum.

## Claims

Most companies insist that claims are made by registered letter (*lettre recommandée*). If a claim is for theft, insurance companies require a copy of the police report (*déclaration de vol* or *plainte*), which you must make within 24 hours. If your car is stolen, an insurance company won't consider your claim until 30 days have elapsed, though you may be loaned a car during this period.

# EDUCATION

Education is a major concern for families relocating to France, and choosing the right school for your child is one of the most difficult decisions you'll face. Don't forget to think beyond school to university and work, as the type of education you choose for your children has important long-term implications.

## French or International School?

If you're able to choose between French and international education,

the following factors may help you to make the best choice for your child(ren).

### International Schools

There are few international schools outside Paris and the Côte d'Azur (for example, there's one each in Bordeaux, Lille and Toulouse), although there are private schools that cater for non-French-speakers in many areas. An international school is ideal if your stay is short term (say up to five years) as it's less unsettling for your children if you return to your home country, or move to another country where there are international schools. The standard of education is generally high and teaching methods and the language of instruction are likely to be familiar, so your children will probably adapt more quickly and easily than to a French school. They won't be under pressure to learn French quickly in order to understand the lessons (but make sure the school offers opportunities to learn the language). Many international schools are 'melting pots' of nationalities – some have pupils from up to 50 countries – making them a unique opportunity to meet people from other cultures.

On the other hand, international schools are invariably expensive (expect to pay at least €5,000 per year for primary school, considerably more for secondary) and there's often a high turnover of pupils, relocating with their parents from one country to another. Some international schools are 'expat bubbles' and don't give children the best chance to learn the local language or mix in with the local community.

> '... education for teachers and pupils is very much a nose-to-the-grindstone affair.'
>
> Nick Yapp & Michel Syrett,
> *The Xenophobe's Guide to the French*

### *French Schools*

If you intend to stay in France long term or if you're uncertain how long you'll be there (in which case it's best to assume a long stay), a French school is likely to be preferable, as your child has a better chance of learning French fluently. If the school is local, your children (and you) become part of the local community. Long-term education and employment possibilities are also better. Education at French state schools is free, and fees at private schools are considerably lower than those charged by international schools.

However, some children (particularly those over the age of ten) find schooling in a foreign language academically and socially difficult. You'll also need to learn enough French to communicate with your child's teachers and understand correspondence from the school – not to mention help your children with their learning.

> **Home Education**
>
> Some 10,000 children are estimated to be educated at home in France. If you choose home education for your children, you must inform your town hall and education authority before the start of each academic year, and it will be subject to regular inspections.

## The French Education System

Education is compulsory from 6 to 16, but most children start school at three. The French education system and teaching methods are similar to those found in Spain and Italy – but totally different from those in the UK and US. Traditionally, almost all learning was done by rote and students were expected to sit in silence and merely 'absorb' information, memorising huge chunks of text and long lists of facts. As a result, pupils had excellent knowledge but little ability to communicate. In theory, this is now changing – the current buzzword in French educational circles is 'communication'. In practice, however, learning is still very much a passive, teacher-directed process, in which children are penalised for their mistakes rather than praised for their achievements.

The French education system is largely centralised and individual schools have less autonomy than those in the UK, for example (inspectors regularly check that everything is as it should be). In particular, head teachers cannot hire and fire staff, and it's almost impossible for a teacher to be dismissed.

> 'Teachers come into school, teach, and then go home. Their responsibility to the student is the giving of information as stated in the yearly *programme*, making sure that they complete the *programme* and checking that the student has retained it. That's all. I was appalled by the lack of pastoral care and guidance expected of me.'
>
> Janet McNicol (British expatriate)

The following aspects of French education may surprise you:

- In theory, children must attend their nearest school (unless having private education) but in practice there are various ways of getting your child into another school, e.g. showing that it's more convenient for you.

- Schoolchildren start in the 11th grade (at the age of six) and end not in the first but in *terminale* (at around 18), though early years are normally referred to by an acronym, e.g. *CP, CE1, CE2, CM1* and *CM2*.

- Children learn to write very differently from their British and American counterparts; not only is the number 7 crossed and the number 1 written with a 'tail', but other figures and letters are written in a more florid style, quite different from printed letters, which can make French handwriting difficult to read

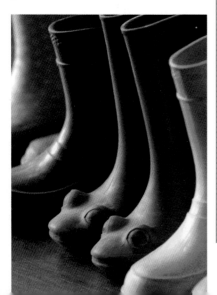

– and, for French people, foreign handwriting incomprehensible.

- Schools organise few extra-curricular activities, such as drama or inter-school sports – some 60 per cent of pupils have no access to a sports ground or gymnasium.

> 'The curriculum allows very little, if any, time for music or art, and children are never asked to write creatively. There is no disputing, however, the solid grounding they have in the "three Rs".'

- There's little streaming in schools and most classes are of mixed ability.

- Although schools readily accept non-French-speakers, most offer them little support – the onus is on students to learn French as quickly as possible.

- Language learning (both French and foreign languages) is grammatical – students learn the names of all grammatical terms and are expected to take dictation.

- Schoolchildren learn philosophy.

- Schools make little use of computers and all homework must be handwritten – on squared paper; calculators aren't used until secondary school (age 11).

- A comma is used to separate whole numbers from decimals and a full stop (period) used to denote thousands, e.g. 10,123 means 'ten point one two three', not 'ten thousand one hundred and twenty-three'.

- Children learn to sing in primary school, read music (*solfège*), and to play the recorder and other instruments in secondary school.

- Few French teachers speak good English – except English teachers, of course.

- Pupils' marks are combined into an average (*moyenne*), which is all-important.

> 'Right from primary school, children and parents are encouraged to buy cahiers de vacances. These are small books full of exercises based on the last yearly programme in each subject, which are used either to catch up on what hasn't been understood or to revise and prepare for the following year's programme.'
>
> Janet McNicol (British expatriate)

- At the end of *3ème* (age 14-15), pupils must sit a national exam called the *brevet*, which tests them in maths, French and history/geography.

- Pupils can be required to repeat a school year (*redoubler*) – usually *6ème* – if they haven't reached the required standard. This means that they spend the rest of their schooldays with children younger than themselves, although this practice is nowadays discouraged and parents must be in agreement.

- State schools don't have uniforms, although some private schools do.

- There's no 'prefect' system in France and discipline can be badly lacking – particularly in inner-city schools.

- Although state education is free, parents must buy pens, stationery and sports equipment, as well as some books (**all** books at a *lycée*).

- Shortly before the beginning of each school year, parents are issued with a list of items required for *la rentrée*, which can run to three A4 pages, causing a crush in the supermarkets.

- Schools provide elaborate lunches (even for three-year-olds), whose menus are posted outside so that parents can consult them.

- Most children have no school on Wednesdays – when there may be sporting activities instead –

The four-day school week dates back to the separation of church and state in 1905, after which parents were expected to arrange religious instruction for their children on Wednesdays.

but some have Saturday morning school (though some have shorter holidays in order to avoid Saturday classes); this means that working parents must find child-minding facilities on Wednesdays – but many *crèches* are closed on that day – and that children have an excess of homework on Monday and Thursday nights (for the following day).

- Age groups for sports activities are given names – such as *senior*, *junior*, *cadet*, *minime*, *benjamin*, *poussin* ('chick'), *mini-poussin* and *ultra-poussin*. The amount of sport in the curriculum diminishes with age – at a *lycée*, children may do no more than two hours of physical activity a week.

- School holidays are among the longest in the world; summer holidays last between 10 and 12 weeks.

- Not all schoolchildren have the same holidays; those in winter (usually February) and spring (usually April) are staggered across the country to avoid overcrowding in ski resorts.

- At the end of each term there's a *conseil de classe* – a meeting of teachers and parents' and pupils' representatives – at which each class and each pupil are assessed.

- A free school bus system operates in most rural areas, so it's unusual for parents to drive their children to and from school.

- Children aren't permitted to wear any sign of religious affiliation to school, e.g. crosses or (Muslim) headscarves.

- Homework isn't common in primary schools but is onerous at secondary level, pupils having at least two hours' homework each day.

> 'It is supposed to be possible to obtain permission from the Mayor to have your children attend school in a neighouring town. However, towns are granted money to run the schools based on the number of students they serve, and no Mayor wants to surrender precious state funds to another town.'
>
> Beverly Laflamme (American expatriate)

- There are few boarding schools in France.

- Children are expected to bring home a lot of books each evening and few schools provide adequate lockers.

## University

- There's no university entrance exam other than the *baccalauréat*, with the result that universities are overcrowded, under-funded and of a generally poor standard. In contrast, the ludicrously competitive *grandes écoles*, which produce 90 per cent of France's 'top' people, are possibly the world's most elite learning institutions.

- A high proportion of university students drop out before they've completed their courses.

- Young people with high aspirations attempt to get into one of the *grandes écoles* or *écoles supérieures*, but competition is fierce.

- Degree courses last at least four years.

- A high number of students take longer than the specified course length to finish their degree, e.g. six years instead of four, and the average university leaving age is 29.

- Grants are available only to those on low incomes and there are no loans 'designed' for students.

- Most students go to a university in or near their home town and live at home during their studies.

- Even at university, there are few extra-curricular activities (other than the pursuit of love) and no 'unions' or even student bars.

## COUNCIL SERVICES

### Refuse Collection

Refuse collection arrangements are made locally and therefore vary widely, but services are usually efficient, and even in rural areas

> 'American students see university as a privilege, French students see it as a right. Students pay practically nothing to go to university, so they don't appreciate how lucky they are.'
>
> Ann Koepke (American expatriate)

---

**Home Collections**

Many communes arrange an occasional (e.g. quarterly) collection of encombrants, i.e. objects you want to get rid of but cannot (or cannot be bothered to) take to the tip — such as old washing machines, refrigerators and armchairs. Certain items won't be collected, however, including old cars and motorbikes (or their parts) and hazardous material.

---

there may be three collections a week: two for waste and one for recyclable material (see below). Collection times also vary.

In some areas, every house or apartment block is given a wheelie bin, while in others black plastic bags are simply left by the side of the road. Refuse collectors (*éboueurs*) take domestic rubbish only and anything else (e.g. furniture or rubble) is left behind.

Non-collectable and non-recyclable rubbish can be disposed of free of charge at a tip (*déchetterie*), which are found in all but the smallest communes and clearly signposted. However, you may use only your local tip and must obtain a permit from your town hall or *mairie*. Check the opening times,

### Recycling

France has recently introduced various recycling (*recyclage*) measures and facilities, although not all French people 'bother' to make use of them. As with rubbish disposal, arrangements vary from town to town, but in many areas there are weekly collections of recyclable material, which must be left out in the containers supplied, e.g. yellow bags.

Not all recyclables are collected, however, and some such as glass, books and magazines must be taken to recycling points (*éco-point*), which are plentiful, and usually include blue bins (for paper, including newspapers, magazines and cardboard) and green bins (for glass).

Out-of-date or unwanted medicines should be taken to a chemist.

## UTILITIES

Arrangements for the connection and supply of power and other services aren't always straightforward. Here's a summary of the main points to look out for.

### Electricity

The domestic electricity supply market hasn't yet been liberalised, so you have no choice but to sign up with the state-owned monopoly Electricité de France (EDF). You do, however, have a choice of the supply (depending on your consumption) and charging system, so it's worth going to an EDF office and discussing your requirements with an adviser, which can save you a lot of money.

### Supply Problems

Power cuts are frequent in many areas of France, where power lines run overhead, although EDF is in the process of burying cables throughout the country. If your commune still has overhead cables, expect 'micro-cuts' (*micro-coupures*) whenever there's strong wind, as well as cuts of several hours (or days) when a tree falls on a line. If you live in an area where cuts are frequent and rely on electricity for your livelihood, e.g. for operating a computer, you may need to install a back-up generator (*groupe électrogène*).

Power surges occur occasionally and you may wish to install a power surge protector for appliances such as TVs, computers and fax machines, without which you risk having equipment damaged or destroyed. Electricity companies pay compensation for power surge damage, but it's up to you to claim (and prove) it – and you still suffer the inconvenience of having equipment repaired or replaced.

If the power keeps tripping off when you attempt to use a number of high-power appliances simultaneously, e.g. an electric kettle and a heater, it means that the power rating (*puissance*) of your property is too low and needs upgrading. This is a common problem in old houses.

## Gas

Mains gas (*gaz de ville*) is available only in some 80 cities and large towns and, as with electricity, there's only one supplier nationwide: Gaz de France (which is part of Electricité de France). In rural areas, bottled gas is commonly used – 1,100kg tanks for heating and small bottles for cooking.

> A stère is 1m3 of stacked wood, including the spaces between the logs, which normally account for between 20 and 40 per cent of the volume, depending on the size of the logs and how neatly they've been stacked. In any case, a measuring tape is never used to calculate quantity, and piles of wood are 'measured' by eye.

> There are several makes of gas bottle, e.g. Antargaz, Butagas, Primagaz and Totalgaz, each a different colour, and the supplier of one make won't accept an empty bottle of another make. Check before you unload your 35kg bottle.

## Wood

Almost a quarter of France is covered by forest (and the area is increasing), and some 7m homes rely solely on wood-burning stoves (*chauffage au bois*) for heating and hot water, particularly in rural areas, and millions more homes have wood fires for effect.

Wood for fuel is measured in *stères* (see box) and costs between around €20 and €40 per *stère* depending on the quality (e.g. oak is more expensive than poplar).

## Water

Water is supplied by a variety of private companies but the infrastructure is owned and managed by communes, so in fact you have no choice of supplier and prices vary widely across the country.

Most properties are metered, so you pay for what you use, but the price per cubic metre depends on whether you're connected to mains drainage or have a septic tank (see **Sewerage** below) – the former costing around four times as much as the latter.

There are rarely water shortages, although recent 'droughts' have led to water restrictions in certain areas, particularly in the south.

### Quality

Mains water is supposedly safe to drink throughout France, although it contains fluoride and other chemicals and can taste awful. Many people prefer to drink bottled water, though it's recommended that you change brands regularly, as each contains a concentration of certain minerals.

## Sewerage

Urban properties are usually connected to mains drainage (*tout à l'égout*), whereas most rural properties have a septic tank (*fosse septique*), which should be emptied every four years or so – though not completely, in order not to destroy the bacteria that enable the tank to function. You shouldn't use flush bleach and other strong cleaning products or antibiotics down the sink, as these can have a detrimental effect; it's possible to buy various products that supposedly improve the efficiency of a tank (a dead rat is

the traditional ingredient) and reduce unpleasant smells.

## Telephone

Telephone services are generally good and most of the country is served by landlines and/or mobile phones, with broadband (*haut-débit*) due to be available nationwide by the end of 2007.

France Télécom is currently the only company that can install a telephone line, which takes a few days in urban areas but up to a month (sometimes more) in rural areas, and costs around €110.

> A favourite topic of conversation among the French is the workings (or non-workings) of their *fosse septique* – they can go into detailed descriptions of how it became blocked and/or overflowed and the consequences – often over dinner.

There are currently around 20 telephone service providers and the choice of 'call plans' is mind-boggling.

All French telephone numbers have ten digits and you must dial all ten, even when phoning your next-door neighbour. Numbers beginning 06 are mobile numbers; those beginning 08 could be free or expensive.

There's no longer a single number for directory enquiries (the service has been privatised), and you must choose your 'provider' and usually endure a barrage of advertising before you're given the number you want. It's quicker and cheaper to use the internet.

> 'Watch French TV, even if you don't understand it at first. Not only will it help you to learn the language, it will give you invaluable insights into the French psyche.'
>
> Bruce Epstein (American expatriate)

## STAYING INFORMED

Even if your knowledge of French is good enough to understand the French media, you may occasionally (or often) hanker after some TV, radio or press in your own language. The good news is that this is relatively easy to obtain in France, particularly for English speakers.

### Television

French TV isn't renowned for its quality, although it's generally no worse than what's on offer in other countries. Programmes generally consist of the ubiquitous game shows, chat shows (which really are chat shows – everyone talking at once), gossip shows and 'reality' shows, with the addition of soaps (French and dubbed imports) sports coverage and the occasional documentary. Most foreign films are dubbed into French and most channels carry advertising.

There are plenty of bums and boobs on French TV and while adult (over 18) films, including soft porn, are shown only after 10pm, films unsuitable for young children are often on in the afternoon. If you have young children, watch TV with them and have the remote control **very** close by – or put on a dedicated satellite channel such as Tiji.

There are no English-language channels broadcasting in France so for programmes in English your only option is videos/DVDs or satellite TV – many parts of France can receive over 200 satellite stations (e.g. Sky) broadcasting in a variety of languages. Before paying for a satellite dish, however, check whether you need permission from your landlord, community (if you live in an apartment block) or council; some have strict regulations regarding the size and location of dishes.

### Radio

The French aren't particularly keen radio listeners (they'd rather be talking) but the quality of radio programmes is generally high. The main national stations are:

● **Classique** – Classical music (with advertising);

- **France-Bleu** – Light and 'easy-listening' music with regional features and interviews;

- **France-Culture** – Highbrow (some would say pretentious) discussions and interviews on the arts;

- **France-Info** – All news;

- **France-Inter** – News, current events, discussions, light music and plays, with bulletins in English during the summer;

- **France-Musiques** – Mainly classical music (without advertising) but also jazz and 'world' music as well as other cultural programmes.

There are umpteen regional and local stations, especially in the Paris area, but English-language stations are limited to the Côte d'Azur, the south-west and the *département* of Lot. The BBC World Service is broadcast on short wave on several frequencies simultaneously, and you can usually receive a good signal on one of them. The Astra satellite (Sky) also receives the BBC World Service. If you have cable or digital TV you should be able to receive foreign-language radio stations.

## Newspapers

The French aren't great newspaper readers, and would rather read about regional and local news than national or international news. In fact, there are no truly national papers, and the biggest-selling daily is *Ouest-France*, published in Rennes in Brittany. There's no popular tabloid or 'gutter' press, as dumbing down is anathema to the French, who also have little interest in the goings-on of 'celebrities'; there are, however, a couple of weekly 'scandal' sheets and two weekly satirical papers, including the (in)famous *Canard enchaîné* ('chained duck'). Most newspapers cost over €1.

France's main newspapers are:

- *Le Monde* – published in Paris with the following day's date and the most widely read; editorial is centre-left and intellectual.

- *Le Figaro* – more conservative but not extreme right-wing;

- *Libération* (known as *Libé* – the French love to abbreviate) – co-founded by Jean-Paul Sartre, and once fashionably left-wing. Now unfashionably left-wing.

- *L'Humanité* (known as *l'Huma*) – official organ of the French Communist party;

- *L'Equipe* – devoted to sport.

There are countless local papers, some covering just a few square kilometres, and free newspapers are widely distributed.

Many foreign newspapers are available in the main cities by the afternoon of the publication date or the following morning, and two English-language papers containing French news are published in France: *The Connexion* and *French News* (see **Appendix B**) – both monthly. *Le Monde diplomatique* is a monthly English-language supplement to *Le Monde*.

## BANKING

Banking in France, like many things French, is a baffling mixture of the ultra-modern and the antiquated. Online banking is widely available, but most banks charge you to use a service that saves them man-hours and facilities. New cheque books are issued automatically, but you're expected to collect them from your branch and must ask for them to be posted to you.

The following are some of the main characteristics of French banking.

- **Bank charges** – If you want an overdraft (*découvert*) facility, you must normally pay a monthly 'service' charge of around €5, and there may be a charge to bank online (part of the French antipathy towards faceless communication). Most banks charge around €30 for you to have a bank card (*carte bleue*); otherwise day-to-day banking is free.

- **Bank managers** – French bank managers are generally personable and approachable – many know most of their clients by name and personally monitor their accounts. On the other hand, they have limited authority and must refer to regional or national offices for major decisions such as granting mortgages.

- **Cash** – At many banks, cashiers don't handle cash (except small amounts) and you must deposit and withdraw cash using a machine.

- **Cash machines** – Instructions are usually available in English and other languages. If you make a cash withdrawal from a machine that doesn't belong to your bank there's usually a charge.

- **Cheques** – There are no cheque guarantee cards in France, where cheques include your address. Once a cheque has been sent, there's no way of 'stopping' it unless it's lost or stolen. If you

> Most banks have double entrance doors; you must wait for the outer one to close before you can open the inner one (or vice versa if you're leaving).

don't have sufficient funds in your account to cover a cheque, you can get into big trouble. Many retailers have cheque-printing machines, so all you have to do is sign (after checking the amount). When you pay a cheque into your bank, you **must** sign it on the back; no one has any idea why.

- **Credit cards** – Credit cards (*cartes de crédit*) are an unfamiliar concept to the French, where most bank cards are debit cards. Foreign credit cards with a magnetic strip – and often 'chip and PIN' cards – cause consternation and distress – to you as well as the French.

- **Deposits** – When depositing cash with a cashier, you may have to ask for a receipt.

- **Opening hours** – Bank opening hours in towns are generally Tuesdays to Saturdays 9 or 9.30am to 5.30 or 5.45pm, with a lunchtime closure between 12 or 12.30 and 1.30 or 2. Village banks may open for only a few hours a week.

## TAXES

As you would expect in a country with millions of bureaucrats, the French tax system is inordinately complicated and most French people don't understand it. However, it's essential to be aware of which taxes you should pay and when. Before you move to France, take expert advice, preferably from someone with knowledge of the tax systems in France and your home country, so that you can benefit from the advantages of tax planning. Once in France, it's best to employ an accountant (*expert-comptable*) to handle your tax matters, especially if you're self-employed.

Although French income tax isn't particularly onerous, social security contributions are; the two together can amount to half your income if you're self-employed or running a business.

The French tax year is the calendar year, and tax payments are usually made in arrears. France has no PAYE income tax system (where tax is deducted at source), and the onus is on the taxpayer (i.e. you) to file a tax return and make payments

- **value added tax** (*taxe sur la valeur ajoutée/IVA*) – automatically added to most transactions;
- **wealth tax** (*impôt sur la fortune*) – payable by ... wealthy people.

> The French tax authorities offer a 'reward' to anyone who denounces a tax dodger; make sure you avoid paying more tax than you need to but don't evade taxes.

on time, although it's possible to set up a direct debit (*prélèvement automatique*).

The main taxes in France are as follows:

- **capital gains tax** (*impôt sur les plus-values*) – payable on the sale of a second home under certain circumstances;
- **income tax** (*impôts sur le revenu*) – payable by all wage earners except those on very low incomes and those with **lots** of children;
- **inheritance & gift tax** (*droits de succession* and *de donation*) – to penalise you for giving to those you love;
- **property tax** (*taxe foncière*) – payable by all homeowners at widely varying rates across the country (oddly, the lowest rates are in Paris);
- **residential tax** (*taxe d'habitation*) – payable by whoever is occupying a property on 1st January;

# 4.

# BREAKING THE ICE

One of the best ways of getting over culture shock and feeling part of life in France, is meeting and getting acquainted with French people. Making new friends anywhere is never easy, and the language and cultural barriers in France make it even harder. This chapter offers information on important aspects of French society and the expatriate community, and advice on how to behave in social situations, topics to steer clear of in conversation, and dealing with confrontation.

> 'To understand French attitudes to sex, it is first necessary to understand that considerations of love and marriage are completely irrelevant where sex is concerned.'
>
> Donald Carroll, *Surprised by France*

## SEXUAL ATTITUDES

France seems to be a progressive and modern country with liberal attitudes to sex and partnerships. For example, same-sex couples can enter into a *pacte de civile de solidarité* (*PACS*), which gives them most of the same rights as married couples; politicians' and celebrities' extra-marital affairs aren't the subject of newspaper headlines and cause for public enquiry. When extracts from Jacques Chirac's biography, *Stranger in the Elysée*, were published in a weekly newspaper, the French were more interested in the revelation of his love of Chinese art than in that of his extramarital affairs. Ex-president François Mitterrand went as far as to have two households (at taxpayers' expense) and two families; when asked about this unusual situation,

he famously replied: '*Et alors ?*' (So what?).

The age of consent is 15, although it's likely to be raised in the near future. Prostitution is legal – there are an estimated 15,000-20,000 prostitutes in France – although solicitation and procuring aren't. The country has liberal laws on the sale of pornography (to anyone aged 18 or over), although extreme and violent forms of pornography are illegal. Nudity isn't regarded as something shameful or 'naughty' but simply part of life, and naked bodies – both male and female – regularly appear on television, in advertising and in 'family' magazines and even stage shows. Although films are graded by censors, ratings rarely take much account of nudity.

Scratch the surface, however, and a strongly traditional society emerges in which men and women have clearly defined roles. This is particularly true in small towns and rural areas, where time-honoured Catholic values remain firmly in place. In your encounters with French people of both sexes you can expect to experience both traditional and progressive attitudes – sometimes in the same person.

The French belief in *égalité* may extend to the legal and social status of men and women, but it stops short of psychological and behavioural equality, as the whole point of there being men and women is that they should be as different as possible, as difference creates interest in life; sameness is tedious.

> Personal grooming, such as applying make-up and combing hair, is expected to be done at home and not in public, although many French people do so while driving – often dangerously. Nevertheless, many French men and women have poor hygiene and body odour is common.

## Men

French men generally see themselves – and are seen by most French women (see below) – as head of the family, breadwinner and hero. Mediterranean *machismo* is an element of their make-up – increasingly so the further south you go. Their traditional role – working, looking after (or hunting) animals, and building and maintaining the home – is still very much the norm, and few French men shop, cook,

clean or look after the children, although this is slowly changing. The exclusive preserve of men in the home is the wine cellar, and they will buy, serve and usually drink all the family's wine (surprisingly few French women drink alcohol and even fewer drink wine).

The corollary to this is that French men prefer women who are submissive, who don't challenge their authority or wisdom, and who are happy to look pretty and do 'women's things'. There are, of course, exceptions, but in general French men aren't attracted to foreign women – particularly northern Europeans and Americans. The opposite is also true: British and American women tend to find French men overbearing, arrogant and boring.

What of the Frenchman's reputation as a great romantic? Sadly, this is largely a myth (propagated by French men, of course), and most French men's idea of romanticism is in fact a blueprint for seduction; though many foreign women mistake their tactics for genuine emotion. As we've seen, in France the heart is ruled by the head – and women are ruled by men. In particular, French men like 'their' women (i.e. wives, partners and girlfriends) to look good, and put pressure on them to keep their figures and dress appealingly – which often results in mutton-dressed-as-lamb grotesquery, with parts of the body inadvisably exposed.

Sexual harassment is common (although it often isn't regarded as harassment by French women – see below), and married men will often fondle their wives or even engage in mock intercourse in front of others, with the implication that their sexual powers are at their peak. Crude jokes full of sexual innuendo (or even outright vulgarity) are the order of the day, even in mixed company – children notwithstanding. It's as well to take such behaviour in good humour – as do most French women.

## Women

Surprisingly, most French women are happy to accept their traditional role of housewife and sex object – even career women often exploit their sex appeal to get ahead. Women's bodies (usually naked or semi-naked) are used to sell

> 'Do not make the first move. Some Frenchmen will interpret "Would you like to go out for a drink some time?" as "Do you want to get married and have six children?" The maiden-in-distress act works especially well.'
>
> Sonia Blaney (British expatriate)

everything from cars to garden hoses and few advertisements are defaced by feminist objectors.

French women have always been 'behind' their European counterparts when it comes to civil rights: not only did they not get the vote until 1944, but until 1923 they had to have their husbands' permission to open letters addressed to them, ask their approval to have their own passport (until 1938), and until 1968 required their authorisation to open a bank account.

Without being obsessive about their weight or size, French women

> 'If you should happen to imagine that the first pretty French girl who smiles at you intends to dance the can-can or take you to bed, you will risk stirring up a lot of trouble for yourself – and for our relations with the French.'
>
> Instructions for British Servicemen in 1944

In one of their few manifestations of rebelliousness, French women will openly discuss their sexuality, and have few qualms about showing a man they're attracted to him – which won't necessarily indicate that they have marriage on their minds – or even in revealing to their partners that they're attracted to another man. Flirting is often quite open but may be nothing more than an 'innocent' game. Or it may not.

are generally careful about what they eat and drink – mindful perhaps of their partners' wishes in this respect (see above) – and like to dress to advantage.

Outside the cities, French women rarely go out together without being accompanied by men, as this is seen as provocative – two or more women alone in a bar or cafe will generally be assumed to be 'on the pick-up'.

In the home, it's invariably the woman who shops and cooks and cleans, as well as taking care of social engagements – no good asking most French men whether they're free for dinner on a particular date.

French women aren't generally talkative and are happy to let men do the talking – even if they're saying things the women disagree with or object to. They may have strong opinions but will rarely voice them – at least in 'public'. On the other hand, they can be bossy, particularly towards their partners.

## Homosexuals

The years between 1945 and 1960 saw a decrease, rather than an increase, in tolerance of homosexuals in France, the latter year seeing the denouncement of homosexuality as a 'public scourge'; not until 1982 was the age of consent for homosexual sex reduced from 18 to 15, the same as for heterosexual sex. Legally, homosexual couples remained disadvantaged until the introduction, in 1999, of the *PACS* (see above), though they still cannot marry. Although attitudes have generally moved in the same direction as legislation, as recently as 1997 (according to a poll conducted by *Le Nouvel Observateur*) 23 per cent of French people believed homosexuality to be 'a disease to be cured' and a further 17 per cent 'a sexual perversion to be fought against'.

Homosexuals (*homosexuels* or *gais*) still have a fair way to go before being accepted as 'normal' in French society – particularly in rural areas – and it's common for French men to make jokes about gays (using the derogatory abbreviation *homos* or the insulting *pédé* – short for *pédéraste*) to demonstrate their 'normality'.

> The current Mayor of Paris, Bertrand Delanoë, who was elected in 2001, is openly gay.

The homosexual scene isn't restricted to 'gay Paree' – where the Marais neighbourhood has recently become the city's unofficial gay centre, but there are gay-oriented associations and activities in most *arrondissements*, often including 'straight' people. Other cities also have thriving gay communities – especially Annecy, Avignon, Biarritz, Grenoble, Montpellier, Nantes, Nice, Toulouse – and various resorts have 'gay-designated' beaches, including l'Espiguette (near Montpellier), Hossegor (near Biarritz), Saint-Tropez and Les Vaches Noires (near Caen in Normandy).

## MEETING PEOPLE

Many expats complain that it's difficult to establish friendships with French people, particularly Americans and Britons, who are used to establishing 'friendships' quickly and are often frustrated by the social hoops that must be negotiated before a French person will accept them as a friend. However, patience is rewarded and once you've befriended French people they will do almost anything for you and expect nothing in return – though, of course, if you're a friend you will treat them the same way.

Apart from the obvious language barrier, there are cultural obstacles to be overcome. The French are private people and guard their privacy. Their houses are often obscured from view by high walls, gates and hedges, and many old houses have their backs or their ends to the road. This makes it doubly difficult to meet and get to know your neighbours. But, like all people, the French are also curious and will want to know who you are, where you've come from and what you're like – foreigners are the object of intense curiosity, especially in rural areas where they're few and far between.

However, the onus is on you to take the initiative, as few French people will make an effort if you don't – and this is easier said

> 'The daily schedule of an average French family doesn't leave much room to meet other people, and the little time that is left is often spent within the family.'
>
> Peter Nowottnick (German expatriate)

than done, particularly if you're introverted or unused to making the first move. Meeting other expats is often easier and friendships may develop more naturally. Nevertheless, going out to meet local people is the first step to enjoying your time in France and lessening the effects of alienation and culture shock.

This means going to local functions, using local shops, visiting the town hall or *mairie* regularly and generally being 'out and about' in order to maximise your chance of bumping into neighbours. It also gives you the opportunity to practise your French and start adapting to French culture – receiving a greeting from *Monsieur le Maire* or the baker makes you feel you've 'arrived'.

There are various other ways of meeting French people and other expats, including the following:

● **At work** – Meeting people isn't a problem if you're an employee, and among your colleagues may be several potential friends. You may have to take the initiative, however. By all means ask others to join you for lunch or coffee, but don't expect regular Friday evening drinks as is common in some countries. Office parties aren't common either, although many companies organise Christmas lunches and get-togethers for employees leaving their jobs. Social arrangements can be vague – someone may suggest going out on a Saturday night but make no specific arrangements. Foreigners are often disappointed or offended when nothing materialises, but this is normal and part of French people's laid-back attitude.

● **Expatriate networks** – There are expats in most parts of France, even if expat enclaves are limited to parts of Brittany, Dordogne and the south. One way of finding them is to contact local English-language schools, which normally employ native speakers. Bear in mind, however, that not all expats want to associate with other expats, even of their own nationality, and you shouldn't expect them to go out of their way to be friendly just because you've arrived in the area.

- **Language lessons** – These provide an ideal environment to meet other foreigners and, possibly, French people learning English. Language schools and teachers usually organise regular social events. Setting up a language exchange (whereby you teach English to someone who teaches you French) often leads to new friends.

- **Local clubs** – Find out about clubs and societies in your area. Town halls and local newspapers are good sources of information, and there may be a 'club day' (usually in September) when representatives of each club set up a stand where you can find out information and become a member. If you play a sport, consider joining the local club – tennis leagues and golf competitions (not to mention the club house) are ideal for meeting people and keeping fit at the same time.

- **School or childcare facilities** – These provide plentiful opportunities for contact with other parents, especially when collecting children. Look on the school notice board for news about forthcoming events and meetings. Most schools have a parents' committee (*comité des parents*), which is worth joining and always welcomes offers of help.

## INVITATIONS

On a first encounter, limit yourself to a '*Bonjour, Madame/Monsieur*' and, if the occasion permits, perhaps a comment about the weather (a topic of equal fascination among the French as among the British). Once you've seen the same person two or three times, you can introduce yourself, although it's polite to wait until you're told a person's name rather than to ask it; but it may not

> 'Many French people think they are open-minded but even though they might encourage you to talk about yourself and about your experiences in France, they won't perceive you in a positive way if you are very different from them. Just give the impression of being almost like them, with some slight differences. This will make them feel comfortable and pleased, as you have enriched them with some exotic flavour while leaving them to their quiet life.'
>
> Dung Rahuel (Vietnamese expatriate)

be until the fourth or fifth occasion that it will feel right for you to invite him (and his spouse or partner or children, as appropriate) round for aperitifs – or, of course, you may be invited yourself.

## Making Invitations

Inviting French people to your home for aperitifs (*inviter à prendre l'apéritif* – always in the singular) is usually the best way to start a friendship; lunch or dinner invitations shouldn't be made until later in the relationship.

### *Aperitifs*

Inviting people for aperitifs (often abbreviated to *l'apéro*) is usually similar to offering aperitifs before a meal (see below). Although it's an informal affair, certain conventions apply, as follows:

- Pre-lunch aperitifs generally start between 11am and 12 noon; pre-dinner aperitifs at around 6 to 7pm, but don't fix an exact time (e.g. 6.20) or expect guests to be punctual.

- Don't offer anyone a drink until all the guests have arrived (or have confirmed that they aren't coming).

- Drinks that may be offered include white wine, fortified wine (including port), whisky (a favourite with the French), rum, *pastis* and soft drinks. It isn't usual to offer cognac, armagnac or calvados (which are generally served after a meal) or red wine. A favourite aperitif is *kir*, which consists of white wine with a *fond* (literally 'base') of fruit liqueur – usually blackcurrant (*cassis*), but it's usual to offer a choice, e.g. *framboise* (raspberry), *mûre* (blackberry) and *pêche* (peach); a *kir royal* is made with sparkling wine and a *kir normand* with cider.

> If you decide to offer sparkling wine, make sure it's champagne; anything less will indicate that you don't value your guests highly. If you can get hold of a champagne that isn't available in supermarkets (either by mail-order or by going to the region and buying direct from the producer), you'll impress more than if you spend a fortune on a famous brand.

- Drinks should be accompanied by 'nibbles' (*amuse-bouche* or, less politely, *amuse-gueule*) such as nuts, crisps and olives.

If you want your guests to stay longer than an hour or two, but don't feel up to offering them a formal meal, you can invite them to an *apéritif dînatoire* – which, as the name suggests, is a cross between aperitifs and dinner. In this case, you'll need to provide some more substantial fare, such as canapés, rolls of cream cheese and smoked salmon, mini-sausages, and blinis spread with pâté or fish eggs – enough to ensure that your guests don't need to eat when they get home.

In any case, it's wise to have 'back-up' food available, as aperitifs can often become *dînatoire*. If this happens, you should be flattered, as it means your guests are enjoying your company.

### Lunch & Dinner

When you've got to know people a little, you can invite them for lunch or dinner, although dinner is more usual. Sunday lunch is a family occasion in France and during the week most people are at work and/or prefer to eat at home.

As with aperitifs, set an approximate arrival time, but expect guests to arrive up to half an hour late. Don't welcome them with a drink, but wait until all guests have arrived, even if some are very late. Even then, it's common for friends to stand around talking for a good while before worrying about eating or drinking. After all, the purpose of the occasion is to converse and enjoy one another's company – not merely to 'fill up' with food and drink.

Expect to be offered gifts. If these are flowers or plants, put them on display immediately rather than hiding them away in a back room. If you're offered wine, write the name of the person who gave it to you on the label and set it aside for drinking on a suitable occasion – to his or her health.

Aperitifs should be as detailed above, but obviously not so copious as to leave everyone with no room for the meal itself. It's common for everyone to have two or three drinks, over which they take up to an hour and a half, before being ushered to the table.

You should seat everyone, preferably alternating men and women. It's advisable to work this out in advance, and you can even write a name by each place setting, though make sure you spell them correctly; no one will sit down until you do, so don't disappear immediately to the kitchen, leaving your guests stranded.

### Courses

French meals follow an almost invariable pattern: a starter, a main course, cheese, dessert and coffee. The starter should be light, and the main course focus on the meat dish, with only a 'decoration' of vegetables.

> Most French people will expect meat, and even fish is seldom served. If you're vegetarian, you should warn your guests when you invite them.

The cheese course, which always precedes dessert, should consist of three or four contrasting cheeses, and should be the only course that isn't home made, unless you're serving an elaborate dessert bought from a *pâtisserie* (not the supermarket). A green salad – with a French dressing, of course – may be served before or with the cheese course. It's quite usual to offer two or even three desserts for guests to choose from – many will have some of each. Don't assume that your guests will want cream or ice cream with their dessert but ask.

Since homemade French cooking is usually excellent, your guests may have high expectations of your cuisine. If you aren't a great cook, it's acceptable to have food supplied by a professional caterer (*traiteur*), especially if it's something elaborate such as a seafood platter, although this is an expensive option and you may be thought to be showing off.

Avoid spicy recipes and unusual dishes, as the French have delicate palates and conservative tastes – they generally won't appreciate, for example, typical British fare such as steak and kidney pie and spotted dick.

It's usual for the same knives and forks to be used throughout a meal, rather than clean ones for each course, but you should have some spare cutlery in case guests give theirs up with their empty plates. You should clear away the salt and pepper before serving cheese.

### *Drink*

Wine and water are usually the only possible drinks to accompany a meal, although cider may be appropriate with, say, *galettes* and *crêpes* in Brittany or Normandy. You should offer both white and red wine (rosé is usually drunk only outdoors in summer, though a strong rosé such as a Tavel may be offered at other times), although most French people prefer red and will drink it even with fish dishes and salads. If you know your wine, you can serve a different one with each course (the French often drink sweet wine with *foie gras*, for example), but don't prevent anyone from drinking red

> Getting drunk, or even tipsy, in France is considered the height of disrespect – for yourself as well as your guests or hosts – so make sure you always remain in control.

when you'd planned white, or vice versa.

Avoid serving non-French wines, however good you think they are, as few French people will accept that anything is as good as their own wine. Generally, the French prefer Bordeaux to Burgundy (or other) wines, but this very much depends on the region. The important thing is that you've thought about the wine and prepared it well in advance of the meal, and not merely grabbed a few bottles off the supermarket shelf a few hours beforehand. Don't worry too much about the temperature of wine, as the French commonly drink both white and red wine at around 18C. It isn't usual to have even a 'wine cooler' on the table, let alone an ice bucket.

Bottled water should be in constant supply, but there's no need to provide water glasses, as most French people will use their wine glass also for water. Your guests won't serve themselves with wine – some not even with water – so it's up to you to keep an eye out for empty glasses and offer a refill.

Coffee should be 'real' and not instant, and be served strong and black, though with milk and sugar on the table. You can offer herbal tea (*tisane*), as a number of French people prefer this to coffee, but not 'ordinary' tea (and certainly not British-style tea). A constant supply of sliced (French) bread should be available from first course to cheese, though you don't need to offer butter, even with cheese.

## Receiving Invitations

The French are generally house proud and you should consider it a privilege to be invited to a French person's home – even more so to a social occasion such as a wedding, which is usually reserved for family and close friends only.

> 'As often as not, friends in English-speaking countries are little more than upgraded business associates, golfing partners, classmates ... In France, by contrast, friends are those select few who have earned your trust, respect, and loyalty. You're committed to each other, and you participate in each others' lives.'
>
> Donald Carroll, *Surprised by France*

Vegetarians are rare in France. If you're a vegetarian (or have any other dietary requirement), don't expect even the most well meaning hosts to cater for them. For example, many French people don't class chicken, ham or bacon pieces (*lardons*) – let alone fish – as meat.

### Dress Code

Your outfit will depend on your hosts and the occasion. For aperitifs or a meal at friends' houses, smart-casual is the order of the day – some French people will even turn up in jeans (usually 'designer' jeans) but you aren't advised to do the same. For a christening or wedding, it's usual to dress up, although a surprising number of French people don't. It's rare for men to wear a suit and tie to any function.

### Gifts

You should take your hosts a gift to thank them for their hospitality. Flowers or a plant are the most common gift and are offered to the hostess (the host will handle them like a hot brick).

It's acceptable to offer your host a bottle of (good, French) wine but don't expect him to open it for the occasion, as he will have planned the wine for the meal and will know that wine needs time to recover from a journey in the boot of a car.

The best gift is a personal one – something you know will appeal

A French person's home is a sanctum and you may never be invited to a 'friend's' house. This isn't an affront to you, but usually because they're embarrassed to let you see their home, which is either 'too small' or 'too untidy' or, most usually, 'in the middle of restoration' (which invariably continues for decades). Never press French people for an invitation to their home and don't appear unannounced on their doorstep unless you know them extremely well.

Invitations usually extend to your partner or spouse, but if your hosts aren't aware that you have a partner, it's acceptable to ask for him or her to be included. If you have children, you shouldn't bring them unless your hosts specifically invite them.

You aren't expected to arrive exactly at the appointed time (if there is one) but between around 10 and 20 minutes later. If you're going to be more than half an hour late, it's polite to let your hosts know.

to your hosts, such as an addition to their collection of ornaments (many French people collect a particular type of ornament) or a book on a subject they enjoy.

> There are many theories and supposed conventions regarding the offering of flowers – such as no chrysanthemums, no yellow flowers, always an odd rather than an even number – but more important is to offer something you know or believe your hostess will like; often the local florist will know.

### The Meal

When eventually you're offered an aperitif (see above), wait for your hosts to raise their glasses and say '*Santé*', then do likewise and clink glasses with each person in turn, taking care to look them in the eye and not to cross arms with any other clinkers (considered to bring bad luck).

At table, keep both hands visible at all times but avoid putting your elbows on the table. Use cutlery from the outside inwards, but if there's only one knife and fork expect to keep these for the whole meal rather than give them up with your empty plate after each course. (Wipe them discreetly with a piece of bread before setting them back on the table cloth.) Americans should note that it isn't done to switch your fork to your right hand in order to put food in your mouth. Don't eat any bread until the first course is served and don't clean your plate with bread. If possible, eat everything you're served.

Unless you know your hosts particularly well, stay seated while the meal is served and don't pour yourself wine or even water, but wait for it to be offered. During or after the meal, don't clear anything away or offer to help – few French people like strangers to see their kitchen.

## CONVERSATION

Although the French have a reputation for aloofness, they're among the easiest people in the world to engage in conversation (provided you speak French), as they love to talk and, even more so, to give their opinion on something – on anything. But French conversation, like most French conventions, follows a particular pattern and is to a large extent an end in itself. Its aim isn't so much the exchange of information as intellectual exercise. You must therefore be prepared to flit from subject to subject, to be interrupted and to interrupt

others, and to avoid holding forth, which will merely bore the French. Conversation may degenerate into argument, but nobody is trying to win; the interest is in the argument itself.

Nevertheless, the French are essentially private people and keep themselves very much to themselves – they tend to rely on their close family for help with personal problems and rarely mention these to 'outsiders'. As a result, even if you've worked with someone for years you'll probably know very little about his life outside the workplace. Although the French can and will talk for hours, topics of conversation with anyone other than family or close friends are usually of a neutral or general nature – with one notable exception.

> 'A bad liver is to a Frenchman what a nervous breakdown is to an American. Everyone has one and everyone wants to talk about it.'
>
> Art Buchwald (American humorist)

The one personal topic the French love to discuss is their health – or lack of it. If you ask about someone's health – and even if you don't – expect to be given chapter and verse on the symptoms, treatment and consequences of a current or recent illness, injury or ailment. It pays to mug up on medical vocabulary if you wish to converse with the French.

Unless French people offer personal information – other than about their health – it's best not to ask, as you risk offending them (see **Taboos** below). On the other hand, the French love to talk about other people (i.e. anyone not present), and will be surprisingly blunt and critical when referring to mutual friends – so you can imagine what they say about you when you aren't around. With this in mind, you might prefer not to provide too much information about your own life and you should certainly avoid bragging about anything, as this is considered in poor taste.

## Taboos

The French are generally relaxed and accommodating of foreigners' *faux pas*, but there are certain taboo subjects of conversation, which it's wise to be aware of. These include the following:

### Work & Money

To say that the French don't like to discuss work and money would be an oversimplification. A Frenchman will happily discuss his work, explaining in detail what he does, as most French people take pride in their work. He will also happily talk about money and particularly about the cost of recent or intended purchases or expenditure. What few French people will do is mention work and money in the same breath – and hardly any will tell you how much they earn. The implication is that one doesn't work for money; one works for a sense of achievement and fulfilment. Money is an almost unintended spin-off of work, which should be put to good use, i.e. exchanged for things of lasting value.

You must therefore be careful how you raise the topic of work and how you refer to money. To ask a French person what his position in a company is, for example, is unwise, as this immediately gives an indication of his salary. To ask him his line of business, on the other hand, is quite acceptable.

If in doubt, avoid both topics unless they're raised by someone else.

> '... one reason the French don't like talking about money is that it might not be in their interest for outsiders to start counting it.'
>
> Donald Carroll, *Surprised by France*

### War

The French have a poor war record, having lost far more wars than they've won – especially in the last 150 years. It's therefore prudent to avoid the subject altogether. References to the Second World War and the Algerian War of Independence in particular, are generally taboo. The Norman invasion of England in 1066 is safe territory and, if you're British, the French will invariably raise the subject of Joan of Arc (*Jeanne d'Arc*) being burned by the English (the French generally make no distinction between British and English, using the word *anglais* for both) – though this is usually tongue-in-cheek and not worth arguing over (she was in fact condemned to death by Bishop Cauchon of Beauvais).

Similarly, it's best not to start a discussion about Napoleon (except with reference to his administrative achievements) or General de Gaulle, who is unequivocally regarded as a hero.

### Religion

In spite of the fact that France is officially a secular state and that only some 60 per cent of French people claim to be practising Catholics, France is still very much a Catholic country and (Catholic) religion plays an important part in society. Many French people have been christened and had their first communion in the Catholic faith, and many have (Catholic) church weddings and baptise their children in the Catholic faith. It's therefore best to avoid expressing negative opinions or making 'jokes' about religion, the Catholic church or the Pope.

### France & French Customs

The French are fiercely proud of their country and its way of life, and generally find it hard to take criticism, particularly from foreigners. When you're with French people, avoid negative comments about France and French customs – keep these thoughts to yourself or share them only with other expats – and don't join in a conversation between French people about France unless you have something good to say.

Similarly, avoid talking about – let alone extolling – your own country's values and way of life. If asked about them, put forward a balanced view, with negative points as well as positive.

## EXPATRIATE COMMUNITY

Few parts of France are now without an immigrant population, although most foreigners are concentrated in Paris and in a few 'enclaves', such as those in parts of Brittany, Dordogne and Provence. In only a handful of towns and villages does the foreign population outnumber the locals.

If you move to an area that's popular with other people of your nationality, the lack of cultural and language barriers makes socialising much easier. Paris and some other cities have well established expat networks, and fitting into these is often straightforward. But you should beware of becoming too dependent on expatriate society, which can be unstable (expats tend to come and go) and claustrophobic, particularly in small communities where little goes on and everyone knows everything about everyone else. Try to extend your contacts further afield and make an effort to meet the locals too – getting to know French people will add variety and interest to your social life, and open new doors to you.

### Advantages

- It's easier to fit in with people of your own nationality.
- You get the chance to relax and speak your own language.
- It's a means of letting off steam after the stress of culture shock.

### Disadvantages

- Spending too much time with expats may mean you don't accept your move as definitive.
- Time spent with other expats could be spent fitting into life with the French.
- Many expatriate groups are little more than an excuse to complain about everything French – this may accentuate your own negative feelings towards France and doesn't help you settle in.
- Expat groups tend to be a varied bunch of people, perhaps not necessarily those you would mix with in your home country – you're drawn together by circumstances more than by genuine interest – and you may find yourself socialising with people you don't like much.

## CONFRONTATION

The French are generally set in their ways and don't take kindly to criticism, or even suggestions that things could be done a different way. If you disagree with them, they're more likely to simply repeat their opinion than to accept your point of view. Moreover, they love to discuss and debate – without necessarily ever reaching a conclusion, agreement or compromise. All this can be intensely frustrating for a foreigner and easily lead to confrontation, although the French generally avoid open arguments or rows.

As far as possible, it's best to remain calm and avoid confrontation – little or nothing is achieved by it and you may earn yourself the unwelcome reputation of being a difficult foreigner. If you fall out with a French person, it can be terminal; he may never say more than '*Bonjour*' to you again.

## DEALING WITH OFFICIALS

Given the bureaucratic nature of French society, you're likely to have frequent encounters with officials, who vary unpredictably from knee-jerk *non*-sayers to couldn't-do-more-for-you helpers. Whichever type you come up against, there are certain codes of behaviour appropriate to the situation (see below).

### Golden Rules for Dealing with Officials

● Dress smartly.

● Don't expect officials to smile – many have an innate ability to remain poker-faced in any situation.

● Always use the *vous* form of address, and don't forget to add *Monsieur* or *Madame* to your greetings and goodbyes.

● Never interrupt them and always state your case clearly and concisely; don't waffle.

● Never lose your temper.

### *Police*

As in other countries, the police in France aren't renowned for their intellectual acumen, diplomatic subtlety or intimate knowledge of the law. Nevertheless, it's wise to show them deference and not try to play the wise guy.

> 'Never ask a French person to deviate from a daily routine.'
>
> Ian Pickering (British expatriate)

If you're stopped by the police for any reason – they may simply wish to check your identity or vehicle documentation – be polite and use vous and Monsieur or Madame. There's little point in being obstructive or arguing, which may in fact make things worse for you. If you think you've been stopped or fined illegally, make a complaint at a police station afterwards.

### *Civil Servants*

French civil servants hold the key to many essential permissions, such as your residence (and work) permit, social security card and driving licence, and your encounters with them are likely to be frequent. In your dealings with civil servants, be as polite and calm as possible and

**always** thank them for their help. Few civil servants speak English and you shouldn't expect them to – take an interpreter if your French is poor.

As with the police (see above), don't expect civil servants to know the law – you're likely to get a subtly different 'interpretation' of it from each official you ask. The trick is to latch onto the one whose interpretation most closely matches your wishes – or the one who seems most likely to bend the rules in your favour.

# 5.
# THE LANGUAGE BARRIER

**B**eing able to communicate with French people, and knowing what to do and say when you meet them, are priorities when you move to France, especially when you first arrive. Although virtually all French people learn English from the age of 11 (and often earlier), few can speak it fluently and hardly any with confidence; they've been taught primarily to read, write and understand, and have an inbuilt fear of making mistakes and looking foolish. You therefore shouldn't expect to be able to communicate with French people in English, but should make every effort to learn French – starting if possible well before you leave home.

There are a few expat enclaves where the *lingua franca* is invariably English and you may be able to get by without a word of French, but unless you learn French, there will be a strong tendency to rely heavily on other expats for your needs. This can be costly – in more ways than one; in some areas there are unscrupulous expats who prey on their fellow countrymen, offering services they're ill-qualified to supply at inflated prices, and sometimes disappearing with the proceeds before they have completed the job.

'We had only O Level French and quickly discovered that the French didn't speak O Level French.'

Audrey & Charles Fleming
(British expatriates)

Learning to speak a foreign language is never easy and full of potential pitfalls – all expats have stories to tell of when they said 'the wrong thing', often with embarrassing consequences.

To help keep your own collection of anecdotes as small as possible, this chapter offers tips on learning French, recognising false friends, getting to grips with forms of address and greetings, and telephone and letter etiquette, and some hints on body and sign language.

## LEARNING FRENCH

Relocation and culture shock experts generally agree that one of the best ways of settling into a foreign country where your language isn't spoken is to learn the local language as soon as possible. This undoubtedly applies in France. Even a basic knowledge of a few key phrases when you arrive will help you feel more in control (or less out of control) in everyday situations. Expatriates with no language knowledge tend to feel vulnerable,

| English | French |
| --- | --- |
| coffe | le café |
| juice | le jus |
| computer | l'ordinator (m) |
| office | le bureau |

as all they can do is nod and gesture – some people also feel a strong sense of ridicule when they have no tools of verbal expression. The benefits of mastering the basics are enormous and it will do wonders to boost your self-esteem and sense of achievement when you first set foot in France.

The French alphabet has the same number of letters as English, but k and w appear only in a few borrowed words. There are also a number of accented letters, only some of which affect pronunciation – for example *de* and *dé* are pronounced differently but *du* and *dû* sound the same. To make matters worse, the French themselves generally have little idea which accents should be used where, and a shocking number of them spell the word for 'very' *trés* instead of *très*.

There are a number of regional languages and dialects in France (see below) but all French people speak 'standard' French, albeit with varying accents. (The 'best' French is said to be spoken in and around Tours.) You will therefore have no difficulty being understood if you speak text book French. On the other hand, you will discover that French people don't speak the sort of French you learnt at school, and a good deal of adjustment will be required before you understand the natives. To give just one obvious example: few French people use the word *ne* in conversation, so that what you learnt as *je ne comprends pas* will actually be said *je comprends pas* – or more likely '*shcomprends pas*'.

What's more, you shouldn't expect French people to speak slowly or clearly or to use simple words and phrases to help you understand. Most won't. This isn't out of unfriendliness or indifference to your predicament, but rather that they simply don't know how to alter their way of speaking. As far as they're concerned, French should be spoken a certain way and only certain words and phrases are 'correct' in each context; to use any others or, for example, to separate words rather than eliding them is to violate their language – an unpardonable sin.

> 'In Paris they simply stared when I spoke to them in French; I never did succeed in making those idiots understand their language.'
>
> Mark Twain (American writer)

To make matters worse, the French will correct you and even make fun of your mistakes. Their obsession with exactitude makes them almost incapable of tolerating 'abuses' of their language – even by other French people. If this happens, there's only one thing for it: grit your teeth, learn from your mistake and remind yourself that sooner or later your French will be far better than most French people's English, which will make you the object of universal admiration.

## Why French is Essential

- In an accident or emergency, knowing what to say in French could save your (or someone else's) life.

- Your chance of finding a job or making a success of being self-employed increases dramatically.

- You save time and money on translations and don't need to rely on others to help you.

- Culture shock and the sense of being a stranger in France diminish.

- Locals will appreciate your efforts and this will help you fit in more easily.

- French culture is easier to appreciate if you speak some French.

- Your circle of friends will be widened beyond other English-speaking expatriates.

- Joining a language class is an excellent way of meeting people.

French is one of the world's most widely spoken languages and some 300m people in over 50 countries speak it as a first or fluent second language. It's an official language in 41 countries, including Belgium, Canada, Haiti, Luxembourg, Monaco, Switzerland and most

> 'The French find it impossible to speak slowly, not to use contractions or idioms, and to avoid cultural references, yet when speaking English they expect you to speak slowly, not use contractions or idioms, and avoid cultural references.'
>
> Bruce Epstein (American expatriate)

North and West African countries, as well as France.

## Know Before You Go

To give yourself the best chance of hitting the ground running, start learning French well in advance of your departure – at least six months before if possible. Don't believe anyone who claims that the best way to learn a language is to go to the country and 'immerse yourself' in it. While this is a good way of improving existing knowledge, experts generally agree that this is the worst way to learn a language from scratch – not only are you under stress from the logistics of

your recent relocation, but you're also prone to picking up errors in the language, which are difficult to correct later. It's far better to gain a grounding in the basics before you leave; knowing how to ask for things and understanding something of what is being said will make settling in easier.

Make your language learning as intensive as possible. Specialist language schools are available in many large cities and the Académie Française ( www.academie-francaise.fr) has over 1,000 centres in 138 countries.

A list of words and phrases you might need during your first few days in France can be found in **Appendix D**.

> 'You have to be fluent in French to register for a French class.'
>
> Martina Nowottnick (German expatriate)

## Once in France

When you arrive in France, make sure that you commit yourself to some sort of learning method as soon as possible, preferably within the first week, rather than merely hoping that you'll 'pick it up as you go along'. There are hundreds of language schools throughout the country with French courses (*cours de français*) to suit all levels and budgets. Shop around to compare tuition fees and teaching methods, and if a course is expensive, ask whether you can have a free trial lesson before you commit yourself.

Private teachers are readily available. Advantages include individual attention and tailored learning, which should lead to faster progress, but private tuition is considerably more expensive (expect to pay at least €20 per hour, more in large cities). A cheap alternative (or supplement) to language classes is a 'language exchange' with someone keen to practise his English (or your native tongue). Arrange to meet on a regular basis and spend half the time speaking English (or another foreign language) and half speaking French. This is also a good way to make friends. You can advertise for a private teacher or language exchange in local newspapers, on bulletin and notice boards (in shopping centres, supermarkets, universities, clubs, etc.), and through your or your partner's employers.

> 'Although I had had some French classes in Brazil, I realised that I didn't speak it at all when I arrived here. And it wasn't because it is more complicated, but because of its peculiarities.'
>
> Kelly Amorim (Brazilian expatriate)

## Why French is Difficult

At first glance French seems a relatively easy language for English-speakers, as around half of English words are derived from French (thanks to William the Conqueror) and are immediately familiar. Unfortunately, many of them have changed their meaning in one or both languages over the last millennium and become 'false friends' (see below). This is one of several subtle traps lying in wait for the unwary learner.

It's often said that French has only around half as many words as English and this may be true, but what is seldom mentioned is that the vast majority of English words are never used (glance through a

Scrabble dictionary will confirm this), and that most French people in fact use a much wider and richer vocabulary than their English-speaking counterparts.

Unlike English and many other languages, which are used primarily as tools of communication, French is an art form in itself; French people love to use 'flowery' language (especially in writing), which can be difficult or impossible to understand, as it invariably cannot be directly translated. For this reason, they're generally reluctant to use 'simple' language to help foreigners understand.

As with any language, the first thing to learn is which sounds are redundant 'fillers' – such as the English er, well, you know and sort of – so that you can ignore them and concentrate on the sounds that matter. Common fillers include *euh*, *alors*, *donc*, *quoi* (at the end of a phrase), *enfin* (often shortened to '*fin*'), *eh bien* (usually abbreviated to '*bain*' and sometimes combined with *bon*, '*bon bain*' having nothing to do with a good bath), *en fait*, *du coup* and *c'est vrai que* (which often sounds like '*serrer que*').

> If something is *offert*, it's free or 'complimentary'. *Gratuit* also means free of charge, whereas 'free' meaning unoccupied (e.g. a toilet) is *libre*.

### Elision

You may have learnt that in French a final consonant is sounded when it's followed by a word beginning with a vowel or silent h. For example, the

phrase *pas encore* (not yet) would be pronounced *pazencore*. In fact, some French people pronounce it like this and some don't, which can make comprehension difficult. Fortunately for foreigners, the current tendency is not to elide.

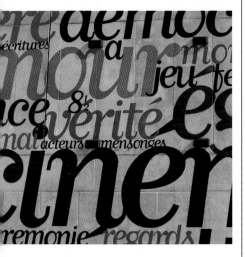

A particular problem is posed by words beginning with h, some of which must be elided and some must not. For example, *un hôtel* is pronounced *unôtel* whereas *un homard* (a lobster) is pronounced *un omard*. In other words, although the letter h is never actually pronounced, as in English, it sometimes acts as if it's being pronounced – and there's no rule for knowing when; you simply have to learn how each word beginning with h behaves.

### False Friends

French is a minefield of *faux amis* (false friends) for English-speakers and it would be impossible to list them all here. Strangely, there appears to be no current dictionary of false friends in English, but a useful French publication is *Les faux amis de l'anglais* by Frédéric Allinne, published by Belin (🖥 www.editions-belin.com).

### Franglais

Despite their inordinate pride in their language, the French cannot resist the temptation to borrow words from English, which is considered *cool*. A new borrowing is made almost every day and there are at least 600 English words in common use. But far from making comprehension easier for English-speakers, this 'Franglais' presents yet another obstacle to understanding, as words are invariably pronounced differently (though sometimes *à l'anglaise*) and often have different meanings from their English equivalents. Some are even a different part of speech, e.g. *cosy* is a noun meaning a child's car seat, and *speed* an adjective meaning 'hyper'.

> It's a myth that the Académie Française safeguards the purity of the French language. In fact, it's a paper tiger, with no authority to oblige anyone to use particular words, except in some cases as brand names. All it can do (and does, fruitlessly) is publish lists of 'unacceptable' words and guidelines as to 'correct' use – which 63m French people blithely ignore.

### Formality

French is a highly formal, rhetorical language, and French people

often use words and phrases in conversation that would normally be used only in formal writing in English, such as *au contraire* (on the contrary), *ceci dit* (that being said), *ceci étant* (that being the case), *cependant* (however), *d'autre part* and *en revanche* (on the other hand), *il n'en reste que ...*and *néanmoins* (nevertheless), *ne serait-ce que ...* (were it not for the fact that), *or* (moreover) and *pourtant* (however).

Conversely, the French use far more colloquialisms and slang than most English-speakers (see **Slang** below), much of which cannot be found in a standard dictionary. They're particularly fond of abbreviating words, usually by cutting them in half and adding *a* or *o* to the end, if one isn't there already – rather in the Australian English manner – e.g. *ado* (for *adolescent*), *apéro* (for *apéritif*), *compta* (for *comptabilité*, meaning accounts or accounting), *frigo*

(*réfrigérateur* – fridge), *rando* (*randonnée* – hike) and *sympa* (*sympathique* – friendly).

The French also have a mania for acronyms – partly due to the fact that the names of their organisations are inordinately long – but partly just for fun. Acronyms that crop up in everyday conversation include *BD* (*bande dessinée*, comic strip), *EDF* (Electricité de France), and *GDF* (Gaz de France), *FNAC* (a chain store selling books, music and IT equipment), *HLM* (tower block), *PACS* (a civil union), *PDG* (*président-directeur-général*, managing director or CEO), *PV* (*procès verbal*, fine – for parking, speeding, etc.), *RER* (a high-speed adjunct to the Paris *métro*), *SAMU* (the national ambulance service), *SMIC* (minimum wage), *SNCF* (French railways), *TGV* (high-speed train), *TTC* (*toutes taxes comprises*, i.e. including VAT), *TVA* (value added tax or sales tax), *VO* (*version originale* – of films, i.e. not dubbed) and *VTT* (mountain bike) – *FNAC*, *PACS* and *SAMU* are pronounced as words while the others are 'spelt out'.

> 'The French are more polite than most of us. Remember to call them "Monsieur, Madame, Mademoiselle", not just Oy!'
>
> *Instructions for British Servicemen in France 1944*

### Pronunciation

Perhaps the most difficult aspect of French is the fact that so many letters aren't pronounced, unlike, for example, German and Italian and, to a lesser extent, English. This means that one sound can have several possible meanings and the only way of knowing which applies is the context – but if the surrounding sounds can also have several interpretations, it requires considerable mental gymnastics to make sense of what you hear.

For example, the words *cent* (a hundred), *sang* (blood), *sans* (without), *sent* (sense or smell) and the word combination *s'en* (as in *s'en aller* – to leave) are all pronounced exactly the same, as are *au* (at/to the), *eau* (water), *haut* (high) and *os* (bones).

### Synonyms

The French are precise in their use of words and won't use a general word when a specific one exists. In many cases, there are two or three French words where there's only one in English. If you use the wrong one, you will usually (but not always) be understood, but you will need to recognise each word if you're to understand what's being said.

For example, for 'window' there are *fenêtre*, *vitrail* and *vitrine*; for 'door' *porte*, *portail* and *portière*; for 'fence' *barrière*, *clôture* and *grillage*. Whereas most English-speakers might loosely refer to a 'deer' or a 'goat', the French will often use a word that specifies the type of animal and its sex.

## Tips for Learning French

- **Stay motivated** – Take every opportunity that comes your way to speak and hear French, even if it's just asking a waiter the time.

- **Don't set yourself impossible targets** – Expect to learn gradually and be prepared for the 'plateau' at intermediate level, where you've learnt the basics but seem to make no progress for weeks.

- **Practise your pronunciation** – The three main things to practise are 'gargling' or (depending on where you are in France) rolling your r, distinguishing between *ou* (as in *vous*) and *u* (as in *tu*) and differentiating *on* from *en*. Practise while sitting in traffic jams and instead of singing in the shower.

- **Don't obsess yourself with the subjunctive** – a difficult concept for a native English-speaker to grasp. Try to learn the most common uses of it (e.g. after *il* *faut*), but if you don't use it or use it wrongly people will still understand you (even though they may pretend not to).

- **Learn at least ten new words a week** – Learn groups or families of words, such as parts of the body or types of clothing, or related words such as *venir, revenir, devenir*, etc..

- **Laugh at your own mistakes** – If you can't beat 'em, join 'em.

- **Take pride in your progress** – Pat yourself on the back when you manage to communicate something successfully or understand part of a conversation, reminding yourself how far you've progressed since you arrived.

- **Persevere** – Don't give up, even if you have to put up with mockery and ridicule of your strange accent or poor grammar along the way. You will learn, sooner or later.

> 'Boy, those French: they have a different word for everything.'
>
> Steve Martin (American humorist)

## Children

If you're relocating as a family to France, your children also need to learn French. For most children, studying in French isn't such a handicap as it may at first appear, particularly for those aged below ten. The majority of children adapt quickly to a new language and most become reasonably fluent within three to six months. However, not all children cope equally well with a change of language (and culture), particularly children aged over ten, many of whom have great difficulties during their first year. Children who are already bilingual (in two other languages) usually have little problem learning French, while monolingual children tend to find it more difficult. French children are generally friendly towards foreign children, who often acquire a 'celebrity status' (particularly in rural schools), which helps their integration.

Before you leave, arrange language classes for your children and ensure they learn the basics. This is especially important if you plan to send your children to a French school – just being able to say '*Salut, je m'appelle Megan*' and count up to a hundred does wonders for your child's confidence on that difficult first day. Once you've arrived, keep up language classes outside school until your children can fend for themselves. Children in a French school will need extra lessons initially to help them settle into their class and make friends.

Foreign children are tested and put into a class suited to their level of French, even if this means being taught with younger children. Children who don't read and write French are often set back a year to compensate for their lack of French and different academic background. Once a child has acquired a sufficient knowledge of spoken and written French, he's assigned to a class appropriate to his age. Some state schools provide intensive French lessons ('bridging classes') for foreign children, although this is by no means the norm. It may be worthwhile enquiring about the availability of extra French classes before choosing where to live.

If your local school doesn't provide extra French classes, your only choice will be to pay for private lessons or send your children to another (possibly private) school, where extra French tuition is provided. Some parents send children to an English-speaking school for a year, before enrolling them in a bilingual or French school; other parents believe it's better to throw their children in at the deep end rather than introduce them gradually to the language. It all depends on the character, ability and wishes of the child.

**Whatever you decide, it will help your children enormously if**

> **All children should learn to say their telephone number and address in French as soon as possible.**

**they have intensive French lessons before arriving in France.**

## OTHER LANGUAGES

France has a number of regional languages, including Alsatian (spoken in Alsace), Basque (in the south-west of Aquitaine), Breton (Brittany), Catalan and Occitan (in Languedoc-Roussillon) and Corsican, not all of which are related to French. You won't need to learn any of these, as all speakers also speak French (and there's little anti-French feeling, as there's anti-Spanish feeling in Catalonia, for example), although picking up a few

words and phrases will help your integration.

The political division of the country led to a separation of the language into the *langue d'oïl* in the north and the *langue d'oc* in the south – *oc* and *oïl* being the respective words for 'yes' – the former becoming modern French, the latter Occitan, which remained the everyday language of most of the rural population of southern France until well into the 20th century and survives in some 20 departments today. It's estimated that there are as many as 3m speakers of Occitan, around a third of whom use the language daily; it's also spoken in parts of Spain and Italy, where the related languages Catalan and Provençal are in use.

Even among French-speakers there's a pronounced north-south difference, southerners speaking

with a 'twang' – usually called *l'accent du Midi* – and often sounding letters that are silent in the north. For example, *vingt* may be pronounced '*veng*'.

### Dialects & Accents

Like most languages, French is spoken with an infinite number of accents, which vary from one region to another and often even within a region. It's generally accepted that the easiest accent to understand is that of central France, i.e. in and around Tours, where the 'best' French is said to be spoken.

Roughly the southern half of France has a distinctly different accent from Paris and the north, with a pronounced 'twang' on certain vowels and often a rolled instead of 'gargled' r. There are also numerous regional dialects (*patois*), although these aren't widely spoken and you're unlikely to be addressed in *patois* – unless your French is so good that you're mistaken for a native.

> '**Many Provençal words have been absorbed into the local language and the more extreme cases of local *patois* can be virtually unintelligible.**'
>
> Martin Hills (British expatriate living in

## SLANG & SWEARING

Like all languages, French has a rich vocabulary of slang and swear words (there are said to be at least 100 words for 'money'), the use of which depends on the company and the context. Even highly educated and 'respectable' French people, however, will pepper their speech with colloquialisms and slang (*argot*), so it's as well to learn the most common expressions at an early stage. These include the following:

| Standard French | Slang | Meaning |
|---|---|---|
| argent | fric or pognon | money |
| chaussures | godasses | shoes |
| enfant | gamin or môme | child |
| femme | gonzesse or nana | woman |
| francs | balles | francs (still used in conversation) |
| homme | mec | man |
| kilomètres | bornes | kilometres |
| manger | bouffer | to eat |
| médecin | toubib | doctor |
| police | flics | police |
| balade | promenade | drive or walk |
| travail | boulot | work |
| travailler | bosser | to work |
| voiture | bagnole | car |

Unless your French is proficient, however, it's best to avoid using slang – it's usually the case that only native speakers know when it's appropriate to use which expression – and especially swear words. All too often foreigners make terrible *faux pas* by swearing inappropriately or using slang in the wrong context. There are innumerable guides to

French slang, some of which are listed in **Appendix B**.

## BODY & SIGN LANGUAGE

While certain types of body and sign language are more or less universal, each people has its own 'vocabulary' of wordless expressions – and the French are no exception.

### Gestures

Although not as fond of gesticulating as the Italians and Spanish, the French often talk with their hands and use a number of gestures with recognised meanings, including the following.

It isn't wise to imitate them until you're proficient in French or it may be thought that you're mocking – the classic French shrug is certainly best left to the natives – and the art of gesticulation is as full of pitfalls for the unwary as the spoken language. Here are a few tips that could help you avoid a *faux pas*:

- Never point with your index finger, which is considered rude, but use an open hand (which should also be used when 'thumbing' a lift).

- Similarly, beckon with your four fingers, palm down.

- The thumb is used to mean 'one' when counting, not the index finger, so the sign for two is thumb and forefinger, not forefinger and middle finger.

- As in many other countries, raising the middle finger is obscene, as is doing a bicep

| Gesture | Meaning |
|---|---|
| Rubbing thumb against fingers | Expensive |
| Rubbing cheek with back of fingers | Boring |
| Kissing the tips of the fingers | Exquisite |
| Shaking a hand up and down | Surprising or impressive |
| Revolving a fist in front of nose | Drunk |
| Miming throwing something over shoulder | Unimportant |
| Making a circle with thumb and forefinger | Worthless or useless (not 'okay') |
| Pulling down top of cheek (just below eye) with index finger | 'My eye' (i.e. disbelieving |
| Tapping forearm with fingers while raising hand slightly | Sudden departure |
| Blowing out cheeks and puffing | 'Bof' (see chapter 2) |

'curl' with the opposite hand on the elbow joint (known euphemistically as a *bras d'honneur*).

## Personal Space

Like Italians and Spaniards, the French like to move in close to their conversation partners, and keep tight up to the person in front of them in a queue. If you feel that your personal space has been encroached upon or even threatened by this closeness, don't take offence and try not to react as if you've been insulted – take a discreet step backwards (or forwards if you're queuing).

## FORMS OF ADDRESS

As the French language tends to be formal, so are French forms of address and you should take care to use the appropriate terms when speaking and writing to French people.

### *Tu* or *Vous?*

In common with many other European languages (but not English), French makes a clear and important distinction between the formal or polite (*vous*) and informal or familiar (*tu*) modes of address, similar to *usted* and *tú* in Spanish, and *Sie* and *du* in German. As English has only one word for you, native English-speakers often find it difficult to decide when to use *vous* and when to use *tu*. The decision is important, because if you address someone as *tu* when you should have used *vous*, you may offend him or it may be taken as a sign of disrespect,

person has switched to *tu*, he may switch back and you may never be able to call each other *tu*.

Children should follow the same rule, except that they must get to know adults really well before they can start addressing them as *tu*. If they've learnt some French in your home country and haven't used the *tu* form much, get them to practise it so that they can talk to their classmates.

## Names & Titles

A potential source of embarrassment is whether to use the word *Monsieur* or *Madame* when being introduced to someone whose name you don't know. In a formal situation (e.g. a business meeting) it's best to use it, e.g. *Bonjour Monsieur/Madame*, even with young adults, but in an informal setting (e.g. at a party) it isn't usually appropriate except with elderly people and you can simply say *Bonjour*. Similarly, when you say goodbye – unless by then you know the person's name. (See also **Greetings** below.)

It's common to use first names with neighbours and other acquaintances from the word go, even if you address them as *vous*, but it's polite to address older

although most French people make allowances for foreigners.

As a general rule, *tu* should be used only when addressing people you know well, children, animals and gods; *vous* should be used in all other circumstances. Note, however, that the plural of *tu* is also *vous*, so you would address more than one person as *vous* even if they were close friends or children, and *tu* is **only** used in the singular.

As in other countries where there are polite and familiar forms of address, the use of *tu* among people who don't know each other well is on the increase, particularly among younger people, but you should always start with *vous* and switch to *tu* only when prompted by the other person – who might say something like '*On se tutoie ?*' (Shall we call each other *tu*?) or simply start using the *tu* form. It's important to pick up on the change from *vous* to *tu*; if you continue to use *vous* when the other people as *Monsieur x* or *Madame x*.(*Mademoiselle* is rarely used.)

French people often have double-barrelled first names (e.g. *Marie-Christine* or *Jean-Pierre* – or even *Jean-Marie*) and you should **never** use only one of these names (e.g. just *Marie* or *Jean*) unless invited to do so – which is rare. Similarly, the French seldom abbreviate names, e.g. *Dominique* (which, incidentally, can be a man's or a woman's name) to *Dom* or *Sidonie* to *Sido*.

Note that the French word *surnom* doesn't mean 'surname' (which is *nom de famille* or simply *nom*) but 'nickname'.

## GREETINGS

When you're introduced to a French adult, you should shake hands and say '*Bonjour*' or, in a formal situation and with older people (see above), '*Bonjour Monsieur/Madame*'. It's also polite to say '*enchanté(e)*' ('pleased to meet you'). With children, simply say '*Bonjour*'. The usual informal greeting is '*Salut*' ('Hello' or 'Hi') – the reply is normally the same.

It's customary to say *Bonjour* on entering a small shop or a waiting room if there are other people waiting to be served; you should say *Bonjour Monsieur/Madame* to the shop assistant or receptionist.

*Bonjour* usually becomes *Bonsoir* around 6pm or after dark, but don't be surprised if a French person responds with *Bonjour* when you've said *Bonsoir* – or vice versa. *Bonne nuit* is used only when going to bed or leaving a house in the evening.

After a meeting or on leaving a shop, you should say '*Au revoir*' – or '*Au revoir Monsieur/Madame*' if you used this form of greeting. You may be wished *bonne journée* (have a nice day) or variations such as *bon après-midi, bonne fin d'après-midi, bon dimanche* or *bon week-end*, to which you may reply *vous aussi, vous de même* or *et vous*. In fact it's usual to wish people a 'good' something when leaving them, whether it's a holiday (*bonnes vacances*), trip (*bon voyage*), car journey (*bonne route*), journey home (*bon retour*), or simply the continuation of whatever they were doing when you met (*bonne continuation*). To wish someone luck with something he's about to do, say *Bon courage*, not *Bonne chance* (which implies that he hasn't a hope in hell).

There are a number of informal alternatives to *Au revoir*, including *A la prochaine* ('til the next time), *Salut, Bye* and *Ciao*. If you've arranged to see the person again, you can say *A demain/dimanche/etc.*; if you're likely to meet again soon (usually within a few hours), *A bientôt, A plus tard, A plus* (colloquial) or *A tout à l'heure*.

> 'I've often wished I could walk in accidentally on two people making love, just so that I could discreetly close the door again, leaving them with a polite "bonne continuation".'
>
> Stephen Clarke, *Talk to the Snail*

## Handshaking & Kissing

When you're introduced to a French adult, you should shake hands (a single pump is enough – neither limp nor knuckle-crushing), although some French people will kiss you on a first meeting and young children will expect to be kissed.

Kissing (*faire la bise*) is something of a social guessing game – even among the French. You may be halfway through a handshake when the other person decides to kiss you; you **never** know which cheek to kiss first; and how many times you kiss depends on where you are in France and how well you know each other. It's therefore best to take it slowly (clashes of spectacles and even heads aren't uncommon) and to take your cue from the French.

The 'kiss' isn't usually a proper kiss, more a delicate brushing of the cheeks accompanied by kissing noises, although some extroverts will plant a great wet smacker on each side of your face.

When appropriate, men kiss women and women kiss women but men don't kiss men unless they're relatives or very close friends. If a woman expects you to kiss her, she will lean forward instead of holding out her hand.

As to how many kisses to give, you should again let yourself be guided by the natives. Two is the standard number, although many people kiss three or four or even six times. It depends partly on where you are in France. (The British travel agent Thomas Cook recently published a *French Kissing Guide*, according to which, four kisses are the norm in northern France, three in the mid-west and southern central areas, and two in the west, east and extreme south; a single kiss is acceptable only in the department of Charente-Maritime – although such generalisations are unreliable.) However, much also depends on how well you know the person concerned: even in the same area, acquaintances might kiss twice or three times, friends four times and old friends six.

Handshaking and kissing usually take place again at the end of a meeting, though in some cases you might kiss a person you initially shook hands with. In an office and at school, everyone shakes hands with everyone else on arrival at work **and** when they depart. It's also customary to kiss everyone in sight – including the men if you're a man – at midnight on New Year's Eve.

## TELEPHONE, LETTERS & EMAIL

The use of email is becoming increasingly common in France, but the telephone is still the preferred means of communication for the vast majority of people (after face-to-face meetings, of course), both in a business context and for private communication. Letters are often used, particularly in business – and here French formality is at its most intimidating.

### Telephone

As in many other countries, telephone communication is increasingly by mobile (*portable* or *mobile*). When you answer the telephone, whether formally or informally, you should say '*Allô*' – this isn't the normal word for 'hello' but is used only when answering the phone. Some people answer with '*Oui*', although this may be regarded as rude.

### Email

Email culture is gradually creeping into French society, although a surprising number of businesses and professionals, let alone individuals, have no email address. Oddly, the French have yet to agree on a word for email, calling it variously *courriel* (short for *courrier électronique*), *mél* (short for *message électronique*), *mail*, *e-mail* and *email* (pronounced more or less as in English).

Most emails, formal and informal, start with *Bonjour* followed by the name of the recipient, although for formal business messages you

Don't be surprised if you phone a business and are greeted not formally with the name of the company, etc. but simply with '*Allô*', '*Oui*' or even '*Je vous écoute*' (I'm listening) – especially when the business is in Paris.

should use the same greeting as for a letter (see below).

### Letters

#### Salutation

Formal letters start with simply *Monsieur* or *Madame* even when you know the person's surname. If you're on friendly terms, you can write *Cher Monsieur* or *Chère Madame* but it isn't usual to add the surname. For friends, write *Cher/Chère* and the first name.

> '**Letter-writing in French is another of those skills that makes you feel as though you've been transported back in time to the court of Louis XIV.**'
>
> Stephen Clarke, *Talk to the Snail*

### Addresses

Addresses are usually written as follows:

| | |
|---|---|
| Name of recipient (surname first, in capitals) | DUPONT Michel |
| Street number and name | 24 rue de l'Eglise |
| Post code and name of commune. | 29000 BREST |

If you're writing to a family, you can put *La famille Dupont* or *Les Dupont* (no s at the end). There's no need to include the *département* or region name. Note that French window envelopes have the window right of centre, as this is where the address is usually written.

You should write your own name and address on the back of the envelope under the word *Expéditeur* (sender).

### Date

Dates are usually written in full and often include the day of the week, e.g. *mardi 6 octobre 2007* – if you omit the day, it's usual to replace it with *le*, e.g. *le 6 octobre 2007*. You may also come across the numerical form, which is written the British and not the American way, e.g. *6/10/07* for the above date and not *10/6/07*.

### Signing off

Formal letter endings (i.e. the equivalent of 'Yours faithfully' or 'Yours sincerely') are one of the most complex areas of the French language, where minute variations in wording convey subtly different tones, as follows:

- *Je vous prie d'agréer, Monsieur/Madame, l'expression de ma considération distinguée* or *Je vous prie de croire, Monsieur/Madame, à l'expression de ma considération distinguée* (neutral);

- *Veuillez agréer, Monsieur/Madame, l'assurance de ma considération distinguée* (formal);

- *Veuillez agréer, Monsieur/Madame, l'expression de mes sentiments distingués* (polite);

- *Recevez, Monsieur/Madame, l'expression de mes salutations distinguées* or simply *Recevez, Monsieur/Madame, mes salutations distinguées* (when making a complaint);

- *Salutations distinguées* (for short letters or emails);
- *Sincères salutations* (for someone you know well);
- *Meilleures salutations* (for a colleague or close associate).

Informal letters are usually ended with one of the following (in order of formality):

- *Cordialement* (the equivalent of 'Regards' and usually used at the end of informal business emails);
- *Bien cordialement* ('Kind regards');
- *Bien à vous* ('Warmest regards');
- *Amicalement* ('Best wishes');
- *Amitiés* ('Love');
- *Je t'embrasse* (literally, 'I kiss

'... few conversations, however successful in practical terms, are without a pang of frustration at knowing that speaking a second language means reducing to basics everything we say – and, to an even greater extent, write. Without subtlety and nuance, it is so much harder to get across the little things which reveal our true personalities.'

Roger Moss (British expatriate)

you' and the equivalent of 'With love');

- *Bises* or *Bisous* (literally, 'kisses' and the equivalent of 'Much love');
- *Grosses bises* or *Gros bisous* ('Lots of love').

You can also end an informal letter or email *Salut* (Bye) or *A bientôt*, etc.

Lake St Hélène, Savoie

# 6.

# THE FRENCH AT WORK

One of the most common mistakes foreigners make when coming to France to work or start a business, is to assume that they can continue working the way they did in their home country, particularly if they had a successful business there. Many expatriates completely underestimate the dramatic differences in business culture between the French and the British or Americans, for example. Working in France usually involves a fairly steep learning curve for a foreigner – professionally, linguistically and culturally.

'The thing that's wrong with the French is that they don't have a word for entrepreneur.'

George W. Bush
(US President)

This chapter provides information on working for or with the French, setting up a business and business etiquette.

## WORK ETHIC

The French work to live rather than live to work, and a job is viewed mainly as a means of earning money to spend in your leisure time rather than a way of fulfilling ambition or talent. This doesn't mean that the French aren't hard workers, but they don't believe a person is better for working harder and longer, and cannot understand why employees in some other countries are prepared to forgo their family, holidays and free time in favour of their job. When a French person goes on holiday, he leaves work behind; he isn't contactable – even in an emergency.

If, as Napoleon famously said, Britain is (or was) a nation of shopkeepers, France is a nation of *artisans* – only loosely translated by the English term 'tradesmen', as it incorporates the all-important word '*art*'. The very traits that make them reluctant to work together – their individualism and *hauteur* – tend to propel them to excel in disciplines where creativity, pleasure and personality are more important than procedure and efficiency. As a result, the French are world leaders in fields such as gastronomy, fashion and the arts.

The French working mentality is possibly unique (perhaps an illustration of the famous *exception française*), in that like the Spanish and Italians, as well as North Africans and Indians, for example, they have little respect for authority; however, unlike those people they also have little adaptability, i.e. the ability to deal with changing conditions or unfamiliar situations,

> 'The French are much like cats: highly independent, difficult (if not impossible) to organise and manage, and set in their habits.'
>
> Bruce Epstein (American expatriate)

(The British, Germans, Chinese and Japanese tend to have low adaptability but high respect for authority, while Americans and Scandinavians score highly on both counts.) Of course, French workers don't blatantly ignore or insult their superiors, but they're suspicious (if not downright contemptuous) of managers and generally unwilling to follow rules and procedures, preferring to 'find their own way' of doing things.

Add to this general mindset several traits that seem endemic to the French – inertia, aversion to taking risks (except when driving), ineffectiveness at project management and dislike of taking decisions – and it will be seen that working with or for the French can be challenging, unpredictable and frustrating. But in order to understand the French business environment, it's essential to remember that French people are socially oriented: they love to meet and discuss – and decisions put an end to discussion. An old joke is that a Frenchman will ask: 'It may work in practice, but will it work in theory?'

The average French middle manager spends all his day (French managers tend overwhelmingly to be male – see **Women in Business** below) in poorly organised meetings where topics are discussed at great length without any sensible conclusion being reached. Since they cannot make any progress during the 'normal' working day, managers often have no choice but to work late (but never at weekends). And that's when things get interesting; as one high-level manager admitted, 'Officially, we work from nine to six, but most people stay later, because stuff happens after about seven.'

French business traditions, including management styles and working habits, have evolved under the assumption, if not overt acknowledgement, of these conditions. And French labour

> 'It is still thought that the later you stay in your office the better a worker you are.'
>
> Janet McNicol (British expatriate)

laws are designed with them in mind: since the French are naturally unmanageable, it must be made doubly difficult to fire them – otherwise, most of the population would be out of a job.

## Bosses

French bosses act differently from most of their foreign counterparts. While their work and career are important, these aren't generally the focal point of their lives and they aren't particularly motivated by money. Since salary in many organisations is tied more to qualifications and length of service than rank, French managers, except at the highest levels, often don't earn much more than their subordinates. They generally have no inclination to change companies or even positions within the same company except to be promoted, since their social status depends on the cachet of their employer and the size of their department.

This philosophy can have unexpected consequences, such as when managers implement strategies that protect their 'fiefdoms' but are harmful to the company as a whole. It isn't unusual for even strategically critical projects to fail for no reason other than that the person leading them was seen to be representing a 'competing' group within the company; for most managers, it's more important to protect their turf than to ensure the success or even survival of the company.

In general, French management displays many of the characteristics of the former aristocracy. The typical manager considers himself superior to his staff – in fact, if he attended a *Grande Ecole*, it has been drilled into him that he is part of the ruling elite. As a result, French managers tend to maintain a substantial distance from their staff, and communication remains formal or one-sided – which in turn means that managers often have little idea about what's really happening in their department, and may not even care.

Concepts that are taken for granted in British or American companies, such as customer satisfaction, employee motivation, quality of service, efficiency and profitability, are noticeable by their absence from the daily preoccupations of a typical French manager.

> The Quality Manager of a well known French company once remarked, 'We would be making a high quality product if it weren't for our customers and their unreasonable demands.'

There are three main types of French boss:

- ladder climbers;
- calendar watchers;
- entrepreneurs.

The ladder climber, or Fast Track manager, is invariably someone who went to a *Grande Ecole* but has no particular management expertise (it isn't necessary). His goal is to be noticed (favourably) so that he can be promoted as quickly as possible to a more prestigious position. His management style is likely to be directive, since he doesn't have the patience to convince his subordinates, and doesn't intend to be around long enough to need to establish any sort of collaborative working relationship. The best strategy for dealing with him is to simply stay out of his way (after all, he'll probably be promoted soon); if this isn't possible, do what you can to make him look good so that you'll be rid of him sooner.

At some point, however, even the Fast Trackers fall off the track (or realise that they'll never get on it), and they become calendar watchers.

These managers (who might be as young as 30) are doing whatever they can to preserve their position until the day they can retire (which may be as early as 55). As opposed to the Fast Trackers, their goal is **not** to be noticed, especially not to 'make waves'. These managers will avoid taking decisions of any kind, and when forced to do so, will find someone to pin the blame on should the decision turn out to be a bad one. The best way to deal with them is to help them avoid problems – or solve them quietly yourself. If a decision must be taken, it must be presented as the only safe course of action (or the least dangerous). What these managers fear above all is being relegated to the *placard* (cupboard).

In large organisations, managers can become labelled as 'troublemakers', often because they refused to pay homage to the hierarchy, or they chose the wrong side in an intra-company political battle; or sometimes because they took a risk that failed in a way they couldn't hide or blame on anyone else. As a result, they're shuffled off the organisation chart to a harmless

> 'Customers seem to be an inconvenience to the French, who prefer to prepare for their annual vacations, and make detailed records of anything and everything, collected in dossiers, so that if something goes wrong, they cannot be blamed.'
>
> Larry Davis (American businessman)

position such as 'special consultant' or 'special projects coordinator', where they have no specific responsibilities – but no prestige either.

It's rare for managers to rehabilitate themselves out of the *placard*, so there they stay until either they retire or, if they retain some self-esteem, find a job at another company. It's even possible for an entire group of managers to fall from favour and end up in the *placard*.

The third type of boss is the one who had the wherewithal to create his own business. These men (again, the vast majority of them are male) are personally invested in their businesses (not just monetarily) and, in general, are more willing to take risks (but only if they have to – even French entrepreneurs are risk-averse), as well as devote the attention necessary to develop their subordinates. Despite historical resistance to small business owners, this model is becoming not only more acceptable but also more prevalent in French business.

But beware – there's also another type of French entrepreneur.

This person is well connected politically and has learned to milk the government subsidy trough for all it's worth, without bothering to produce a viable product or service. Some even go as far as to pretend to be working in another region of France in order to collect more subsidies – when the government auditor shows up, they simply go there for the day as if it were a normal business location. Needless

Hundreds of thousands of unemployed young French people and frustrated would-be entrepreneurs go abroad each year to work, particularly to the UK, where they flourish in the less regulated working conditions and countless business opportunities. A million French people have left France in the last few years – London, for example, is now the seventh-largest 'French' city in terms of French residents.

to say, working for such a boss can be a frustrating experience.

## Tradesmen

As has been intimated, French tradesmen are 'artists' (*artisans*) rather than traders, and therefore take great pride in their work but also suffer from an artistic temperament and a lack of commercial nous. In short, they're often a law unto themselves. Many are almost impossible to get hold of, not even having answering machines, let alone messages that give their name or the name of their business; if you do manage to leave a message, it's unlikely to be returned (or even listened to – in fact, it's seldom worth leaving a message); when you finally get hold of a tradesman, he's likely to be *débordé* (literally 'overflowing' with work) and unable to do any job for you for days, weeks or months – the more specialised his craft, the longer you normally have to wait, having a long waiting list being regarded as a sign of expertise rather than of inefficiency.

Once you've made an appointment, don't expect him to turn up at the agreed time – or even at all; nor should you be surprised if he doesn't phone to tell you he isn't coming, or to apologise for not coming or make another appointment – after all, you're a mere customer. Finally, when the work has at last been done, the tradesman may be unable to tell you how much it will cost (unless it has been subject to a written quotation) and you may receive a bill a week later, or a month later, or in some cases never.

> 'Builders are either wonderful or awful; there is no in-between. They only do the job they are trained for and they always arrive two days late.'
>
> William Jaques (British expatriate)

Naturally, there are exceptions to the above, and some French tradesmen are models of efficiency; but as a rule you must exercise extreme patience and persistence to

get a job done in France – no wonder the French themselves often DIY. On the other hand, if you manage to get a job done, it will invariably be well done.

## PERMITS & PAPERWORK

As you would perhaps expect, the pernicious red tape for which the French are notorious rears its ugly head highest when it comes to working in France, particularly if you're a non-EU citizen and/or plan to set up a business. Setting up a business is fraught with bureaucratic obstacles for the French, let alone foreigners, and the process can take several months, if not over a year. Obtaining a work permit (non-EU citizens only) is extremely difficult in most areas, as preference is given to EU citizens for any job vacancy.

The maxim 'patience is a virtue' is never more true than when getting a job or starting a business in France.

Whatever field you're looking to break into, there's undoubtedly a professional organisation (association) which you can join for a token fee, as a means to establish or increase your network.

## FINDING A JOB

The key to finding a good job in France is personal contact – this is a country where the right connections go a long way towards finding you employment. Casual jobs and jobs at the bottom of the employment ladder are relatively easy to find, particularly in areas where unemployment is low, but if you aspire to something better you need to know people. Many expatriates find it difficult and frustrating to break into the job market because a large proportion of vacancies are filled through personal recommendation or internally within a company.

Although it obviously helps considerably if your father is best mates with the director, personal contact works at all levels, however low, and networking (*faire du network*) is essential. Make sure your name, face and aspirations are well known: visit companies in person to hand in your CV; phone a few days later to follow up your application; be prepared to attend an interview at any time; and make sure all your friends and acquaintances know what sort of job you're looking for and what your qualifications are.

## Speaking French

Unless you plan to work solely within the expat community, where your job and career possibilities are severely limited, you need to speak good French. Outside popular expat destinations, there are virtually no job opportunities for non-French speakers other than manual labour such as fruit picking and teaching English (or another language). The better your French is, the better your employment prospects.

### Qualifications

In theory, any EU qualification is recognised in France; in practice the certification (*certification* or *agrément*) process is mired in red tape and typically takes several months (at least). If your job hunting success depends on your qualifications being recognised, apply for certification well in advance of your arrival in France – though some French consulates may provide information on the process. It may be some consolation to know that it isn't just foreigners who have to go through this – newspapers

frequently include articles about French people who have achieved high qualifications abroad but have been unable to obtain recognition of these in their own country.

If foreign qualifications aren't recognised (either officially or unofficially), foreigners – especially women – often end up working in positions well below their abilities.

## Applications

French curricula vitae – the French use the same term, whereas the American English word *résumé* means 'summary' – are written and presented in a particular way and you shouldn't simply have your existing CV translated into French.

> 'In the eyes of a French human resources officer, even if someone has set up their own company, made a small fortune and sold out to a multinational, their experience will not count for as much as s two-year course at a business school.'
>
> Stephen Clarke, *Talk to the Snail*

Your CV should be accompanied by a letter (*lettre de motivation*) explaining why you're eminently qualified for the position.

As qualifications are everything in France, you should take particular care to specify your educational and business qualifications, giving French equivalents where appropriate. For example, the names of standard North American university degrees, Bachelor's and Master's, **don't** translate into the French words *baccalauréat* and *maîtrise*. The *baccalauréat* is a high school diploma (equivalent to British A Levels), and a *maîtrise* is a four-year degree.

It isn't usual in France to start working immediately after school and to obtain further educational qualifications at a later stage. If, for example, you obtained a degree (BA/BS or MA/MS) part-time while working, be prepared to explain why at an interview.

Any CV submitted in France should be in French as well as in English (which is considered an asset for most jobs), but however good your French is it's essential to have it translated by a **professional** translator, as most French people have a shaky idea of spelling and grammar.

## Employment Agencies

### *Government*

It may come as a surprise to discover that the government employment agency (the Agence Nationale Pour l'Emploi/ANPE) does relatively little to help you find a job. Offices post job vacancies – you're expected to browse through these – and if you're registered as unemployed you may receive the occasional phone call from the agency with details of a job offer or a training session, but don't expect to. Some agencies are better than others and recent government initiatives have implemented measures to try to make the agencies more 'effective', but you cannot rely on an agency to find a job for you: the onus is on you to do your own job hunting.

Several websites serve the French job market; among the better known are ⌨ www.apec.fr and ⌨ www.cadremploi.fr (for cadre positions), and ⌨ www.anpe.fr for all positions listed with the government employment agency.

### *Private*

Head-hunting and recruitment agencies exist in France, although to a lesser extent than in the UK and US, but their activities are mainly confined to the major cities. Other agencies, such as the multi-nationals Adecco and Manpower, are allowed by law to handle only temporary employment (*travail temporaire/ intérimaire*); most towns and cities have one or more agencies.

## Selection Process

The job selection process in France usually involves several tests and interviews, particularly if you're applying for employment in a large company. The tests (*tests psychologiques*) are used to ascertain your intelligence, aptitude (for a particular job) and personality: some companies expect candidates to sit several tests, which range from multiple-choice to essay format. In some cases, you must take tests before being interviewed – large companies tend to rule out 80 per cent of job applicants based on their CVs and test results – but in others you're tested after the interview stage. It isn't uncommon for a prospective employer to ask for a handwritten text sample, in order to perform a handwriting analysis (*graphologie*).

The number of interviews you have depends on the company (and your success at interviewing), but expect at least two and possibly as many as half a dozen, spread out over several days or even weeks. A surprising number of employers don't ask for references from your previous employers, but most want to see copies of your qualifications and CV (which should all be translated into French).

If you apply by letter or email, it's always wise to follow up with a telephone call. The French are notoriously bad at responding to correspondence, but this is for the simple reason that they would much rather talk to you – on the telephone or, preferably, face to face.

## Salary

Unless you're lucky enough to secure an executive post, where salaries are on a par with those in other northern European countries, the chances are that your wages in France will be lower than in your home country. The legal minimum wage is around €1,250 per month and many salaries aren't a lot higher.

> The French notion of 'net pay' often causes confusion among foreigners. As income tax isn't withheld at source (as it is in almost all other industrialised countries), you must bear in mind that you could receive a sizeable tax bill later.

On the plus side, many employees receive 13 or even 14 salary payments a year (if you manage to get a job in a bank, you may receive as many as 16) – an extra month's salary in December and another in July before the summer holiday period.

### Benefits

In addition to salary, all companies with more than 20 employees are required to provide an allowance for commuting costs (in Paris, for example, this is generally 50 per cent of your monthly or annual public transport pass), and provide either a subsidised *cantine* or restaurant tickets (*Tickets restaurant*, similar to luncheon vouchers in the UK). Most companies also provide complementary health insurance cover.

## Discrimination

Under French law, racial and sexual discrimination is prohibited, meaning that theoretically anyone who meets the employment criteria has an equal chance of getting a job. In practice, this isn't always the case: France is 'a man's world' and a country where employers are still sometimes reluctant to take on young married women (for fear they'll fall pregnant and take 26 weeks' maternity leave) or coloured people (racial prejudice runs deep in some company veins). White European men generally encounter the least discrimination – although the French would **always** rather employ a Frenchman.

If you think a job wasn't awarded to you owing to discrimination, you have the right to appeal, but your case may be extremely difficult to prove.

## CONTRACTS

French labour law strongly favours the employee, and once a worker has signed an indefinite-term contract (*contrat à durée indéterminée/CDI*) it's difficult and costly for an employer to fire him. Not surprisingly, this means that employers tend to favour a temporary contract (*contrat de travail temporaire/intérim*), which may only be awarded in specific circumstances, or a fixed-term contract (*contrat à durée déterminée/CDD*), valid for up to two years.

Nevertheless, all contracts (whether *CDI* or *CDD*) begin with a trial period (*période d'essai*) during which the contract may be terminated by either party without notice and without compensation. The length of this period varies by profession, but is generally between one and three months, and is usually renewable for a second period.

In an attempt to reduce unemployment by making it simpler for employers to hire (and, especially, fire) workers, the government introduced the *contrat nouvelles embauches* (*CNE*) in August 2005. Although technically a *CDI*, this contract, which applies only to people over 26, can be revoked for almost any reason within the first two years. Encouraged by the success of this initiative (over 400,000 workers were signed up in the first eight months), the government introduced the *contrat première embauche* in April 2006. Essentially the same type of contract but limited to those under 26, the *CPE* aroused storms of protest, not only from the young it was supposed to help find jobs (who demonstrated violently and destroyed university buildings), but also from unions and anyone opposed to the current government. The ensuing political crisis saw the President instructing the Prime Minister to repeal the *CPE*, leaving the government with a copious amount of egg on its face, and France's youth facing the continuing prospect of one of the highest unemployment rates in Europe.

## Collective Agreements

Employment conditions are wholly or partly determined by collective agreements (*conventions collectives*), approved annually between management and unions. Collective agreements, which cover working conditions and salary scales, apply to virtually the entire salaried workforce, including civil servants.

## STARTING OR BUYING A BUSINESS

The secret to setting up a business in France is research and more research, together with a generous dose of patience as you plough through the inevitable red tape. Don't be tempted to by-pass the bureaucracy and start trading without registering and obtaining the necessary permissions. This is illegal and you'll probably be found out – there's a good chance that a competitor will report you; why should you get away with dodging

the system when they had to do things properly (even if they didn't)? The authorities impose large fines on illegal traders and you'll find it difficult or impossible to set up a business afterwards.

Most foreign entrepreneurs find that financing a business in France is the most difficult part of setting up (more so than the paperwork), and even an extensive business plan for a potentially highly profitable business won't necessarily tempt financial institutions into lending you 'seed' money.

> 'France is just crazy about categorising people and businesses into regimes.'
>
> Beverly Laflamme (American expatriate)

## Loans

French banks have traditionally been among the world's most cautious, and they still aren't keen to lend to small businesses; however, this is changing and banks are becoming more generous with unsecured loans at low interest rates – albeit with relatively modest sums. Foreigners are even less likely than the French to receive approval for a business loan – even those who are resident and have some collateral (e.g. a property in France). Business plans need to be detailed and cover every conceivable aspect of a proposed business; some banks want to see 'evidence' that it's viable – a tall order if you're at the setting-up stage. Most banks require a guarantor, but sometimes even a multi-millionaire behind you isn't enough. This is one area in business where personal contacts aren't effective, as branch managers don't have the authority to approve loans – this is done at regional level.

If you do manage to squeeze a loan out of a bank, the repayment period will be relatively short – between five and seven years.

## Grants

In theory, grants are available at many levels including EU, national, regional, departmental and local, as well as from charitable organisations. There are around 250 grants and subsidies available to individuals, but most of them (with the exception of research grants) are intended to provide support for businesses that are already up and running, and relatively few are available for starting a new business or taking over an existing business – some of these are listed on ⌨ www.apce.com.

Furthermore, obtaining approval for a grant and getting the money

paid into your bank account is another matter altogether. The application process typically takes months, if not years, and there are numerous incidences of grants arriving several years after a business was set up. It's worth requesting as many grants as you're eligible for, but don't factor the grant money into your financing.

## Premises

Most business premises (*local*) are leased or rented. It's possible to buy premises outright but they're usually in short supply (most owned business premises are handed down through a family), and it may be difficult or impossible to obtain a mortgage.

It's rare to find empty business premises (*local vide*), as a business activity or 'going concern' (*fonds de commerce*) is normally sold with its premises, and there may be a separate price for each.

If you rent premises, you must usually buy a lease (*bail*), which may cost almost as much as the freehold and usually restricts the type of activity you may undertake.

On top of that, you must pay an

Even if you find empty premises, there may be restrictions as to the type of business you can set up, and you should always check – even if the premises are advertised as '*toute activité possible*' – whether you'll be able to run your intended business before entering negotiations to buy or rent.

annual rent (*loyer*). It's possible to rent business premises without buying a lease (usually on a nine-year contract), but you may not have much legal protection.

### Working from Home

Under French law you cannot set up just any business in your home: there are extensive regulations (and paperwork) concerning what you're permitted to do. Broadly speaking, these are designed with neighbours in mind, and activities that interfere with 'normal' life are prohibited or restricted. This being France, however, rules and regulations vary from one *commune* to another – some councils allow some businesses in some areas while others don't allow any. If you're considering working from home, visit your local town hall and find out what regulations apply.

## Self-employment

As in many countries, being self-

employed in France is financially wearing, particularly in the first three years – in fact, the third year is usually the hardest, as many taxes are 'delayed' for the first two years and then you must pay for three years at once. Social security contributions are astronomical, as you have no employer to make at least half of them for you – and you're entitled to few benefits, which means you must take out (expensive) private insurance if your earnings are to be guaranteed in the event of serious illness, accident or disability, for example.

For this reason, although there are many small businesses in France, most of them are handed down from father to son, and setting up a new enterprise is relatively rare – especially as the French don't like risk.

## Marketing

The French concept of marketing (they use the English word) is radically different from the usual American or British notion. Indeed, to most French people the idea of selling is anathema, as it's undignified and requires putting oneself at the service of a potential customer and – horror of horrors – discussing money. What counts in France is a good reputation, which is a far more effective marketing tool than any number of adverts or expensive publicity campaigns. A business with a good reputation doesn't need to sell or market itself, as most French people ask relatives and friends for a recommendation when they need something, rather

than responding to advertisements or publicity material. The French marketing credo is: 'If I have a good product or service, people will come to me' and many business owners literally sit back and wait for customers to come through the door.

But even when customers come through the door, the French seem reluctant to close a sale; if it happens, it happens, but it isn't their primary objective. In business, the French are reactive rather than proactive, and the customer must often insist on buying if he isn't to go away empty-handed.

If you're setting up a business, you should therefore ensure that you provide a good service and nurture your contacts – good ones should be taken out for coffee and lunch and phoned regularly. Have plenty of business cards and hand them out at every opportunity, but avoid 'hard selling' which will generally get you nowhere.

## BLACK ECONOMY

As in any other country, there are locals (and foreigners) who work 'on the black' (*au noir* or *au black*) in order to avoid paying taxes and social security contributions, although this practice isn't as prevalent as in Italy and Spain. Few people work entirely on the black but, given the French propensity for rule-breaking, many do the odd 'cash' job when the occasion arises.

You should, of course, be wary of both paying for goods and services 'under the table', which means that you have no guarantee, and providing goods or services without putting them through your books; both are illegal and you can be heavily fined if you're discovered. The authorities are clamping down on illegal activity, particularly in employment and tax declaration. Note also that if you work illegally, you have no rights and are entitled to no benefits.

## WOMEN IN BUSINESS

Officially, France is not only a colour-blind but also a gender-neutral society, which is supposed to extend into the workplace. Indeed, there are several well publicised cases of major companies headed by women, and generally French men don't have a problem working **with** women. That is, a woman already in a position of authority is treated with the respect she deserves.

On the other hand, there's a reluctance to promote women to positions of authority in the first place. Eventually, most women either resign themselves to the fact that they'll never crack the 'glass ceiling', or start their own businesses.

It's also well documented that when women do manage to attain the same level as French men, they're typically paid substantially less. Partly this is to 'compensate' for maternity leave. Although officially a company is required to reinstate women returning from maternity leave (which can last a year or longer – paid and unpaid) in their old jobs, the reality is much more complicated. Often, the position doesn't exist any more, due to a reorganisation; in the case of senior positions, most companies find it virtually impossible to reallocate responsibilities 'temporarily' during such an extended absence. In any case, many bosses take the opportunity of maternity leave to 'reposition' women in 'more appropriate' posts. (While it's theoretically possible for men to take a similar amount of paternity leave, very few do so.)

Unlike their counterparts in some other countries (such as the US), French women in the business world remain first and foremost women. That is, they're proud of their femininity, and succeed not by mimicking men, but by exploiting their attributes – in interpersonal relations, for example. French women in general are unashamed of their bodies, and businesswomen are frequently seen wearing outfits that would be labelled 'provocative' in socially conservative countries such as the US: tight-fitting dresses with high hems and plunging necklines, for example. This should be considered neither as an invitation nor as a provocation, but simply as an expression of pride in appearance. This isn't to say that French businesswomen are dainty or fragile creatures – not by any means. It isn't uncommon to hear a businesswoman using language just as coarse as her masculine counterparts, or appreciating (or even telling) an off-colour joke.

On the other hand, if you're a foreign woman doing business

> In 2007 Anne-Sophie Pic became the first woman for over a decade – and only the fourth ever – to receive three Michelin stars for her restaurant, La Maison Pic in Valence, which she had inherited from her father and completely restyled. On receiving the award, Pic commented, not without irony: 'A woman who takes the reins in the kitchen, that had never been seen before.'

with the French, it's important to understand certain dynamics. French businessmen are used to dealing with strong, independent women who are also thick skinned. Don't take offence at the jokes, 'compliments' or insults; these are generally harmless pleasantries. On the other hand, if the behaviour crosses the line into personal attacks or propositions, then of course you must protest. Also, although you may have endured a long struggle to reach your position, don't make too much of it or flaunt your achievements; the French will find it pretentious.

## BUSINESS ETIQUETTE

In the workplace, as in any other environment, there are unwritten rules that must be observed if you're to avoid upsetting others – particularly the French – and be accepted by your colleagues and clients. Indeed, etiquette is a vital component of business behaviour in France – after all, the French invented it.

The business day starts with the ritual handshake. Each person who arrives is expected to make the rounds of the office to greet others who are already there. Then, throughout the day, each time you run across someone for the first time, there's a '*Bonjour*' and handshake; the second time you see a person, you don't say *Bonjour* again but go straight into what you have to say. How the French remember who they've already seen on a particular day is a source of amazement among foreigners. Although many women

> An American woman with a PhD once insisted that her French colleagues refer to her as 'Docteur', a stance which completely backfired; rather than commanding their respect, she was intentionally treated with disdain.

will greet each other and 'familiar' male colleagues with kisses, it won't be appreciated if you do likewise until you've been 'initiated'.

The French prefer personal contact – face to face is the best option, if it's available, otherwise the telephone. Note, however, that it's difficult to reach a French manager during the working day; since very few arrive early in the office, the best bet is to try calling in the evening, after 6pm. If the manager has provided his mobile phone number, it may be considered an open invitation to call him out of hours; if he doesn't wish to be disturbed, he'll switch off his phone.

Letters are reserved for official correspondence. If you must write a letter, bear in mind that the language must be formal and almost never 'direct' (the French will

take offence). Email is beginning to become an acceptable form of business communication but is nowhere near as prevalent as in other countries and is normally used only after the two correspondents have met; the French are reluctant to answer emails from people they don't know.

Working lunches are a rarity in France; although the tradition of the two-hour lunch is disappearing in some regions, the dining hour is sacrosanct and many French workers go home rather than out for lunch. If you're asked to go to lunch with colleagues, don't expect to talk business exclusively. And don't be surprised to see the alcohol (especially wine) flowing freely, even in the company *cantine*.

Also, the French may love small talk but not about personal subjects (e.g. family or home). If, like most Americans, you're averse to discussing politics and religion (topics the French adore), safe subjects are hobbies, sport (but not baseball, American football or cricket), travel and holidays (another favourite French topic).

The French maintain a strict separation between business life and personal life. In general there's no mixing business with family activities; it's rare indeed to receive an invitation to a colleague's home, and French workers' offices rarely have home comforts such as pictures on the walls and family 'souvenirs'.

The value accorded to personal life also shows up when planning business trips; the average French manager would leave or return home

in the small hours of the morning rather than spend a night (or an extra night) in a hotel. This is to be borne in mind especially when scheduling meetings that start on Monday morning or end on Friday evening; don't be surprised to have large numbers of people arrive late on Monday or leave early on Friday. It's also out of the question to schedule work-related activities at weekends or on bank holidays or during any of the frequent school breaks.

A memorable scene in the recent film *Marie Antoinette* typifies the importance of protocol in the French psyche: the young Dauphiness is standing stark naked and shivering in her boudoir surrounded by her court, while the ladies of the court defer, each in turn, to a higher ranking member of the nobility before the dressing process can proceed. In many ways French business etiquette has scarcely evolved since Marie Antoinette's day.

## Appointments

Don't expect to see anyone in France without an appointment – even those with empty diaries will have a full agenda of invented activities when you turn up unexpectedly to see them. Make an appointment at least a week in advance, preferably by telephone or fax. Don't, however, expect secretaries or assistants to make appointments for their managers, as they rarely have access to their diaries – or know what they're doing from one day to the next – and, even if they do, they may not have the authority to arrange meetings without their approval.

Equally, don't expect to see the person you've made an appointment with, even if you ring to confirm the day before, as it's common for meetings to be cancelled unilaterally – and the onus will be on you to rearrange it.

When you arrive for an appointment, don't expect to be offered coffee or tea, or indeed anything (so if you're dying for a coffee, have it **before** your meeting).

The words *ce* (this), *prochain* (next) and *dernier* (last) can cause confusion when referring to dates. When an English-speaker says 'next Friday' (for example), he usually means 'Friday of next week', but when a Frenchman says *vendredi prochain*, he is referring to the **first** Friday after today (which an English-speaker would have called 'this Friday'). Similarly for months: *avril dernier* means the most recently occurring April, and *juin prochain* is the next occurring June, even if today is 31st May. It's therefore strongly advised to specify the month, date and even year to avoid confusion. Also, bear in mind that the French normally use the 24-hour clock when arranging meetings or timetables – *am* in French means *après-midi* or afternoon – and that, rather than 'a week' and 'two weeks', they will say 'eight days' and 'fifteen days' (e.g. '*vendredi en huit*' means 'Friday week').

## Business Cards

When you introduce yourself for the first time, be sure to have plenty of business cards. Not only do the French consider a large collection of cards to be a measure of their own importance, but having your name printed helps avoid misunderstandings (apart from pronunciation) due to language difficulties.

## Business Gifts

Although token gifts are greatly appreciated, it's best to avoid

around two hours and for alcohol to be served and consumed.

## Dress

Until recently, the French have dressed conservatively for work – even in summer it wasn't unusual to see men wearing dark suits and ties – but this is changing. Although still the case in traditional businesses (banking, industry, law, etc.), in sectors dominated by creativity or the younger generation (e.g. high-tech and 'creative' disciplines), dress tends to be more informal. In any case, the French pay particular attention to accessories such as shoes, ties, jewellery and scarves, which are a means to express their individuality. Note, however, that it's considered in poor taste (in some cases even illegal) to wear items of 'conspicuous' religious significance.

It isn't usual for men to remove their jackets and loosen their ties in meetings – even when it's stiflingly hot.

personal gifts unless you're sure that you know the recipient's tastes – in which case a book or music recording will show that you're interested in culture. Otherwise, practical gifts with corporate themes (pens, mugs, paperweights, card holders, etc.) are generally safe options. Note also that many large corporations have official policies limiting the value of gifts that employees are allowed to accept; it's best to enquire before offering an expensive gift.

## Business Lunches

Lunches in France are long affairs and business lunches are no exception. However, business may not be discussed at all during the meal, which is usually seen as an opportunity to get to know a client or supplier. Don't start a business discussion with a French person, even (or especially) if you're trying to sell him something, but wait for him to do so. Expect the meal to last

There are two types of 'deadline' in France: *une date butoir,* which literally means a 'butting' date, which (in theory) cannot be exceeded; and *une date cible,* a target date. Most French deadlines are *dates cibles.*

## Timekeeping

Timekeeping and punctuality are relative concepts in France, where few events (other than the most important things in life, such as football matches) start at their advertised time. However, if you're trying to sell a product or service, you should arrive on time – or even five or ten minutes early. This shows that you're serious (*sérieux*) and wish to be taken seriously. If you're going to be late, you should phone and say so. Don't expect your counterpart to be on time, however – 15 to 30 minutes late is considered acceptable – and, unless he's extremely late, don't expect an apology or explanation.

Like time, deadlines are flexible and are rarely met. France famously disregarded the Maastricht treaty's requirement to 'balance its budgets' by 2004 – and infamously got away with it. The fact that something gets done or arrives a few days late isn't a cause for concern, but is accepted as part of normal business life – you'll **never** get an apology for tardiness.

## Meetings

The given starting time for a meeting or other appointment is only approximate. Don't be surprised to have to wait 20 minutes or longer beyond the appointed time for a meeting to start – and even then there may be a good deal of general chitchat before any business is addressed. Similarly, don't expect to complete meetings on time – unless a key participant has a plane to catch.

Despite the Revolution and their belief in *égalité*, the French still operate in a hierarchical structure – especially when it comes to meetings. It's best not to speak until explicitly invited to do so, and then

to start by addressing the highest-ranking manager present. On the other hand, business meetings tend to be undisciplined affairs, with everyone talking at once (and not necessarily on the main topic or even on the same topic), or answering their phones or even getting up and leaving at random moments.

Meetings are generally seen as an opportunity to exchange ideas and receive information. Few decisions are made, as time is needed to mull over the ideas expressed.

### First Meetings

The French like to do business with people they know and trust, and they consider that the key to successful business dealings is a solid personal

Most meetings have an official agenda and you may receive a written copy of this. However, the agenda isn't cast in stone and may be followed roughly, in part or not at all, depending on the course the meeting takes. Bringing the agenda to people's attention is *mal élevé* ('badly brought up').

relationship. Few French people do business with strangers whom they've met briefly or know little about. First meetings are therefore used mainly for getting to know each other, and are often taken up entirely with building the foundations of a relationship, rather than actual business. Don't be surprised if most of an initial meeting is taken up with 'small talk' and don't try to force a business agenda at the first encounter. Take the initiative from the person you're meeting and follow his cues.

### Language

English is taught to virtually every French schoolchild for at least five years but this doesn't mean that all French people speak English – and even those who do are generally reluctant to do so in front of native speakers for fear of appearing foolish. You should certainly never assume that a French person can speak and/or understand English. Expect a meeting to take place in French – take an interpreter with you if your French isn't good enough. If you need a meeting to be conducted in English, start by greeting the person in French and politely ask if he speaks English.

If a meeting is in English, speak slowly and clearly until you gauge the other person's level of English. Even if it's high, avoid metaphors and cultural references, especially those based on sports idioms. The French have no idea what 'a country mile' or 'a New York minute' might mean; they have no concepts equivalent to 'the ball's in your court', 'hit one out of the park', 'take a rain check', or 'drop back and punt'. Similarly, many everyday English phrases can incite hilarious reactions, even when analogous expressions exist in French. For example, 'the shoe's on the other foot', 'it's raining cats and dogs', 'to have other fish to fry' or 'to throw in the towel'. Beware also of using 'sloppy' contractions such as 'gonna', 'wanna', 'woulda', 'shoulda', 'kinda', 'sorta', 'dontcha' and 'gimme', which also makes it difficult for non-native speakers to understand.

Note also that while the French may have learned to read and write English, their instruction in spoken English often didn't include learning to count or pronouncing the names of the letters, so if you speak any French at all, it's best to use it for numbers and letters. But make sure you know your French alphabet. In particular, remember that the names of the letters g and j are the almost exact opposite in French (a source of innumerable misunderstandings) and that i is pronounced like e (and

e is pronounced 'euh'). Telephone (and many other) numbers are given in pairs, e.g. *vingt-deux, trente-six*, etc., and not singly, so you'll need to practise your numbers too – especially those from 70 to 100.

Needless to say, you should use only the *vous* form until your counterpart explicitly invites the *tu* form. This may not ever happen – in some organisations, even long-time colleagues address each other as *vous*. Also, it's advisable to refer to everyone simply as *Monsieur* or *Madame* (not even using their surnames) until you've broken the ice.

Finally, a few business-related *faux amis* to watch out for:

- *complexe* & *compliqué*: although in English 'complex' and 'complicated' are virtually synonyms, in French they're quite distinct. A situation that's *complexe*, while challenging intellectually or technically, is surmountable; whereas when it's *compliqué* it's pointless to expect to make any progress – as, for example, when it requires navigating a morass of contradictory regulations, or convincing a large number of people to do something they have no desire to do.

- *délai*: an untranslatable word meaning 'the amount of time before something happens', e.g. *Pour cette voiture il y a un délai de six mois.* (There's a six-month waiting list for that car.) delay: *retard*.

- *rendez-vous* is a noun meaning 'meeting' and not a verb; the French won't understand the phrase 'Let's rendezvous on Friday'.

- RSVP, which in English stands for *Répondez, s'il vous plaît* but is used as a verb (e.g. 'Could you RSVP this'), isn't used in this way in France, where people don't 'RSVP' but simply reply (*répondre*).

There are many other common business terms that cause confusion, as their meanings in French and English are quite different – much narrower or much broader or simply not the same at all. These include to achieve/*achever*, to complete/*compléter*, to control/*contrôler*, to dispose/*disposer*, diligent/*diligent*, elaboration/*élaboration*, important/*important*, interesting/*intéressant*, planning/*planning*, precision/*précision* and punctual/*ponctuel*.

Needless to say, the French use the metric system – after all, they invented it – so references to feet, yards, miles, acres, ounces, pounds, stones, pints, quarts, gallons and

Grand Arche, Paris

Fahrenheit are unlikely to be understood. There's one possible exception: inches (*pouces*), in which television and computer screens are measured.

## Decision-making

If there's one area that can cause insurmountable problems for foreigners – particularly Americans – when dealing with the French, it's the decision-making process. Here the French love of debate is often misleading, giving the appearance that the various options are being considered and evaluated while in fact being nothing more than a smokescreen for avoiding or postponing a decision.

Although in theory decisions are taken at the top rather than by consensus and should therefore be quickly implemented, in practice the decision-making process is slow – or non-existent. As mentioned above, the French are naturally averse to taking risks. Since a decision represents a risk of making the wrong choice, they're especially reluctant to take decisions. If you require a decision, there are three stratagems you can put into practice, although all three require a certain degree of politicking or lobbying (and thus risk-taking in their own right).

The first option targets the decision-maker himself. Bearing in mind that he'll never expose himself to public criticism, you must ensure that the decision is made in private. Arrange a one-to-one meeting with him, present him with the choices, outline the pros and cons (making it absolutely clear which option is preferable), and then give him plenty of time to get accustomed to the 'decision' before he has to present it publicly. A larger meeting can then serve as a forum for presenting the choices to those concerned, despite the predetermined outcome – thus providing at least a smokescreen of procedural propriety.

If the decision-maker is unapproachable, a second strategy targets his subordinates. Following the same principles as the first strategy, you lobby each of the subordinates individually (after all, they're often 'clones' of their boss) until you reach 'critical mass', where enough of the subordinates present the same idea to the boss that he cannot help going along with it.

The third strategy is the riskiest and should be used as a last resort; it's what the French call *faire du forcing*. Essentially, it involves going over the head of the decision-maker, convincing his boss, and thus 'forcing' the decision.

## Negotiating

Here's a common scenario: you spend hours (or even days) pitching your idea; all along, the French show interested attention and asked pertinent questions, so you think the deal is done, right? Wrong. Once you've finished your pitch, someone will drop the bomb: 'Have you considered …?' and he will have identified a one-in-a-million case that jeopardises the whole deal. Or, after all, they simply reply, 'Thanks, that's an interesting idea, we'll consider it' – which simply translated, means 'No thank you.' Note that the French will never actually say '*Non.*'

Maybe negotiations have stalled and you're trying to find out the latest status of the project. Either nobody responds to your repeated phone calls or emails, or you get bland statements such as 'Thank you for your enquiry, we'll investigate and get back to you.'

But let's assume that somehow you overcome these obstacles and agree to a deal. You may receive a contract that looks good at first glance but actually provides lots of room for backing out (the French

> If you're asking the French to do something for you, it's likely that their initial reply will be '*Non*,' followed by 'maybe' or 'perhaps if …' You'll probably never receive an unqualified '*Oui.*' (If you do, it's best to be suspicious; often the French will say yes just to get you off their backs and have no intention of doing what's requested.)

love contracts, though rarely respect them).

Then you discover that a key milestone has slipped because it was scheduled during a bank holiday or school break – which are hard to avoid (see **Holidays** below) or because there has been a strike somewhere in the supply chain, or simply because France have reached the World Cup final … Finally you take delivery of your hard-earned product and discover that it wasn't what you'd agreed to – at which point, the French will either feign ignorance of the 'agreement', fail to understand what you're talking about or claim that somehow it's **your** fault.

If, on the other hand, the French have purchased your goods or services, you'll need to come to terms with another important French business practice: to delay payment. In fact it's an accepted French 'custom' to force suppliers to send frequent reminders that payment is (over)due – for which the term is *relancer* (literally, to relaunch).

When negotiating a business deal with a French person, also bear in mind the following:

- The French have little respect for those who boast – be self-effacing in your description of your company's achievements and products.

- All business dealings are based on mutual trust, therefore a French client might prefer to make a small initial order to see if you fulfil expectations before taking things further.

- Be patient at all stages of negotiation: the French hate rushing (except when they're behind a steering wheel) and dislike others hurrying them. Accept that each stage takes time.

### Regional Differences

As in any large country, the significant cultural differences between the regions of France are also present in business, and your experience with a Breton company may be quite different from the way you're dealt with by a business in Paris, Pau or Provence. In general, people in southern France have a more Latin, Mediterranean style and those in the north, including the capital, a more northern European work ethic – relatively speaking – but don't take this for granted.

You also need to be prepared for huge contrasts in business styles and operations between different companies: France is home to dynamic, modern businesses based on US models using the latest technology and management policies, but also to small, traditional companies, often family-run, where little has changed in decades. Even among the large companies, many operate in an 'old-fashioned' way.

These contrasts mean that foreigners intending to do business in France need to be adaptable and flexible and not try to impose a particular procedure – or indeed any procedure – on the French.

## EMPLOYING PEOPLE

Think long and hard before you employ staff in France – it's no exaggeration to say that you'll be stepping into the proverbial minefield. French labour law is one of the most rigid in the developed world and employees with indefinite contracts are among the best protected. Labour legislation is designed to protect employees from exploitation and they therefore enjoy extensive rights – to the extent that many employers complain **they** are the exploited ones and have fewer rights than their employees. Workers

renewable for a further three – while you assess a person's suitability.

### Domestic Help

As in many countries, the vast majority of workers employed in homes, e.g. gardeners and cleaners, work illegally, as few 'employers' offer them contracts and pay their social security contributions as they should. You should be wary of doing this, however, as it isn't uncommon for a maid or gardener to report their employer for not making social security contributions. If you employ someone illegally in your home and he has an accident, you're considered responsible and liable for damages – which can be astronomical. One way round these problems is to use the *chèque emploi service universel* system (where you act as an employer and pay your employee's social insurance), operated by most banks.

## Social Security & Tax

Social security contributions can be financially crippling for a new business – an employer must pay up to 50 per cent of each employee's gross pay. Unlike most other European countries, however, France has no 'pay-as-you-earn' (PAYE) system, so employers aren't responsible for deducting employees' tax.

are entitled to a minimum wage, 13 or 14 'monthly' salary payments, five weeks' paid holiday and up to ten paid public holidays, and employers must pay a significant part of their social security contributions (see below).

## Contracts

Be wary of entering into a permanent contract (*CDI*) with an employee unless you're sure he's the right person for the job and has proved his worth in your business. Employees on permanent contracts are extremely difficult to fire (unless they commit a heinous crime), and if a court rules that the dismissal is unfair – which they usually do – employers must pay huge compensation, i.e. up to two years' salary. Make full use of the trial period (*période d'essai*) – which can be for three months, sometimes

> Oral agreements are valid under French law, and if you pay someone for work you're deemed to have entered into a contractual relationship, even if there's no written contract.

## TRADE UNIONS

France doesn't have a strong trade union (*syndicat*) movement and only some 20 per cent of the workforce belong to a union. Nevertheless, the main union confederation, the Confédération Générale du Travail (CGT), plays a major role in industrial negotiations such as collective labour agreements, and is a key player in national employment policy – thanks to its disproportionate influence in a few highly sensitive and visible sectors, such as railway workers.

Industrial relations have improved hugely over the last few years, although strikes (*grèves*) are still more common in France than in almost any other country.

### Joining a Union

Employees aren't obliged to join a union, but all businesses with 50 or more employees are required to have an employee representation committee (*comité d'entreprise*), which ensures certain benefits, such as free access to legal services, job training programmes, and subsidised holidays and children's summer camps. Union membership, which costs little, is sometimes tax-deductible.

## WORKING WEEK

A controversial law passed in 2002 introduced a 35-hour working week in an attempt to reduce unemployment. As this was a dismal failure, the law has since been 'softened' and most employees work a 37- or 39-hour week, from Monday to Friday. It's rare for managers and the self-employed to work less than 40 hours a week but, under the 35-hour-week rules, employees who habitually work longer hours are entitled to a certain number of compensatory days off. These are usually referred to as *RTT* days (after the clause in the law relating to working time reduction – *réduction de temps de travail*) and often used to make long weekends around bank holidays (see below).

In the past, Saturday was also part of the working week, and it's still officially a working day (*jour ouvré*), with Sunday the only official day off in the week – Sundays and public holidays are highlighted on calendars.

Despite the legal maximums and common perceptions about French working habits, official surveys find that the effective average working week in France – 41.8 hours – is comparable to, though admittedly slightly lower than, that of other European countries such as Spain (43.1) and the UK. (44.8); the EU average is 43.7.

### Coffee & Smoking Breaks

Few companies have scheduled coffee breaks, but most employees are entitled to 30 minutes off during the mornings and afternoons. However, the enactment of anti-smoking laws, whereby employees are no longer permitted to smoke at their desks but must leave the building to satisfy their nicotine addiction, has been calculated to cost over an hour per day in lost work time.

> 'French employees aren't often motivated and excited when it comes to their jobs; they are just trying to get through the day.'
>
> Ann Koepke (American expatriate)

## HOLIDAYS

French workers have more paid holidays than those of any other country, averaging 39 days per year compared with the Germans with 27, the British 24, Canadians 19, Australians 17 and Americans just 14. The French take their holidays seriously and the vast majority of employees take all their annual leave – forgoing part of your holiday in order to work is not only unheard of, it's illegal except for the self-employed.

Employees are generally entitled to five weeks' holiday a year plus public holidays and *RTT* days (see above), and it isn't uncommon to meet 'workers' who enjoy eight or nine weeks' annual holiday in all. Most workers take a whole month off in summer. Whereas the most common period used to be the whole of August, and later either July or August, the period which includes two summer public holidays – the 14th July (*la fête nationale*) and 15th August (*Assomption*) – is now the most popular time for *les grandes vacances*. If you're a new arrival in a company, however, you're unlikely to be able to take your holiday during this period unless the entire company or business closes (as is common in manufacturing and industry), as choice of holiday period is decided by strict hierarchy.

There are certain times of the year in France when it's best to avoid doing business (see below); if you have to, expect things to take **even** longer than usual. In fact, it's often difficult to avoid some kind of holiday. In addition to summer holidays and bank holidays, there are two-week school breaks every two months (at the end of October and the end of December, in mid-February and in mid-April); in May (which the French call *le mois gruyère* – Swiss cheese month) the bank holidays are often 'strung together' to make a two-week holiday, and of course December and early January aren't good times for doing business either…

## Public Holidays

The only public holiday (*jour férié*) that an employer in France is legally obliged to grant with pay is 1st May (irrespective of which day of the week it falls on). However, most collective agreements allow paid holidays on some or all of the following days. (A Pentecost/Whit Monday holiday was officially abolished in 2004 but is still widely observed.)

> '... the French work to live. Or, more precisely, they work to go on holiday.'
>
> Stephen Clarke, *Talk to the Snail*

The number of days the French actually take off work, however, varies from year to year. When

| Public Holidays | |
|---|---|
| **Date** | **Holiday** |
| 1st January | New Year's Day (Nouvel An/Jour de l'An) |
| March or April | Easter Monday (Lundi de Pâques) |
| 1st May | Labour Day (Fête du Travail) |
| 8th May | VE Day (Fête de la Libération/Victoire 1945/Anniversaire 1945) |
| May | Ascension Day (Ascension) – the sixth Thursday after Easter |
| 14th July | Bastille Day (Fête Nationale) |
| 15th August | Assumption (Fête de l'Assomption) |
| 1st November | All Saints' Day (Toussaint) |
| 11th November | Armistice Day (Fête de l'Armistice) |

a holiday falls on a Saturday or Sunday, another day (e.g. the previous Friday or following Monday) isn't usually granted as a holiday instead. However, when a public holiday falls on a Tuesday or Thursday, the day before or the day after (i.e. Monday or Friday respectively) may be declared a holiday, depending on the employer. This practice is called 'making a bridge' (*faire un pont*). If a holiday falls on a Wednesday, it's common for employees to take the two preceding or succeeding days off – especially in May (known as *les ponts de mai*).

All public offices, banks and post offices are closed on public holidays and only essential work is performed. Foreign embassies and consulates in France usually observe all French public holidays, **as well as** their own country's national holidays.

## Special Leave

Employees in France don't receive a quota of sick days as in some countries (e.g. Australia and the US), and there's no limit to the amount of time you may take off work due to sickness or accidents. You're normally required to notify your employer immediately of sickness or an accident that prevents you from working, and to obtain a medical certificate (*arrêt de travail*) from your doctor – being 'off sick' is known as *être en arrêt de travail*.

> Despite decades of falling sales due largely to New World competition, it was not until 2004 that the French wine industry announced changes to its 85-year-old appellation d'origine contrôlée system, but these were not only too late but also too little to put French wine back on the world's supermarket shelves.

# 7.
# ON THE MOVE

**F**rench cities and large towns have good and cheap public transport networks and there are excellent nationwide rail and air services. But in rural areas the only way to get from A to B is usually by car – and the French will think nothing of driving non-stop (except for petrol) three-quarters of the way across France for a weekend visit. When it comes to travelling, the French like to do so in style and comfort but, above all, at speed.

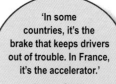

'In some countries, it's the brake that keeps drivers out of trouble. In France, it's the accelerator.'

Stephen Clarke,
*Talk to the Snail*

To help reduce the surprise (and shock) factor of travelling in France – particularly by road – this chapter contains useful tips, including driving and parking conventions (the rules seldom apply) and information on public transport.

## DRIVING

Driving in France isn't for the faint-hearted and although French drivers aren't the worst in Europe, they give the Italians, Portuguese and Spanish a good run for their money, and make most British and American drivers seem like paragons of virtue. Until recently, France had one of the worst accident records in the EU, with over 8,000 road deaths in 2002 (though nothing compared with the country's all-time record of 16,617 in 1972, when there were far fewer cars on the roads). Since then, a government campaign combining scare tactics with more severe (and more often imposed) penalties for dangerous driving has succeeded in almost halving this figure – which isn't to say that the French have suddenly turned into patient, courteous and law-abiding drivers, although they are sometimes, surprisingly, all of these.

When driving a long distance, try to avoid the following popular holiday 'changeover' days, when all of France is on the move: 30th June, 15th July, 31st July, 14th August and 31st August.

## French Drivers

Like Latins (and the French have plenty of Latin blood), French people seem to change personality the moment they get behind the wheel of a car, when even normally laid-back people who will happily spend half an hour chatting with a

drivers are **never** to blame for such 'accidents').

Oddly the French take similar pride in being caught speeding (as is increasingly likely with cameras popping up all over the country and *gendarmes* lurking in lay-bys with *jumelles* – speed cameras), as this proves that any previous tales of indulgence in excessive speed hadn't been mere exaggeration.

Collecting fines, licence penalty points and even driving bans (which are frequently ignored – at the risk of a prison sentence) is also part and parcel of the French disdain for rules, which is evident from their driving behaviour – from their use (or non-use) of indicators to their disregard of traffic lights and parking restrictions.

'Slow'-moving vehicles (which include those exceeding the speed limit by only a moderate margin, but not tractors, which cannot go any faster), and especially foreign-registered cars, are like red rags to a bull to many French drivers, who **must** overtake them – preferably on a blind bend – even if they intend to turn off at the next junction.

To this end they will 'stick' (*coller*) to your rear bumper, even if they have no way of getting past (e.g. there's a constant stream of oncoming traffic or the road has been reduced to a single lane by road works). If you're in front of a tailgater (which you inevitably will be much of the time), leave a large gap between you and the vehicle in front – this gives you and the tailgater extra space for an emergency stop.

friend on the way to the post box, turn into suicidal maniacs bent on reaching their destination (or the next life) almost before they've left home. Many French people seem to be frustrated racing drivers – and not only men. Women, young and old, drive just as fast as men and often as recklessly and it isn't unusual to see great-grandmothers in their 80s and even 90s careering around the countryside with blithe disregard for weather and traffic conditions, and the ability of their vehicles to remain in contact with the road.

'Going into the scenery' (*aller dans le décor*) is a favourite French pastime, and people will gleefully describe their most spectacular 'exits' – particularly if they involved a brush with death – as they pushed their inadequate machines just beyond their limits (French

> 'There's something about the sight of a car in front of them that releases a red mist in the brains of all French drivers ...'
>
> Donald Carroll, Surprised by France

## Roads

The quality of French roads varies greatly – from velvet-smooth motorways (*autoroutes*) to pot-holed minor, and even major, roads. This is partly a question of budgets, as different types of road are the responsibility of different authorities (national, regional, departmental and local), which may have more or less money for maintenance and improvement (or give low priority to such expenditure). In general, however, the most-used roads tend to be the worst maintained.

French motorways are among the least-used roads – largely because most of them are toll roads (*à péage*) and among Europe's most expensive. It pays, however, to find out which sections of motorway are free – generally, but not exclusively, around cities and other busy areas – as not only are they the fastest roads, they're also the safest (relatively speaking).

The classic French road – straight and tree-lined and seemingly never-ending – is fast disappearing, as trees are felled (they 'cause' many deaths when French drivers go into the scenery) and roads are widened into dual-carriageways. Those that remain provide a unique and nostalgic driving experience; in stark contrast to driving in cities and towns, driving on country roads is usually enjoyable.

Always have a good, up-to-date map when driving in France, where road signs aren't to be trusted: if they aren't pointing in ambiguous directions or positioned so that you cannot see them until it's too late, they peter out at the crucial moment (if in doubt, go straight on).

## Road Rules

Officially, driving in France is governed by rules, but these are seldom adhered to by the French. In fact, there isn't a single 'highway code' (*code de la route*) but several, produced by different publishers and each with its own interpretation of the law – which, like most French laws, is impenetrable. Therefore, although all French drivers are required to learn the rules in order to obtain a licence (they must pass a written test before being allowed to take a practical test), these are generally regarded only as guidelines. The notes below indicate

the main areas where common practice deviates from official theory.

### Speed Limits

Speed limits might be thought to be unequivocal. But not in France. The limit on motorways, for example, is 130kph (82mph) except *par temps de pluie* (wet or poor driving conditions), in which case it's 110kph (68mph). The difficulty is in deciding whether weather is 'rainy' or not; does it actually have to be raining, for example, or does a wet road qualify? And if it's raining on and off, can you speed up between showers? Such questions are of mostly academic interest, however, as most French people drive at a minimum of 150kph on motorways, even in thick fog.

Other limits include 110kph on most non-motorway dual-carriageways, 90kph (56mph) on most single-carriageway roads outside towns and villages, 70kph (48mph) on some rural roads and 50kph (31mph) in most built-up areas, including cities, towns and villages. Typically, the French treat these limits as the minimum rather than the maximum, and few even slow down when passing through villages on a main road, let alone drive at less than 50kph.

The authorities know full well that speed limits are rarely observed – despite repeated reminders (*rappel*) – and it isn't unusual to see a temporary speed limit (in operation during road works, for example) that's **higher** than the limit normally in force.

The French have long had an obsession with speed: it was a Frenchman who invented the 'velocipede', an early bicycle, another who built the first steam carriage in 1769, and yet another – the impressively named Comte de Chasseloup-Laubat – who held the first official world land speed record (63.158kph) at a competition held, of course, in France in 1898. The French were also the first to fly (in hot air balloons, in 1783) and pioneered the high-speed train and the supersonic airliner.

### Right is Right

Like all continental Europeans, the French drive on the right-hand side of the road – most of the time. In fact, the French habitually take a 'racing line', which involves cutting corners (even when there are cars coming the other way), hang out towards the middle of the road when tailgating (i.e. often) on the look-out for an opportunity to overtake,

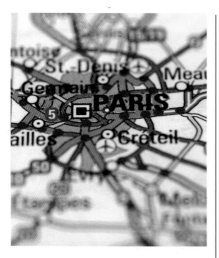

certain 'etiquette' to be observed. As no French driver can reasonably be expected to slow down sufficiently to give way at every junction sporting an 'X' sign, you only really have priority from the right when you arrive at a junction well before the other driver and make it clear – by edging your car forwards – that you intend to assert your rights, and even then those rights may be blatantly ignored. If you simply pull out onto a major road without looking, you're asking for trouble – even though 'technically' you'll be blameless for any resulting crash.

> Take particular care in car parks, where the 'priority on the right' rule applies – most of the time.

and generally wander across the centre line in a disconcerting and sometimes dangerous manner.

This last habit may have something to do with a long-standing French tradition that drivers emerging from a turning on the right have priority over those on the road they're joining, even if this is a major road. Unfortunately, whereas this rule used to be universal and therefore easy to understand, it now applies in some circumstances but not others – and even the French aren't always sure which.

In general, you can assume that drivers on a main road have priority unless you see a triangular sign with a large X in it, which indicates that **all** drivers must give way to the right – this includes at junctions with traffic lights when the traffic lights are out of order or flashing orange, as they often are at night in rural areas.

Note, however, that even where *priorité à droite* applies, there's a

As in many other countries, on motorways and dual-carriageways most motorists ignore 'Give Way' signs on slip roads and pull out (with or without indicators flashing) as if they had priority.

### Roundabouts

Driving on the right means going round roundabouts (traffic circles) anti-clockwise, although most have tyre marks to show that they've occasionally prompted nothing more than a slight deviation from a straight line. Roundabouts are a relatively recent arrival on the French road scene and many French drivers haven't yet got to grips with them.

Most don't indicate, but even if they do it's best to ignore what they

seem to be telling you. Often, for example, the French will indicate left on entering a roundabout when in fact they're going straight on; others will indicate right at some point in their navigation of a roundabout, but not necessarily before the exit they intend to take. To make matters worse, they are taught to use only the outside lane of a two-lane roundabout for going straight on – you will cause consternation and confusion if you use the inside lane for the same purpose – and some believe they should use this lane even for turning left.

Take extra care on roundabouts and be prepared for anything to happen.

### Traffic Lights

French traffic lights change from green to amber to red and straight back to green, without an intermediate red-and-amber stage (which would be pointless, as everyone would ignore it). The French manage to jump lights nevertheless (especially in Paris) by watching for the lights in the other direction to turn red rather than for their own to turn green. As it's common for drivers not to stop if a light has 'only just' turned red, this is a highly hazardous practice.

Flashing filter arrows are rare but sometimes allow a right turn when the coast is clear. At night in rural areas and some small towns, traffic lights automatically switch to flashing-amber mode, which means that 'priority on the right' rules apply (see above).

> French traffic lights are difficult to see, particularly on a sunny day, as they have weak bulbs; keep a sharp eye out for them – especially red ones.

### Overtaking

You're supposed to indicate left when about to overtake (most motorists do so **as** they overtake, which defeats the object) and – on single-carriageway roads only – indicate right when about to pull in again after overtaking. In fact, most French drivers use their left indicators to tell the driver in front 'I intend to get past you and I'd be obliged if you'd pull over to let me do so' or, when in the outside lane of motorways and dual-carriageways, to tell drivers behind 'I've got my foot to the floor and I'm not going to get out of your way until I've finished overtaking everyone in the middle lane between here and Paris [or wherever]'.

If you drive at the speed limit, you're unlikely to need to overtake anything other than tractors, lorries (trucks) and the occasional *sans permis* (see box) – meanwhile every other vehicle will be overtaking you.

### Other Rules

Other rules that should be observed include the following:

- All vehicles must carry a full set of spare bulbs and fuses (available in sets from the vehicle manufacturer or separately in supermarkets).

- All vehicle occupants must wear a seatbelt and children under 13 aren't allowed in the front seat.

- The use of a mobile (unless it's a hands-free set without earphones) is prohibited, as are radar detectors, the use of which can incur a fine of €1,500 and the loss of your licence.

- Motorists are advised (it isn't yet law) to use dipped headlights (low beam) at all times when driving outside built-up areas during 'winter' (i.e. between the end of October and the end of March).

- Hazard warning lights (*warnings*) **must** be used when being towed.

- The permitted blood-alcohol level is 50mg per 100ml and you can be fined up to €4,500 and lose your licence for driving with over 80mg per 100ml – despite which French men (especially) routinely drive when well over the limit, believing that no amount of alcohol impairs their judgement.

A stunning example of the French indifference to road safety is the existence of cars for which no driving licence is required – known as *sans permis*. These vehicles, powered by supercharged lawnmower engines, can seat four people and are capable of speeds up to 90kph (downhill with a following wind). Needless to say, they should be given a wide berth.

## Motorcyclists & Pedestrians

Keep a sharp eye out for motorcyclists, who even more rarely obey speed limits than car drivers and often overtake on the inside, particularly in towns and on dual-carriageways, expecting you to get out of their way whatever speed you're doing. Most dangerous of all are children (as young as 14) on mopeds (usually referred to by the trade name *Mobylette*), who weave in and out of traffic as if on a skateboard and flatten themselves against their handlebars in an attempt to gain a few extra kph. Fortunately (and perhaps for this

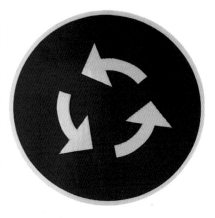

or illumination. You aren't obliged to stop at a crossing unless there's someone on it or a pedestrian is 'clearly demonstrating his intention to cross' (or the light is red); if in doubt as to a pedestrian's intentions, stop – but look in your mirror first to check that the tailgater has time to stop too.

## Documents

Under French law, you must carry the following documents when driving: proof of insurance cover (signed on the back – though it isn't known why); your driving licence; your car's registration document (*carte grise*); and personal identification (e.g. passport or residence permit). Your vehicle must also display, inside the windscreen (windshield), proof of insurance cover and, if the vehicle is more than four years old, a national car test certificate. (A road tax *vignette* is no longer required for most vehicles.) Failure to produce any of the required documents can incur an on-the-spot fine of up to €38 – rising to €135 if you don't produce them within five days.

Here again, however, there are grey areas. First, it isn't clear whether you need to carry the originals of all these documents or whether copies are acceptable. However, it's advisable to carry the originals – although **never** to leave them in the car – as most *gendarmes* will insist on seeing them. Whether *gendarmes*' knowledge of the law is shaky or whether they're willing to use underhand methods to achieve their daily quota of

> 'Don't expect to keep your car scratch-free – the French don't care much about theirs, so why should they care about yours?'
>
> Ian Pickering (British expatriate)

reason) they make so much noise that you can hear them coming even if you don't see them.

Watch out too for pedestrians. Even where there's a pavement (sidewalk), the French prefer to walk in the road – possibly because pavements are often dotted with dog excrement (see **On Foot** below), even with small children and babies in pushchairs. Many have kamikaze tendencies and cross the road without looking, irrespective of whether there's a crossing nearby.

Pedestrian crossings (*passages à piétons*) are often indistinct – they may consist of white stripes on the road or merely some kind of paving stones, and few crossings outside cities and towns have traffic lights convictions (*procès-verbaux* or *PV*), they've also been known to fine motorists €180 for failing to sign the insurance certificate displayed in the windscreen of their car.

## Parking

One of the joys of driving in France is that most small towns have few metered areas and you may park free almost anywhere, provided you don't cause an obstruction. On the other hand, France has no 'park and ride' facilities (as are common in the UK, for example).

Parking in Paris

In large towns and cities, however, it isn't surprising to discover that finding a parking space is both challenging and time-consuming. French people often solve the problem creatively (and quickly) by parking almost anywhere – any space large enough for a car is deemed a parking spot – and pavements, bus stops and driveways are often crowded with parked cars.

> 'The average Frenchman deems it his right to double park in the main street and to ignore No Parking signs, but when an Englishman or German does it, it is cause for aggression.'
>
> William Jaques (British expatriate)

The French are also creative when it comes to making spaces fit their cars, using bumpers for just that purpose – bumping – until an impossible space becomes merely a tight space. Paris offers many spectacles, but one of the most entertaining (and typical) is watching a 75-plated car swing and nudge and jostle its way up against what looked like barely enough kerb to scrape a shoe on.

Official parking spaces include:

- underground car parks – your best bet as they're easy to find and secure, but parking is expensive;

- 'blue zones' (*zones bleues*), where you display a disc showing the time you arrived and the time by which you must depart;

- metered parking (*parking payant*) zones, where you normally take a ticket from a machine to display in the car ( maximum parking time is between 90 and 120 minutes);

- and streets without no-parking signs, usually a blue sign with a red line through it.

## Petrol Stations

Petrol stations (*stations de service*) are plentiful throughout most of

France and are mostly self-service but in rural areas some are manned. In many petrol stations you have a choice between two types of pump: at one type you must pay at a kiosk after filling up (this may be indicated by a sign saying *paiement en caisse*); at the other you pay by debit or credit card (which must have a microchip) at the pump in a complicated and usually lengthy procedure (a sign may say *24h/24h* to indicate that it's open at all times). An increasing number of petrol stations are completely unstaffed and you have no option but to pay with a card at the pump.

Petrol stations have tyre pressure pumps and water supplies, and some have vacuum cleaners and car washes. Many stations sell snacks, drinks, newspapers, confectionary, cigarettes, car accessories including oil, and sometimes local produce. Toilets are available, but some are of the 'Turkish' variety (i.e. a hole in the floor) – standards of cleanliness

> 'The French public transportation system reflects exactly the priorities of its Parisian overseers. Thus it is quick and easy to get around Paris; it is quick and easy to get to or from Paris; it is slow and difficult to get around the rest of France.'
>
> Donald Carroll, Surprised by France

often leave a lot to be desired. Toilet paper and soap are rare commodities.

## PUBLIC TRANSPORT

French public transport varies from outstanding and cheap (especially in Paris and other large cities) to non-existent, i.e. limited to expensive taxis (in remote rural areas). It's therefore impossible to generalise on the subject – except to say that smoking is prohibited on all public transport.

### Buses & Trams

France has no national bus network (which would be far too slow a means of transport for the French) and in most rural areas the only regular services are school buses, although some have 'occasional' services whereby you can book a bus pick-up at certain times and the driver alters his route accordingly. Most towns and cities, on the other hand, have excellent bus services – and many are reintroducing trams (*tramway*).

### Trains & Undergrounds

French trains are world famous – and not without justification. They generally run on time – you're

even told how long a train is to stop at each station and can claim a refund if a train is over half an hour late – and there are few accidents. Most famous is the *TGV* (*train à grande vitesse* – high-speed train), which was launched in 1981 and subsequently set a string of world record speeds – the latest being 574.8kph (357mph) in early 2007. *TGVs* serve most parts of France (the network is constantly being extended) and are a viable alternative to air travel, in terms of cost, speed and comfort.

Other services include 'ordinary' express, local and suburban trains, and there are international services (e.g. to Belgium, England, Germany, Greece, Italy, the Netherlands, Portugal, Spain, Switzerland and Scandinavia) from Paris and cities near France's borders.

Most train tickets aren't dated but are valid for two months and, when used, must be validated (*composté*) by inserting them in a machine on the station platform; failure to do so makes you liable for a fine. If you don't have a ticket (e.g. because the ticket office was closed or you arrived too late to buy one), you must find a ticket inspector onboard and own up; if you wait until he asks to see your ticket, you can be fined. Underground (*métro*) tickets may be valid indefinitely. On *TGVs* and long-distance trains, it's possible to book a (numbered) seat. Tickets are cheaper during off-peak hours, known as the *tarif bleu* as opposed to the *tarif blanc*.

Paris isn't the only French city to have an underground (subway)

system, although the *métro* (other cities use other names) is by far the most extensive. It's also ludicrously cheap: you can cross the city for just GB£1 (US$2). When using it, you must know the number of the line you want **and** the name of the station at the end of the line in the direction you want to go; when changing lines, look for signs reading 'Correspondance'. Lille, Lyon, Marseille, Rouen and Toulouse are among the other French cities with metros. Tickets can be bought in *carnets* (booklets – although in Paris you're simply given ten loose tickets), which must be inserted into a turnstile to gain access to trains.

Over-ground and underground train doors don't open automatically and you must usually depress or raise a lever or press a button, which won't work until the train has stopped.

> 'In the US it's easy to get anything done. France is the opposite. Everything is a struggle – except travelling by train.'
>
> Larry Davis (American businessman).

## Taxis

Taxis are common in large towns and cities and can be ordered by telephone in most rural areas. They're usually 'ordinary', unmarked cars with a 'TAXI' sign on the roof, even in Paris – a white light indicates a vacant taxi, an orange light one that's engaged or not in service. You often have a better chance of finding a vacant taxi by going to a hotel or tourist attraction than by standing in the street. If there are four or more of you, you may have to take two taxis.

All taxis are metered; in cities and towns, they're cheap (Paris taxis are among the cheapest in any European capital) but in rural areas they tend to be expensive. Taxi drivers generally pay no more attention to speed limits or road rules than other motorists; it's usual to tip them irrespective of whether they scare you half to death.

## Planes

Owing to the size of France, it's common for people to take internal flights, which are available from dozens of airports. The principal airline is Air France, which has few competitors and therefore expensive tickets – expect to pay at least €200 for a return flight across France and over €300 to fly to Corsica (or a neighbouring country such as Switzerland).

## BY BIKE & ON FOOT

French men (almost exclusively) are keen cyclists – but for exercise. A bicycle is rarely used purely as a means of getting from A to B. French motorists are nevertheless surprisingly considerate when encountering cyclists, and generally give them a wide berth when overtaking and dip their headlights at night when coming in the opposite direction. Surprisingly, however, there are few dedicated cycle (or roller-skate) paths or tracks, although these are now beginning to appear as part of France's general trend towards 'greenness' – they're sometimes called *voies vertes* (green ways).

Being a pedestrian in France, on the other hand, isn't without its hazards. To begin with, paths and pavements (*trottoirs*) are often dotted with dog excrement (*crotte* – giving rise to the expression '*crottoirs*') – and not only in Paris. That's when there is a pavement – on many rural roads there aren't any – and you must walk in the road and risk being mown down by speeding vehicles (a fluorescent jacket is highly recommended).

At pedestrian crossings, motorists aren't obliged to stop unless there's a red light or a pedestrian is halfway across, so don't start crossing unless the road is clear or oncoming traffic has plenty of time to stop.

Many towns have pedestrian-only zones (*zones piétonnes*) and some have recently introduced 'pedestrian priority' routes, where cars are supposed to give way to pedestrians. Like many innovations, this is a concept the French are having difficulty coming to terms with, and to assert your pedestrian rights is to take your life in your hands.

Nevertheless, the best way to become part of a French community – never mind saving the planet – is to walk whenever possible, as you will invariably bump into people you know (or can get to know) as well as experiencing the various sights, sounds, smells and other pleasures France has to offer.

---

**Parisian Pavements**

In May 2006 Paris (re)launched a campaign to clean up its streets, with the slogan 'Pas de ça chez vous ? Paris c'est chez vous !' (Not in your back yard? But Paris is your back yard!). Owners who don't scoop up after their pooping pooches risk a €183 fine. But according to a town hall survey, 92 per cent already do so – at least that's what the owners themselves claimed; a study based on simple observation revealed that 40 per cent don't.

---

# 8.

# THE FRENCH AT PLAY

**B**ecoming socially adept in a different culture is perhaps the greatest challenge in your bid to 'fit in' abroad, as you're most likely to do the wrong thing when socialising. To help you avoid social gaffes, this chapter contains information about dress code, dining out (and entertaining), and sporting and leisure activities.

> 'The truth is that the French mostly dress like frumps.'
>
> Stephen Clarke,
> *Talk to the Snail*

## DRESS CODE

The French have a reputation for dressing smartly and elegantly. Sadly, it's largely underserved. True, you'll encounter plenty of expensively dressed people on the Rue du Faubourg Saint-Honoré in Paris – and similarly upmarket parts of other cities and towns – but elsewhere the French can be astonishingly badly attired. Not only will they go out shopping in the ubiquitous jeans and trainers or, worse, tracksuits, but they often don't bother to dress up for concerts, parties, weddings and funerals, let alone when entertaining or being entertained at home. If they do decide to smarten up, their dress sense often leaves something to be desired and it's as common to see people in drab or ill-matching clothes as in fashionable outfits.

It's therefore easy to feel overdressed in France, although you should also beware of dressing scruffily. Jeans are widely acceptable provided they're clean and pressed and not the ones you use for gardening. Not that the French normally wear jeans for gardening – or any other household work – and it's common practice to don overalls (usually blue and hence called *bleus*) for any dirty work.

As in many other aspects of life, the French are traditional (or old-fashioned, depending on your viewpoint) when it comes to clothing. Women often wear scarves, for example, and men commonly drape a sweater over their shoulders. On the other hand, men are more inclined to wear bright colours than, say, British men, and ties are rarely worn except at work.

Despite their reputation for sexiness, French women generally dress conservatively and expose less flesh than, for example, women in the UK. In particular, the fashion for displaying six inches of belly between navel and belt has scarcely caught on.

French children wear what children the world over wear and have no more desire to stand out – or to be seen at all – than their foreign counterparts.

Many parts of France have traditional costumes, which are worn on special occasions such as local fairs or religious celebrations. Most costumes are colourful and those worn by women in Alsace, Brittany and the Basque country are particularly eye-catching.

## EATING & DRINKING

Just as the French work to live, they live to eat – perhaps more so than the people of any other country. Not only is there an abundance of mostly inexpensive eating places serving excellent food throughout the country, but the French pride themselves on their culinary skills, and eating at friends' homes can be an even more gastronomic experience than dining in a Michelin-starred restaurant. Eating out is a popular social activity – many French people eat out on Sundays and public holidays, when restaurants are full to bursting.

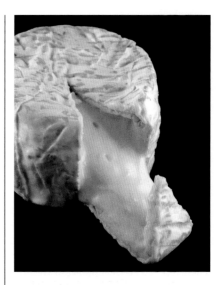

Any and every social occasion revolves around food – whether it's Christmas or New Year's Eve, Epiphany or 14th July, a wedding or a christening or simply a fete. Meals are long. It's usual for aperitifs to last at least an hour and for the meal proper to take a minimum of two hours. Meals that 'start' at eight (meals never start on time) may not finish until two or three in the morning.

This doesn't mean that the French eat inordinate amounts of food, but rather that each course is given plenty of time to be digested before the next is embarked on, so that even after a seven- or eight-course meal you rarely feel 'full up' but rather pleasantly sated. The ultimate compliment you can receive on a meal served to the French is *on s'est régalé*, which literally means 'we ate like kings' – and kings aren't noted for rushing their pleasures.

> 'All countries value their cultural heritage in their own way and with varying degrees of pride. Nobody, however, can match the French for their devotion not only to their own resplendent culture, but also to the idea of culture itself.'
>
> Donald Carroll, *Surprised by France*

Nor do the French drink a lot – surprising as this may seem. To begin with, many women drink no alcohol at all, and of those that do most will consume only one or two glasses of wine with even a long meal. Men generally drink more, but invariably in moderation, and drunkenness is almost unheard of – at least on social occasions. Just as food is to be savoured and not merely to satisfy hunger, so alcoholic drinks are to be appreciated for their taste, rather than used as a means to becoming inebriated.

During your stay in France you'll probably receive invitations to many meals in both informal and formal settings. Knowing which cutlery to use, what (not) to talk about and how to behave at table not only makes you feel more comfortable; it might make the difference between being invited again and ostracised.

> 'The French hate anything that's ugly. If they see an animal that's ugly, they immediately eat it.'
>
> Jeremy Clarkson (English journalist)

## Meals

### Breakfast

French breakfast is invariably of the continental type – coffee and croissants or bread (often *brioche*) served with jam or 'jelly'. An increasing number of French people drink tea or *tisane* (herbal or fruit tea) instead of coffee, and decaffeinated coffee is popular.

Many French have breakfast in a bar or café on their way to work – some city bars open as early as 5am and don't close until the early hours of the morning.

### Lunch

This is the main meal of the day and is eaten from midday onwards. Lunch traditionally consists of three courses: a starter, main course and either cheese or dessert. It's often accompanied by wine. Many French workers eat lunch at home and return to work at 2 or 2.30pm. Those who don't lunch at home tend to go to restaurants or bars serving a set menu (*menu*). Most French people consider it sacrilege to have anything other than a proper meal at lunchtime and few people eat sandwiches – especially not in the street – although an increasing number will settle for a salad or filled pancake (*galette*) instead of a three-course meal.

> '**Everything ends this way in France – everything. Weddings, christenings, duels, burials, swindlings, diplomatic affairs – everything is a pretext for a good dinner.**'
>
> Jean Anouilh (French dramatist)

### Goûter

It isn't common for the French to have 'tea' in the afternoon. Where this is offered (e.g. in hospitals), it's referred to as either *le goûter* (literally 'the taste') or *la collation* – although the latter can be a late-morning snack – and consists of tea or coffee and a buttered roll with jam, a *pain au chocolat* or, in more upmarket surroundings, *petits fours* (miniature cakes that are bought by the kilo from *pâtisseries*). Hot chocolate (*chocolat chaud*) is a popular alternative to tea and coffee.

### Dinner

The French generally dine at around 8pm (often later in summer) and, when not inviting guests, eat a lighter meal than at lunchtime – though still a 'proper meal' rather than a snack.

### Aperitifs

Lunch and dinner are invariably preceded by aperitifs (*l'apéritif* in the singular), which consist of a drink (or three) and nibbles (*amuse-bouche* or, less politely, *amuse-gueule*). You won't be offered either until everyone invited has arrived – which can be up to an hour after the 'official' starting time. You may be offered champagne or a *kir*, for example, or asked what you would like to drink. You can ask for almost anything, including a soft drink, though it isn't usual to drink cognac, armagnac or calvados (which are generally served after a meal) or red wine.

You should wait until your host raises his glass and toasts his guests – '*A votre santé*' or simply '*Santé*' or sometimes '*A la vôtre*' – and drinks, before doing the same. When toasting, it's usual to clink glasses with everyone present (unless there are dozens) while making eye contact, but it's considered bad luck to cross arms while doing so – which can lead to some interesting gestures.

### Cutlery

On a smart occasion you may be faced with an array of cutlery (silverware), in which case you should start at the outside and work your way in. Most of the time, however, there will be just one knife and one fork, which you use

throughout a meal, discreetly wiping them with a piece of bread before laying them on the table between courses. (In some restaurants, staff will insist on your keeping your cutlery if you're having the standard menu.) There's no set way of 'parking' cutlery when you've finished eating; simply leave it tidily on your plate.

Some food, e.g. cakes and fruit, can be eaten with the hands, but you should take your cue from the French.

## Seating

On most occasions, guests are seated alternately male and female, with the hosts at the ends of the table. It's polite to wait for the host to tell you where to sit and not to sit down until you're invited to do so. On big occasions such as weddings or banquets, cards with guests' names are placed on the tables. It's considered impolite to change places before or during a meal, but after dessert guests are free to mingle and sit elsewhere.

## When to Start

It's polite to wait for everyone to be served (irrespective of the formality of the occasion) before starting a meal. At formal meals you should wait for the host to start before you do, unless he gives you permission to start first. It isn't usual for the French to say grace before a meal.

## Bread

Bread is an essential part of a French meal. Except in expensive restaurants, where rolls may be

served, this invariably consists of a sliced *baguette* or *pain*, served in a wicker (or mock wicker) basket. Bread is broken rather than cut and is normally eaten without butter. You shouldn't start on the bread until the first course is served.

Plates aren't provided for bread, which should be put on the table between mouthfuls. Using bread to mop up the remains of a sauce or soup is acceptable at an informal table but you shouldn't do this at a formal meal.

*'Il n'y a pas de mal à se faire du bien.'* (There's no harm in enjoying yourself)

## Table Manners

The following courtesies should be observed when invited to lunch or dinner.

● Eat with both hands above the table but keep your elbows off the table.

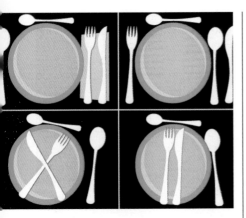

- Don't serve yourself with wine (water is acceptable) but wait until you're served.

- Avoid adding salt or pepper to any dish, as this implies that you find it inadequately seasoned.

- Try to eat everything you're served; if you're offered more but don't want any, say '*Merci*' – preferably followed by a compliment on what you've eaten. Or you can say '*Merci, je suis rassasié*' ('no thank you, I am full/satisfied').

- Use your napkin (serviette) frequently to wipe your mouth.

- Avoid blowing your nose at table.

- Don't offer to help clear away or serve, unless you know your hosts well.

## Conversation

What you talk about during a meal depends very much on the occasion and how well you know your host(s). As a general rule, it's best to let the host lead the conversation and do most of the talking. Stick to neutral topics such as the weather, local events and holidays. Avoid referring to work or money. Although politics, religion and health are favourite subjects of conversation among the French, you should wait until these subjects are raised before discussing them. The French also love to talk about people, including friends, who aren't present, and can be surprisingly frank and even unkind about them. (You can only imagine what they say about you when you aren't around.)

Expect other guests to ask you questions about your home country and your impressions of France – keep to the positive ones. Avoid asking people personal questions unless you know them well, and don't talk about work unless someone else raises the subject. It's polite to compliment your host on the meal.

> French people's conceptions of other countries are often based on out-dated clichés: don't be surprised – and certainly don't take offence – if you're asked strange questions about your country, such as 'How do Londoners cope with the fog every day?' or 'Don't Americans get tired of eating hamburgers all the time?'

## CAFES, BARS & RESTAURANTS

France offers a wealth of eateries – from luxury gourmet restaurants (with matching prices) to humble

---

### Smoking

France has one of the highest smoking rates in the EU and is among the most reluctant members to introduce legislation to restrict or ban smoking in public places. Traditionally smoke-filled, bars, cafes and restaurants have been theoretically obliged for some time to have non-smoking areas but few take the law at its word, non-smokers often being banished to an upstairs or back room, where service is slow or surly (often both). Since the beginning of 2006, smoking has been banned on all public transport and in stations, and in February 2007 the ban was extended to all public places – except bars and restaurants, which in typically evasive Gallic style, managed to obtain a 'reprieve' until January 2008. It remains to be seen whether this too will be wriggled out of.

---

*auberges* serving homely fare for a few euros – as well as its famous cafes and bars.

## Cafes & Bars

British visitors and residents often say that the thing they miss most in France is the pub – or rather pub culture, i.e. spending an evening after dinner drinking with friends. As the French generally dine later and take longer over their meal, and regard drink as an accompaniment to food, 'going out for a drink' is a concept largely unfamiliar to them.

---

'My all-time favourite activity is sitting in a cafe with my café noir, reading and people-watching. I feel like a real Frenchwoman when I do this.'

Ann Koepke (American expatriate)

---

Cafe (and bar) culture is strong in France, although the two are distinct. Cafes (*cafés*), especially those with pavement seating, are used by people from all walks of life to while away an hour or so with a newspaper or book, or perhaps as a romantic meeting place; bars (*bars*) tend to be a male preserve, where friends meet for a drink before or after work. Except in cities and large towns, few bars or cafes stay open after around 8pm. There are no licensing hours, however, and most bars remain open all day.

Bars and cafes with terraces or exterior tables have two tariffs: one for drinks consumed at the bar and one for drinks served elsewhere – and there may be a considerable price difference between the two. At the bar, it's usual to be given a till receipt each time you order a drink, and to pay before you leave. If you choose to sit at a table, you should wait for a member of staff to come and take your order, which will be accompanied by a till receipt.

In Paris and most tourist resorts, where customers aren't trusted, you'll be asked to pay immediately; elsewhere, it's usual to pay on departure. Staff normally expect a small tip to be left.

Most cafes and some bars serve food, although the selection depends on the establishment. Some offer nothing but croissants and sandwiches (invariably containing ham) while others serve full meals at lunchtime and in the evening.

When ordering a beer in a bar or cafe, don't ask for *une bière* (which is rather like asking for *du vin* in a restaurant) or you may get a litre! For a draught beer, say *une pression*, for a small draught beer *un demi* or, even better, specify the brand, e.g. *une Amstel*.

## Restaurants

France is, of course, famous for its restaurants, and foreigners expect to eat well wherever they go. There are, however, some surprises in store for those who – like the French

### Coffee Culture

French coffee is superb and excellent value (as little as €1 in many bars). The main types are:

café express – or simply café or express: small black coffee

café double: twice the normal size

café serré: extra-strong black coffee (serré means 'squeezed')

café allongé: weak black coffee (literally 'lengthened')

noisette: with a dash of milk (and therefore the colour of a hazelnut)

café au lait: coffee made with milk instead of water – normally drunk by the French only for breakfast

(café) crème: black coffee frothed with milk

grand crème: as above but more of it

cappuccino: black coffee with whipped cream

café décaféiné or simply un déca: decaffeinated coffee

café liègeois: cold coffee with coffee ice-cream

– believe France to be a gastronomic Mecca, including the following:

● **Foreign cuisine** – Outside the cities and tourist resorts, non-French restaurants are few and far between, and there isn't the range of cuisines to be found in, say, the UK or US. The most common foreign restaurants are Italian and Chinese, although the former tend to serve little other than pizzas, and the latter limit themselves mostly to non-spicy dishes in keeping with French

tastes. Indian restaurants are especially thin on the ground, and many serve only 'watered down' Indian food (i.e. nothing hotter than a medium curry).

- **French cuisine** – French cuisine can be outstanding and is rarely less than good, but it's almost entirely predictable: the same few starters, main courses, cheeses and desserts can be found on menus from Calais to Cannes, although each region has a few specialities and you're likely to be offered locally made (but never foreign) cheese. What distinguishes even the humblest French restaurant from its British or American counterpart is that everything – from the *tarte à l'oignon* to the *mousse au chocolat* – is home-made, and nothing is prepared in advance or (heaven forbid) heated in a microwave oven.

- **Wine** – Even more restricted than your choice of food is your choice of wine, which will invariably be French, French or

French. Although the occasional Italian or Spanish wine might make an appearance on a wine list, you're as likely to be offered a New World wine as you are a burger and chips with ketchup or brown sauce. Whereas it used to be possible to order a house wine for just a few euros, the cheapest wine on a menu now often costs over €10 – i.e. as much as the entire meal – and the mark-up in comparison with supermarket prices can be 400 per cent. The cheapest, though not necessarily the least good, wine is the house wine (*vin de la maison*), which is often served in a jug or pitcher (*carafe* or *pichet*) of various sizes – from a litre to a quarter of a litre.

- **Water** – If you don't want to pay for mineral water, ask for *eau de robinet* (tap water) or *une carafe d'eau* (a jug of water). Some good restaurants provide mineral water free of charge.

- **Menu** – Most restaurants offer one or more set menus (*menus*) at different prices. The minimum is usually a three-course meal (although there may be an option to have either a starter and main course or main course and dessert), the maximum six or seven courses, although a *menu dégustation* in fancy establishments can consist of up to ten courses. In addition to what's on the menu, you may be offered *amuse-bouche* or an appetizer before the first course, and an interim dish between

the first and second or second and third courses (known in Normandy as a *trou normand* – 'Norman hole') to aid digestion – and give the chef time to prepare the main course. Vegetables may be served as a separate course after the main (meat) course, and salad is sometimes served with the cheese course, sometimes separately. Dessert always follows cheese and is followed by coffee. Many restaurants offer children's menus. Prices range from around €10 for a simple three-course meal to €100 or more in a Michelin-starred restaurant.

Although the word for menu is *carte*, the French don't use the phrase *à la carte*; *le menu* is the set menu.

- **Opening hours** – Most restaurants close one or two days a week, usually Sunday evening and possibly also on Monday. Some, unbelievably, are closed on Saturdays. Many close for holidays in January and August for at least two weeks.

- **Ambience** – Although it's a French word, ambience is sorely lacking in the majority of French restaurants, where lighting is often of operating theatre brightness and music is conspicuous by its absence. To the French, what matters is the food and the conversation: one must be able to see exactly what one's eating and hear what one is saying – no one goes to a restaurant merely for its setting (*cadre*) or atmosphere. Nevertheless, it's considered rude to talk loudly enough to be heard by other diners.

- **Ordering** – Women are expected to order before men, but not the wine, which is a male preserve.

- **Service** – Waiting is a profession in France, where there are few casual waiters (except in beach bars). This doesn't necessarily mean, however, that standards of service are invariably high – or rather the manner of serving staff may be quite unlike what you're used to, especially if you're American. A waiter or waitress may merely approach your table and stand there until you give your order. If you're invited to make an order, it may be with a perfunctory '*Je vous écoute*' (I'm listening) or – the height of politeness – '*Vous avez choisi ?*' (Have you chosen?). A smile is optional. Many don't write anything down,

> '... a 15 per cent service charge is automatically added to all restaurant and café bills, so they don't give a damn whether you get good service or not.'
>
> Stephen Clarke, *Talk to the Snail*

but pride themselves on their ability to remember everyone's order – which can make things awkward if they bring the wrong thing, as there's no evidence of what you asked for.

In smart restaurants, your wine order is dealt with by a different member of staff from your food order and the *sommelier* (wine waiter) will be able to recommend wines to accompany your meal, though they may be served at temperatures you aren't used to – red wine 'cool' and white 'warm'. It's rare to be offered a wine cooler and many restaurants couldn't even produce one if you asked.

- **The bill** – Few waiters bring you the bill unprompted and most have a knack for avoiding your gaze when you want to pay and leave. Don't say '*Garçon*' (this should **never** be used) but '*S'il vous plaît*' and, when a waiter finally arrives, '*L'addition, s'il vous plaît*.' The international gesture of writing on your palm is generally understood and accepted.

- **Tipping** – Restaurant bills include service and there's no need to leave a tip (*pourboire*), but it's usual to leave a few euros

if service has been exceptional – by French standards, that is. Tips should be left as cash and not added to a credit card or cheque payment.

## NIGHTLIFE

The French aren't great nightclub-goers, although there are a surprising number of nightclubs even in rural areas – where they're often housed in impressive buildings such as ancient barns or former manor houses. In major cities and resort areas, there is of course a wide choice of nightlife for all ages, including jazz clubs, cabarets and discos.

Before you sample the French club scene, note the following:

- **Opening hours** – Few nightlife venues open before 11pm and you may get in for less before midnight, when the real action starts. Those in remote areas (i.e. where there aren't any neighbours to complain) stay open until dawn but nightclubs in urban areas must close by 4am.

- **Age** – You must usually be at least 18 and you may be asked for proof of your age before being admitted.

- **Dress code** – Casual dress is the norm for most nightclubs, although most don't allow jeans.

- **Bouncers** – 'Doormen' won't admit you if you aren't properly dressed and may not admit groups of men even if they are.

- **Charges** – Entrance fees (usually from €10) sometimes include a drink; some clubs have no entrance fee and drinks cost from €3 to over €20, depending on the establishment.

> 'While quality time is a modern expression, it only expresses something the French have always held dear – time spent with family and friends.'
>
> Karen Tait, *French Property News*

## CELEBRATIONS

Celebrations form an important part of the French social calendar, as they're the perfect excuse to have an extensive meal and prolonged conversation. Although these centre around the family (often extended to cousins and in-laws), close friends are usually included; if you're invited, you can consider yourself well and truly integrated.

As well as the annual festivals listed below, the most important family celebrations are as follows – with some tips on what to expect and how to cope.

### Birthdays

Birthdays are generally low-key occasions and some French people mark their saint's day rather than their birthday; every day of the year is named after a saint and if you have the same name (or almost) as a saint, that becomes your saint's day.

However, 'landmark' birthdays, e.g. 40 and 50, are often celebrated in style. Fifty or 100 people may be invited, and there may be a theme (sometimes simply a colour) and entertainment – often provided by guests – as well as recorded music or a live band. Join in the entertainment if you can, but don't expect it to be properly rehearsed and be prepared to improvise on the night. The party itself, of course, will centre around food, and the meal may last for five or six hours, with entertainment or singing between courses – get some sleep in the afternoon if you want to stay the course. Children don't usually have birthday parties until around the age of five.

## Christenings & Communions

Adults as well as children are christened or baptised in France to mark their 'admission' to the Catholic faith. If you're invited to a christening (*baptême*), check whether the invitation is for the ceremony only or also the meal afterwards. You should take a gift, especially for a child – ask the parents what's wanted so that you don't duplicate the gifts of other guests. Gifts don't have to have a religious connection.

A child's first communion – when he first 'receives the body of Christ' – is usually held when he's ten, and at 12 he 'professes his faith'. These are group events, normally held once a year – communion around Easter time and *la profession de foi* in May or June – in each parish, all local children of the appropriate age attend together. The latter is usually in two parts: an evening service (for close family only) followed by Mass the next morning. The ceremonies may be followed by private celebrations (i.e. meals) and, as with christenings, you may be invited to the ceremony only or the meal also – though you're more likely to be invited to a *profession de foi* than a *première communion* – and should check what is an appropriate gift.

Dress appropriately for these and other religious ceremonies, i.e. not jeans and trainers.

> The French are increasingly giving their children Anglicised names, such as Audrey, Bryan, Dave, Jennyfer, Joyce, Kevin and Sandy, so depriving them of saints' days.

## Christmas & New Year

The main Christmas celebration is held on Christmas Eve (24th December – known as *le réveillon de Noël* or simply *le réveillon*), when it's traditional for the whole family to mount a nativity scene (*crêche*) and go to 'midnight' mass (usually much earlier, as eating takes priority) before indulging in an extravagant meal. Typical fare includes oysters (*huîtres*), pâté de foie gras (*fois gras*), goose (*oie*) or turkey (*dinde*) and black pudding (*boudin*), washed down with various wines and champagne. Dessert is usually a rich chocolate Yule log (*bûche de Noël*). Most families exchange gifts at this time and children put their shoes by the fireplace for the convenience of

*le Père Noël*, although traditionally Christmas presents were exchanged on 6th January (see below) and some people give them on 1st January. The day after Christmas Day has no name and isn't a holiday in France, although many working people take the week between Christmas and New Year off.

Traditionally, Christmas decorations were low-key in France, but in recent years people have started covering their houses inside and out with all manner of gaudy trimmings, including flashing

Singing Christmas carols from door to door is virtually unheard of in France (far too cold and no opportunity to eat or talk), so be prepared for bewildered reactions if you decide to do so. Similarly, greetings cards aren't sent or given at Christmas but at New Year – and only to people you don't normally see.

lights and climbing Santas. Most households have a Christmas tree (*sapin de Noël*) but it isn't usual to put presents under it.

New Year's Eve (also called *le réveillon* or *le Saint Sylvestre*) is also very much a family affair in France, and follows a similar pattern to most other French celebrations, i.e. a protracted meal. Food is similar to that eaten on Christmas Eve and the meal is interrupted only briefly at around midnight (the exact time is unimportant) – by which time you may have reached only the second or third of half a dozen courses – for everyone to rise from the table and kiss everyone else (the only time it's traditional for men to kiss men) and wish them a '*Bonne année*', before being resumed with renewed gusto. Other possible wishes are '*Meilleurs voeux*' (best wishes), '*Tous mes voeux*' (all my wishes), '*Une très bonne santé surtout*' (above all, the best of health).

New Year's Day (*le jour de l'an*) is sometimes called *le Jour des Etrennes* (Day of Presents/Boxes), when gifts are given to loved ones and families gather for – you've guessed it – an elaborate meal.

## Fête des Rois

As in all Catholic countries, Father Christmas or Santa Claus is a recent foreign (heathen) import and the traditional bearers of gifts are the Three Wise Men or Three Kings (*Rois Mages*), who are believed to have reached the baby Jesus on 6th January with their offerings of gold, frankincense and myrrh. Although few French children can wait that long for **their** presents, the Epiphany is still celebrated – and there are no prizes for guessing how.

The *Fête des Rois* (also called the *Jour des Rois*) is a low-key celebration by French standards, normally taking place in the afternoon of the nearest Saturday or Sunday if the sixth is a weekday, as it isn't a public holiday. The fare consists simply of *galettes* – large cakes consisting of puff pastry with an almond paste filling – and sparkling wine or champagne. (Nevertheless, the celebration is more commonly referred to as *les galettes* than *la Fête des Rois*.) Each *galette* contains a small token (*fève* – meaning 'bean', as this is what was originally used), usually a figurine; whoever finds the token in his or her portion is crowned king or queen – a gold card crown is provided with each *galette*.

*Galettes* are on sale in bakeries and supermarkets from the beginning of the year (and are usually sold off cheaply after 6th) – the French rarely make their own.

The *Fête des Rois* is often a communal celebration and in some villages is a rare opportunity to meet neighbours (the only other may be the *Fête nationale* – see below) and wish them well for the coming year.

## Fête Nationale

What's known in the Anglo-Saxon world as 'Bastille Day', 14th July, is known to the French themselves as *la Fête nationale*. (If you refer to it using the word *Bastille*, you will be met with blank looks.) As its name suggests, it's the day when the entire country lets its hair down, and it marks the start of the month-long summer holiday for many people – ending on the next public holiday, which conveniently falls on 15th August.

The date commemorates the start of the French Revolution in 1789; celebrations invariably end with a firework display – of a spectacular nature, even in the smallest village – no doubt symbolising the explosive events that took place over the next few years. Otherwise, there are no historical references (not even the singing of the *Marseillaise*) but simply – lots of food, drink and merrymaking.

Appropriately, the *Fête nationale* is a communal celebration, virtually all of France's 36,000-plus communes staging a dinner, disco and fireworks at minimal cost to participants but heavily subsidised by local taxes and communal grants. It's an event not to be missed but not to dress up for – there are few flags and no red-white-and-blue outfits, just ordinary clothing.

## Weddings

As in other countries, weddings are a cause for major celebration and one of the few social occasions on which many – but certainly not all – French people *se mettent sur leur trente-et-un* (dress up to the nines). This doesn't mean that weddings are always expensively elaborate affairs – they can be quite simple; the emphasis, as always in France, is on the banquet that follows, which can last well into the following morning.

French newly-weds rarely 'disappear' halfway through the evening and fly off on honeymoon the next morning; they stay until the end of the celebrations and often take their honeymoon several days, weeks or even months later.

Unlike in the UK, for example, hen and stag nights are rare in France and, when they happen, are low key rather than riotous, drunken, sexually charged affairs – definitely not French. If you're invited to an enterrement de la vie de garçon or de jeune fille (literally 'burial of bachelor/spinster life'), you're advised to bear this in mind.

### Invitations

Formal wedding invitations (*faire-part*) are usually sent by post a couple of months before the event. As with christenings and communions, you should check whether you're invited to the meal following the wedding or just to the ceremony itself and the *vin d'honneur* (see below) – there's nothing more embarrassing than turning up to an event you haven't been invited to.

### Gifts

Most couples have a wedding present list (*liste de mariage*), but the invitation seldom includes this or tells you where the selected items can be bought – this would be far too 'commercial' for the French. You should therefore enquire when accepting an invitation. There are shops in most towns that specialise in wedding lists and you may be directed to one of these, where items from the lists of couples about to be married (usually crockery and cutlery) are displayed; give the couple's name and you will be shown the relevant display and a copy of the list. It's possible to buy a single item from a set, or even, in the case of very expensive items, part of an item. You pay for the gift, which is then allocated your name on the list, but you don't take it away with you. If all this sounds too impersonal and you know a couple's tastes, you might prefer to buy something not on the list.

If you know the couple reasonably well, but cannot go to the wedding, you should buy a gift.

## Procedure

A French wedding is normally divided into stages: the official ceremony, which must take place at the town hall of the town or village in which one or both of the participants lives; an optional church 'blessing'; a post-wedding drink-cum-aperitif (*vin d'honneur*); and lunch or dinner (depending on the time of the wedding – though most weddings take place in the late afternoon so that the eating

and drinking can go on all night afterwards).

The bride and groom normally spend the whole day together, as well as the previous day, and there's no tradition of their not seeing each other immediately beforehand and turning up separately to the ceremony.

As France is officially a secular country, it's the civil ceremony that legally makes a couple man and wife, though many couples have a church ceremony as well. The civil ceremony lasts around half an hour (it often starts late) and is only semi-formal – photographs can usually be taken at any time, including during the signing of the register. A church ceremony normally lasts around an hour and includes a blessing and speeches, but doesn't usually include singing.

At both ceremonies, the couple normally exchange rings, which are usually worn on the left hand. Confetti may usually be thrown without worrying whether or not it's biodegradable. There may be a photo session immediately after the ceremony/ceremonies, although this is often conducted at a later (or even earlier) date, as nothing must delay the important part of the day.

The *vin d'honneur* takes the place of the usual pre-meal aperitifs, though in fact differs little from them, and is followed by a four-or-more-course meal. This follows the usual pattern, except that a wedding cake replaces the usual desserts. There may be formal or impromptu speeches, or nothing but eating and drinking – there's no set pattern.

---

**PACS**

Cohabiting partners, including those of the same sex, may sign a pacte civile de solidarité (PACS), which entitles them to similar property rights (e.g. inheritance) and tax benefits as married couples. To make a PACS you must go to your local tribunal d'instance (listed in the phone book). The procedure has added a verb to the French language: pacser – to get PACSed.

---

Guests are often given sugared almonds (*dragées*), attractively packaged, as a memento.

# FUNERALS

You may not – and don't need to be – invited to a funeral, but simply hear of a death in your village or among your circle of friends or acquaintances by word of mouth and wish to pay your respects. Funeral services invariably take place in a (Catholic) church and are lengthy affairs with much talk of God, Jesus and the afterlife, sometimes little or no reference being made to the deceased and his or her life or achievements – which can make them even more than usually depressing affairs, especially for non-believers.

To make matters worse, there's no tradition of mourners repairing to a hotel or relative's house after the burial (cremations are rare in France); everyone merely disperses – often before the actual burial.

To pay your respects, you should approach the family (widow or widower first), shake hands or kiss them and say '*toutes mes condoléances*' (all my condolences). It's usual to take flowers (commonly chrysanthemums) or have them delivered to the church.

Although cemeteries are often adjacent to a church, they're secular and are usually owned by the local authority, which leases burial plots for 15, 30 or 50 years – sometimes indefinitely – after which time the body is moved to a common burial ground.

## Dress

Many mourners wear black to a funeral or memorial service, although this is by no means standard practice and some people turn up in their ordinary clothes. Traditionally, widows and their daughters have worn black for at least a year after their husband's/ father's death – widows sometimes for the rest of their lives – but this is rarely done nowadays.

## 1st & 11th November

All Saints' Day or All Souls' Day (*la Toussaint*) is a national holiday

the flesh of the fruit hollowed out for the previous day's celebration).

The signing of the armistice at the end of the First World War, at 11am on 11th November, is commemorated on the same date (though not necessarily at exactly the same time), whatever day it falls on, and not on the nearest Sunday as in the UK. This too is a national holiday, though shamefully most French people – many of whom had relatives who gave their lives in one or both of the two wars – treat it as an excuse to go hunting or mow the lawn, rather than as an occasion to remember and pay tribute to the dead. Coincidentally, 11th November is also St Martin's Day (*Le Saint Martin*), a day of feasting often resulting in *le mal de Saint Martin* – a hangover.

## CLUBS

Joining a club is one of the best ways to meet local people – especially in rural areas, where social contact can otherwise be sporadic. Social, sports and other clubs and societies exist throughout France, although they may not be easy to trace, as most don't advertise but – like French businesses – rely largely on word of mouth to recruit members. Talk to neighbours and ask at your town hall and those of nearby villages and towns for details of local organisations, which may include music, art and crafts societies, sport and other physical activity (e.g. dance and gym) clubs, twinning associations (*comité de jumelage*), historic houses and heritage organisations,

> 'Although they may be 'christened' by state registrars, and married by civil officials, and during their lifetimes only 8 per cent of them attend Mass regularly, most of the departed French nonetheless have the Last Rites of the Church and then a religious funeral followed by burial in consecrated ground. It's a very French solution to a potentially awkward situation in the hereafter.'
>
> Donald Carroll, *Surprised by France*

in France and traditionally the time of year when the French honour their dead and visit their burial places – although strictly, All Saints' Day should be a celebration of the saints, and the following day *le Jour des Morts* or *la Fête des Morts*. Cemeteries are a hive of activity for most of the day as relatives clean graves and lay fresh flowers – the result is often a spectacularly colourful display – before going home for pumpkin soup (made with and walking and hunting groups. Many communes have associations that organise activities for older inhabitants, principal among which – no surprise – is the annual *repas des anciens* (old people's dinner). Details of local clubs, etc. may be posted outside the town hall or adjoining *salle des fêtes*, where many club activities take place.

Most groups recruit in September – you can usually join at any time but may have to pay for a whole year – when many towns organise shows at which all the local clubs exhibit, and you can talk to the organisers and see which clubs are most appealing. Membership fees vary from a nominal €25 or so (e.g. for a painting group subsidised by the local council) to several hundred euros (e.g. for a private tennis or golf club).

To engage in any activity that involves physical exertion (even stretch classes), you must usually obtain a doctor's certificate; simply ask for a *certificat de santé* and he will check that you aren't likely to suffer heart failure.

All French clubs and societies are governed by strict regulations (no one escapes the paperwork) and must hold elections at an annual general meeting, to which you'll be invited. Although you don't have to

attend, a French AGM can itself be a good way of meeting people and socialising: in typically French style, business is quickly concluded to make time for eating, drinking and conversation.

## POPULAR CULTURE

Although the French have a strong sense of individuality and privacy, they also like to do things *en masse* – or at least *en famille*. This is particularly apparent at the beach or in the countryside in summer, when many French family groups set up mini-campsites with awnings, chairs and tables for a picnic; after all, **anywhere** is suitable for eating and drinking.

Don't expect a cheese sandwich and a flask of tea at a French picnic; whatever the location, tablecloths and serviettes adorn the ground and are piled high with platters of food. In fact, it will come as no surprise that a French picnic largely follows the pattern of any French meal, with aperitifs followed by three or four courses and coffee. The only

> 'The French are great holiday-makers for they have discovered one great truth of holiday life – it is possible to get away from it all and yet take it all with you.'
>
> Nick Yapp & Michel Syrett,
> *The Xenophobe's Guide to the French*

concession to the *al fresco* nature of the occasion might be the drinking of rosé instead of red or white wine.

In times of national celebration, French people of all ages demonstrate on the streets in their thousands – or millions, as when the Champs-Elysées spontaneously became a seething mass of Parisians after the French football team's World Cup victory in 1998. More often, however, such demonstrations (*manifestations*) are a sign of protest, the French being world champions also of the strike (*grève*) – and no strike is considered 'successful' if it fails to bring out the *CRS* (riot police).

## Festivals

Festivals (*fêtes*) form an essential part of cultural and social life in France, where during the summer there are festivals of all kinds in the most unlikely places. If a tiny village has an unusual feature or tradition, it may host a major festival, attracting thousands of people. Needless to say, these are often connected with food (or at least drink) and centre around a meal of some kind. There may also be music (traditional or otherwise), displays or other entertainment and stalls selling local produce. There may be a token admission charge or a charge for parking a car.

France's major festivals include the following (in chronological order):

- **Valentine's Day** (*Le Saint Valentin* – 14th February) – widely observed, with the usual offering of overpriced roses;

- **Shrove Tuesday** (*Mardi Gras* – late February) – celebrated with pancakes (*crêpes*) and, especially in the southern cities of Cannes, Grasse, Menton and Nice, street festivities involving 'flower battles' (*batailles des fleurs*); some argue that the 'real' pancake day is Candelmas (*la Chandeleur*) on 2nd February;

- **Mothers', Fathers' and Grandmothers' Days** (*Fête des Mères/Pères/Grandmères* – not necessarily coinciding with those in other countries) – but, curiously, not Grandfathers' Day;

- **Easter** (*Pâques*) – 'Good Friday' isn't a public holiday, but Catholics are supposed to fast (*jeuner*), though most of them manage only not to eat meat – they have fish instead. Easter Monday (*lundi de Pâques*) is a

holiday, when it's traditional to eat omelette for breakfast and for everyone to wear something new; Easter Sunday is the one day in the year when almost all French people go to church – after the children have found the eggs hidden in the garden.

- **April Fools' Day** (it has no name in French – 1st April) – when innocent tricks are played, the victim being known as the 'April fish' (*poisson d'avril*);

- **May Day** (1st May) – also Labour Day (*la Fête du Travail*), when it's traditional to give those you love a sprig of lily of the valley (*muguet*) to bring them luck (one with 13 flowers brings extra luck);

- **Pentecost** (*Pentecôte* – the 40th day after Easter) – when city-dwellers try to spend two days in the country, enjoying picnics and other outings, although the national holiday was officially cancelled in 2004;

- **St John's Eve** (*Veille de St Jean* – 3rd June) – a strange ceremony dating back to the ancient Druids' celebration of the summer solstice, culminating in the lighting of an enormous bonfire, the remains of which are thought to bring luck or prosperity;

- **Halloween** (*Halloween* – 31st October) – has recently begun to be commemorated in France, children dressing up and 'trick or treating' from house to house, but Halloween parties are rare.

## Music

French popular music is a curiosity. Although most French people listen avidly to the latest (largely) British, Irish and American pop music – as well as classic hits (known as *tubes* – they're particularly keen on a few songs by the '70s group Supertramp) – they retain a fondness for the traditional French *chanson*. So much so that radio stations are obliged, by law, to devote at least 40 per cent of their airtime to French songs and record shops have a separate section,

If you wish to invite French people to a party on the occasion of Halloween, Thanksgiving or Bonfire Night, they will be pleased to attend and join in the traditional activities. You should, however, make some concessions to French cultural norms – don't ask your guests, for example, to stand out in the cold rain with a mug of lukewarm mulled wine watching a measly fireworks display.

entitled *Variété française*, for the genre. Here you'll find the ballads of such archetypically French crooners as Charles Aznavour, Georges Brassens, Maurice Chevalier, Mireille Mathieu, Yves Montand and Edith Piaf, as well as Jacques Brel (Belgian, but widely regarded by the French as 'their' greatest popular singer).

The *chanson* is essentially a sung poem – in many cases more spoken than sung – with a simple, even minimal, musical accompaniment. The melody, harmony and rhythm (almost all are in waltz style) are incidental; what matters is the words – and there are lots of them. A *chanson* can run to seven or eight ten-line verses (sometimes with a refrain between each), which recount a story – usually a love story – in often banal detail (see box). Many French people 'absorb' these songs and can sing dozens of them word for word.

## Sports

The French are less sports-mad than say Americans, Australians or the British, and tend to favour individual sports over team sports – in keeping with their individualistic nature. Nevertheless, watching sport – and to a lesser extent participating in it – is a popular pastime. Most international sports have a keen following in France, which boasts one or two that are peculiar to the country. On the other hand, certain British and American sports, such as American football, baseball and cricket are played only by a small number of fanatics, a large proportion of them expatriates – satellite TV is a must if you want to watch the Ashes or the World Series.

### *Boules*

If France has a national sport, it must be *boules*, which is played in almost every town and village. An apparently simple game (it has uncharitably been described as 'a glorified game of marbles'), *boules* conceals a variety of subtleties – not least the fact that different variations of the game are played in different parts of the country. Regional variants include *boules lyonnaise* (originating, not surprisingly, from Lyon), *le jeu provençal* (from Provence) and *pétanque* – believed to derive from the expression *pieds tanqués* (feet together). The latter owes its name to a certain Jules Le Noir, a champion *je provençal* player who was once confined to a wheelchair as a result of an accident,

> The British claim that *boules* is a derivative of 'bowls', a game invented in England and played with cannon balls (which, incidentally, Sir Francis Drake is said to have been playing when informed of the impending arrival of the Spanish Armada, famously continuing his game in the knowledge that he couldn't set sail until the tide had turned). Needless to say, the French vociferously reject this absurd 'Anglo-Saxon' notion.

and was therefore unable to take a run-up. There's even *boules de fort*, played in central France with square 'balls'.

The game features contrasting techniques, complex tactics and an abstruse vocabulary, including *la belle* (the decider), *le cochonnet* (the 'jack'), *doublette* and *triplette* (games for two and three players), *pointer* (to aim for the jack). To penetrate its many mysteries, visit 🖥 www.petanque.fr.

Unfortunately, though played by young and old alike, *boules* is another activity dominated by men – and not much of a spectator sport either.

### Cycling

The annual Tour de France is reputed to be the world's biggest spectator event – or rather non-event – as some 15m French people turn out along the route to watch the competitors flash by so fast that it's barely possible to distinguish any of them. (Oddly, but not atypically, the French have failed to produce a Tour winner since Bernard Hinault in 1985, and recently had to suffer the

indignity of their race being won by an American – not once, but seven times!) However, the Tour is merely the internationally visible tip of the iceberg of the French infatuation with cycling.

Lance Armstrong, Tour de France winner 1999-2005

This isn't cycling as a means of getting from A to B in order to save money or reduce pollution, nor cycling as an obsessive form of exercise – the French rarely use a bicycle merely as a mode of transport and hardly ever cycle in anything but bright sunshine – but cycling as a cross between healthy activity and social bonding.

French cycling involves joining a cycling club, of which there are two types: those affiliated to the Union Française des Oeuvres Laïques d'Education Physique (UFOLEP) and those affiliated to the Fédération Française de Cyclisme – the latter being for 'serious' cyclists. Anyone over 13 can join a UFOLEP club, which costs around €45 and includes the provision of a 'jersey' (*maillot*), complete with sponsors' logos, that instantly turns ordinary people into high-profile racing cyclists. Clubs organise 'races' every week, usually on Sunday mornings – sunny Sunday mornings. But true to their instincts, the French play down the competitive aspect and exercise their lungs as much as their legs, conversing almost constantly while peddling – at high volume – to compensate for the whistling of the wind and the swish of rubber against tarmac; and they make sure they're home in time for Sunday lunch, which takes up most of the afternoon.

Like *boules* (see above) and hunting (see below), cycling in France is an almost exclusively male pursuit.

### Football

As in many countries, the most popular participation and spectator sport in France is probably football (soccer), although the French are less fanatical about 'the beautiful game' (whoever called it that must have been visually challenged) than the British, Spanish or Italians, for example.

At the lowest level, football (*football* but more usually abbreviated to *foot* – pronounced with a long vowel, like 'boot') is played by schoolboys, many of whom belong to local clubs (there are few school sports teams) – though fewer and fewer boys can drag themselves away from their computer screens and out into the fresh air. There are also local adult teams and then a range of area

amateur teams, the best of which compete in two leagues known as the Championnat de France Amateur (CFA). The higher of these merges with the professional game, which begins with the National League 2 and rises through National 1 and Ligue 2 to Ligue 1, which contains the top 20 or so French teams.

French football 'came of age' in the '70s, when Saint-Etienne achieved international success, but its supremacy is long-since over and it's currently Lyon that dominates the domestic game – so much so that the competition is to decide who will be second in the league. The chasing pack includes Bordeaux, Lens, Lille, Lyon and Marseille (as well as Monaco), the once glorious Paris Saint-Germain now hovering between Ligue 1 and Ligue 2 (there's a three-club relegation/ promotion system).

League games are rarely televised on terrestrial channels and attract relatively little interest (30,000 spectators constitutes a big game) – with the possible exception of local derbies (*derbys*), e.g. between Lyon and Saint-Etienne or Nice and Marseille – though even Ligue 2 matches can be seen on satellite channels.

Of more interest to TV audiences are the two cup competitions: the Coupe de la Ligue (equivalent to the UK's League Cup), contested by clubs in Ligues 1 and 2, and the Coupe de France (FA Cup), open also to other clubs, including semi-amateur sides. These reach their climax in May, and quarter-finals, semi-finals and finals can usually be watched on terrestrial TV.

Admission to top league matches costs from around €15 and from around €45 for the national team (see below). There's little 'trouble' at most matches, but two teams – Marseille and Paris Saint-Germain – have notorious supporters' groups and their clashes (literally) are to be avoided unless you enjoy violence.

Zinédine Zidane

**National team:** France's national team, known as *Les Bleus* on account of the players' all-blue strip, is alternately – and quite unpredictably – a source of euphoria and despair to its millions of fans. After its unexpected triumph in the 1998 World Cup on home soil, the (virtually unchanged) team ignominiously exited from the first round of the 2002 event without scoring a single goal. Then, in 2006, the (still largely unchanged) team scraped through to the final again, only to be beaten on penalties by Italy. Their roller-coaster fortunes – and French national pride – were epitomised by their captain, Zinédine Zidane, hero of the '98 cup-winning side, who only minutes from the final's final whistle (and the start of his retirement from the game) committed one of the sport's most spectacular fouls by head-butting an opponent in the chest, knocking him to the ground. Claiming afterwards that the Italian had insulted him (as if that were sufficient justification for actual bodily harm), Zidane maintained his status as national idol, and continues to earn millions by endorsing products related and unrelated to football.

### Skiing

France boasts some of the world's best ski resorts and the French are avid skiers, many of them starting to ski almost as soon as they can walk,

> **'Sometimes in football you have to score goals.'**
>
> Thierry Henry (French footballer)

## Tennis

Question: What are the four Grand Slam tennis tournaments? Answer: Wimbledon, the US Open, the Australian Open and the French Open. Wrong. The French Open doesn't exist – at least not in France, where it's referred to, like Wimbledon, by the name of the club where it's held: Roland Garros (incongruously named after a First World War fighter pilot). It's an event that grips the nation every May, but the French display little interest in the world's other major tournaments – none of which is played on the same surface (clay).

Tennis is widely played in France, where there are thousands of clubs. These, however, aren't like their equivalents in the UK or US, where socialising is as important as playing; they're mostly mere facilities, where courts are booked by the hour (just like municipal courts) and there's no 'club afternoon' or club tournament or even, in many cases, a clubhouse.

As with skiing, however, French passion for the sport has produced few world beaters. Amélie Mauresmo is currently among the top women players, but the last Frenchman to achieve even fleeting tennis stardom was Yannick Noah, who won Roland Garros back in 1983 – his only Grand Slam title.

and taking at least a week's skiing holiday every year thereafter. In fact, so popular is the sport among children that the winter and spring school holidays are staggered across the country to spread the load on ski resorts. Needless to say, the French rarely visit other countries' resorts.

> Since the early '90s, when the French team began to enjoy international success, most of the top French players have been snapped up by foreign clubs (especially British, Spanish and Italian) and live abroad, so there's little popular interest in their lives.

Considering the popularity of skiing in France, it's surprising that the country has produced so few world champions. In fact, the only French skiing icon is Jean-Claude Killy, the only person ever to win Olympic gold medals in all three major disciplines: downhill, slalom and giant slalom – but that was way back in 1968.

## Hunting

So-called game sports are popular in France, where the Revolution turned hunting (*la chasse*) – previously a 'privilege' of the aristocracy – into

### Sporting Events

The following annual sporting events are the most important in the French calendar:

Football – Finals of the Coupe de la Ligue and Coupe de France (May);

Tennis – Roland Garros (French Open), Stade Roland Garros, Paris (May/June);

Motor racing – Formula One Grand Prix, Magny-Cours, Nevers, Nièvre (June/July) and Le Mans 24-hour race (Les 24 Heures du Mans), Le Mans, Sarthe (June);

Golf – French Open, Saint-Quentin-en-Yvelines (June/July);

Cycling – Tour de France, throughout the country and sometimes abroad, ending in Paris (three weeks during July);

Horse racing – Prix de l'Arc de Triomphe, Hippodrome de Longchamp, Paris (September/October).

a 'right' enjoyed by all and sundry (though mostly men). Although a permit is required to hunt, and certain rules apply (at least in theory), almost anyone over 18 can obtain a gun – and many people who never hunt keep one 'under the bed', just in case. Popular game includes duck (*canard*), hare (*lièvre*), deer (*chevreuil*, *biche* and *cerf*) and wild boar (*sanglier*), though the French will shoot almost anything that moves – including passers-by and each other (dozens are killed in hunting accidents every year).

The hunting season varies according to the area and the game, but is generally from early September to early March. Hunting takes place in many parts of the French countryside, including public land, although it isn't permitted within 150m of any habitation. Areas where hunting isn't allowed are marked by signs saying '*chasse interdite*'. Unless you see such a sign, take care when walking in the countryside during the hunting season.

Hunters claim to be fulfilling a necessary function, i.e. controlling wild animal numbers so that environmental balance is maintained, but many have little concern for the environment and are eager only to boast how many animals they've killed. It's perhaps some consolation – to conservationists if not to the animals – that most kill is eaten.

There are no vociferous national movements against hunting; public opinion is temporarily outraged if a bear or eagle is killed, but the fact that thousands of animals are shot annually doesn't cause national concern. Although many French people are 'against' hunting, it's generally considered to be part and parcel of everyday life. You should avoid voicing strong opposition to hunting unless you're with French people who you know will be sympathetic.

## THE ARTS

To most French people, the word *culture* means the Arts and doesn't embrace popular culture, let alone the many other aspects of culture discussed in this book. Nevertheless, the arts aren't considered high-brow in France, where classical music, theatre and visual arts are simply types of entertainment.

When going to a concert, film or play in France, bear in mind the following:

- **Information** – Details of what's on at the cinema are available only on expensive 0892 telephone numbers providing recorded information in French or via the internet or press; it isn't possible to speak to anyone.

- **Language** – Only a few cinemas in cities and major towns show films in their original language with French subtitles (labelled *VO* for *version originale*), most foreign-language films being dubbed into French (*VF* for *version française*) – invariably badly. Not surprisingly, very few plays are in English.

- **Classification** – Films are classified as *interdit aux moins de*

---

> **La Fête de la Musique & Les Journées du Patrimoine**
>
> There's a national music 'festival' on 21st June, when every town in France turns into an open-air concert venue. The third weekend in September is officially designated 'the Heritage Days', when many historic monuments, castles and houses normally closed to the public must open their doors to the curious. It's an enormously popular occasion, the French turning out in their millions to discover unseen treasures in their local area.

*18/16/12 ans* (not for those under 18/16/12) but classification may be more lenient than you're used to, especially if a film contains 'only' nudity. French plays often contain strong language and nudity but there's rarely a warning to this effect in the publicity; if in doubt, ask before buying tickets.

- **Booking** – France is barely emerging from the Dark Ages when it comes to booking 'systems'. While cinema tickets can often be booked online and collected from a dispenser in the foyer, seats for the theatre,

concerts and other entertainment must often be purchased by post or even in person. Many organisations won't accept credit card bookings by telephone, and the collection of tickets from the box office is often a shambolic affair, even at prestigious Paris venues, as doors open barely half an hour before a performance is scheduled to begin, when several hundred people push and shove their way to a single counter.

- **Finding your seat** – Seat numbering systems are often (intentionally?) confusing, so that you're obliged to ask an usherette (most are women) where to find it; in fact, certain doors (including fire doors) may be locked in order to funnel you towards an *ouvrière*, who

will 'demand' a tip if you don't proffer one. Just to confuse you, in some venues tipping isn't allowed.

- **Start time** – With the possible exception of cinema séances, performances never start on time and are often half an hour late. To the French, this is *normal*.

- **Interval** – While classical concerts normally have intervals, during which you may just have time to buy and gulp down an overpriced drink, most other entertainments don't and you may have to sit for two hours or more without a chance to wet your whistle or spend a penny. Worse still, there may be no opportunity to purchase a drink afterwards.

The Louvre by night

- **Applause** – The French are generous in their applause and often make no distinction between a great performance and an indifferent one. To show their appreciation, they invariably break into synchronised clapping and may stamp their feet and shout '*bravo*' and '*bis*' ('encore').

## Museums & Art Galleries

France has many world-class museums and art galleries housing unique treasures – those on show in the Louvre and Musée d'Orsay in Paris are exceptional. Most cities and many towns have a *musée des beaux arts*, often housing surprisingly famous paintings.

- **Opening hours** – For obscure reasons, most museums are closed on Tuesdays – but some close on Mondays. Smaller museums close at lunchtime and may be shut during August. Most chateaux and stately homes are open during the summer only (e.g. from May to September) and close for lunch.

- **Entrance fees** – Most museums and galleries charge an entrance fee, though these are usually state subsidised and therefore reasonable. Concessions are available for children, students, the unemployed and pensioners, and reduced prices often apply after a certain time. Some museums have free-entry days, e.g. the first Sunday of each month at the Louvre, when they're usually crowded. Season tickets are available for many museums and major cities offer tourist tickets, e.g. the Carte des Musées et Monuments in Paris, which costs between €20 and €40 depending on the number of days' validity.

- **Labelling** – Exhibits may be labelled only in French; if there are English translations or guides, they're invariably unidiomatic. On the other hand, visitors won't hesitate to correct spelling or grammatical errors in the French labelling.

# 9.

# RETAIL THERAPY

**S**hopping in France, where small family-run shops still constitute the bulk of French retailers, is generally a pleasurable experience. Shopping 'etiquette' in France may differ considerably from what you're used to. This chapter provides information about the uniquely French aspects of shopping and other things that newcomers you may find surprising.

> 'You can't go into a store expecting to be entitled to good service; you have to work for it.'
>
> Ann Koepke
> (American expatriate)

## OPENING HOURS

Small French shops are generally closed not only on Sundays but also on Mondays, and most shut for lunch, between around noon and 2 or 2.30pm. Exceptions are bakeries and florists; the former usually open every day and close in the afternoon, while the latter remain open through lunch, as it takes them 20 minutes or more to clear their displays off the pavement and as long again to redeploy them. Some shops close for annual holidays, stock taking or family reasons.

Large stores and supermarkets normally remain open all day every day except Sundays, when only a few open in the morning.

## GREETING

In small shops, it's polite to greet other shoppers when you enter, with a '*Bonjour Madame, Monsieur, Mesdames, Messieurs* or *Messieurs-Dames*' as appropriate. When it's

your turn to be served, greet the shop assistant with '*Bonjour Madame* or *Monsieur*' before stating what it is you want.

On leaving a shop, say '*Au revoir Monsieur* or *Madame*'. If the assistant wishes you a '*Bonne journée*' or something similar, say '*Et vous*', '*Vous aussi*' or '*Vous de même*'.

> 'It didn't take me long to learn that one avoids going shopping, particularly in the *hypermarchés*, on Wednesdays, when most schools are closed.'
>
> Beverly Laflamme (American expatriate)

## QUEUING

The French have an ambivalent attitude to queuing, as they do to any kind of rule that impinges on their individual liberty. Normally, they're happy to stand in a line and wait their turn. In some situations,

however, other kinds of behaviour are deemed more appropriate. These include the following:

- **the informal queue** – In some circumstances, e.g. in post offices and at market stalls, a single file approach either isn't possible or seems unnecessary, but everyone will know who is in front of them in the 'queue' – even reminding them if they forget.

- **ticketing system** – Some supermarket counters (e.g. fresh fish) – as well as government offices – have machines which dispense a numbered ticket, where you must wait until your number is displayed over the counter, though such a regulated system isn't popular in France. Sometimes it isn't obvious that you need to take a ticket or whether a ticket system is in operation; if in doubt, you should ask: '*Il faut prendre un ticket ?*' (Do you have to take a ticket?).

- **sheer impatience** – There comes a time when French people simply have to get to the front of a queue. It may be that they have a genuine reason for being unable to wait – or it may not; whatever the case, it's best to do like the French and take it in your stride – while making a mental note of how they do it.

The most important thing to remember about queuing in France is that the existence of a queue is invariably an indicator of quality; if you want to know which of several *boulangeries* is the best, look to see which has the longest queue.

## CUSTOMER SERVICE

Business in France has traditionally focused on production rather than marketing – selling isn't a recognised profession – the idea being that if a product is of high quality it will sell itself without the need for the businessman to stoop to the level of a common salesman. Although this ideology is changing, it's still surprisingly prevalent and customer service (*service clientèle*) or after-sales service (*service après-vente* or *SAV*) is a concept alien to many shopkeepers in particular, for whom the customer is merely a necessary nuisance.

It's especially difficult to obtain satisfaction over the telephone, as the French regard a ringing phone as an unwelcome intrusion on whatever activity they're currently engaged in (even if it's merely chatting), and are consequently predisposed to rebuff any request for help.

When shopping you should therefore expect to come across the surly indifference for which the French are infamous – you'll then be pleasantly surprised on the many occasions when you encounter couldn't-do-more-for-you attentiveness. In some shops it can be difficult to get a 'thank you' out of the assistant; in others, you can spend a pleasant half-hour chatting, even if you don't buy anything. If you receive poor service, take your custom elsewhere, as complaining will rarely get you anywhere.

An agreeable surprise in store for many foreign shoppers – especially the British – is that French shop assistants know their stuff. Even in a DIY supermarket or furniture superstore, staff aren't school-leavers who can barely direct you to the product you want, but experienced people with detailed knowledge in a particular area

(you'll need to ask for the relevant person – *le responsable du rayon*), who will not only tell you which product best meets your needs but also how to use, store and maintain it.

If the item you want is out of stock, however, don't bank on its being replenished the next day or even the following week – let alone on anyone contacting you to tell you it has arrived. If you want it, you must be prepared to ring, remind, pester and chase.

## Wrapping

One of the delights of shopping in France is the fact that almost everything – from flowers to cakes to books to the most insignificant trinket – is gift wrapped. In a *boulangerie*, for example, anything other than a loaf of bread will be packed in a box and tied up with ribbon – even if there's a queue halfway down the street; buy a single stem from a florist and he will make it look like an elaborate offering with cellophane, stickers and ribbons – not to mention instructions on how to make it last.

If you acquiesce to the question *C'est pour offrir ?* (Is it a gift?) or *Vous voulez un paquet cadeau ?* (Do you want it gift wrapped?) you'll be treated to a highly skilled display that can take several minutes and for which there will be no charge.

> 'Accept the fact that life is more expensive here. It's worth it.'
>
> Bruce Epstein (American expatriate)

## SALES & BARGAIN SHOPPING

Sales (*soldes*) are strictly regulated in France. They may be held only twice a year – between mid-January and mid-February and between July and August (the exact dates vary from year to year); items in the sale must show the lowest price offered during the previous month as well as the sale price; goods mustn't be bought in specifically for a sale; and stock mustn't be changed during a sale.

Although sales are popular, the French aren't generally discount-mad – bargain shops (*discounts*) aren't common and charity shops rare. On the contrary, the French value quality and are willing to pay for it; they're much more likely to tell you how much something cost if it was expensive than if it was cheap.

### Car Boot Sales

Surprisingly, given their love of quality, the French are keen on car boot sales. Sales (called *vide-grenier* in the south and *foires à tout* in the north) are held at weekends from February to June and from September to November in towns, villages and fields up and down the country; they feature everything from worthless junk to collectors' items and new goods (clothes, jewellery, CDs and DVDs, tools and craft objects), sold by professional traders as well as individuals having an annual clear-out.

Car boot sales are generally more relaxed affairs than their British equivalents, and are a good place

to find authentic French artefacts at bargain prices – but they're dangerously addictive.

Do as much of your shopping as possible in local shops. This gives you the chance to practise your French and become part of your community, giving you a sense of belonging.

## TYPES OF SHOP

With the appearance of supermarkets and hypermarkets, discount warehouses, and shopping centres housing dozens of chain stores open all day throughout the country, the face of French shopping has changed dramatically over the last decade. In most French towns, small, traditional shops are struggling to compete and some have been forced to close. Many still survive, however, thanks to the French love of tradition and quality, and specialist shops offer beautiful and often unique goods as well as a 'real' French shopping experience.

Among the many typical French shops are the following:

- *boulangerie* – where the French go for their daily bread (sometimes twice a day), especially if they have to queue outside, because that means the bread is the best in town; often combined with a *pâtisserie*, selling cakes;

- *charcuterie* – sells cured meat products, though often combined with a *boucherie*, selling fresh meat;

- *chocolaterie* – as the name indicates, sells chocolates by weight (you make your own selection from the flavours on display) but also other sweets – all home-made, of course;

- *fleuriste* – no ordinary flower shop but a riot of colour and fragrance; the French love to give flowers and think nothing of spending €30 or €40 on a bouquet or potted plants when invited to dinner.

- *mercerie* – a haberdashery, where you can buy individual buttons, ribbons and braiding by the metre, and tights and socks

Many flowers are believed to have particular significance in France: crocuses signify worry, carnations are believed to bring bad luck, and chrysanthemums are associated with death and are taken to funerals and placed on graves. Love can be expressed by black tulips (ruinous love), red roses (to distraction), pink roses (tenderly) or white roses (wordlessly), but yellow roses betray unfaithfulness. Violets indicate that you're too timid to express your love and narcissi show that you love yourself. However, you shouldn't worry too much about all this; simply trust a florist to give you a bouquet suitable for the occasion.

for women and children. Some also sell lingerie.

- *pâtisserie* – a cake shop whose window display is enough to make any one with a sweet tooth go weak at the knees; often combined with a *boulangerie*, selling bread;

- *pharmacie* – sells mainly medicines but also health-related products; identified by a large green cross, which flashes when the shop is open – note that many everyday health-related products cannot be bought in other stores (e.g. supermarket);

- *quincaillerie* – not just ironmongers, but treasure troves of household and DIY items, where you can buy nails and screws (by weight) and small domestic appliances, have keys

cut, and obtain expert advice on how to fix something;

- *(bureau de) tabac* – a unique institution in France, which therefore doesn't have an accurate English translation. They aren't merely tobacconists – as well as being the only licensed vendors of tobacco and cigarettes, *tabacs* sell stamps, sweets, lottery tickets, postcards, stationery, spirits, and tax and other official forms (e.g. for contracts). They're often combined with a bar.

## Markets

Markets (*marchés*) are a regular feature of French towns and larger villages, appearing on one or two days a week to offer all manner of goods, but principally food and clothing. In a village, the market may consist of just one or two stalls selling local fruit and vegetables, whereas in a large town it may take over the main square and adjoining streets. Some markets have 'specialities', such as livestock.

> 'Somehow the idea has got around that stallholders in French markets object to having their produce handled or sniffed. This is nonsense. In some cases they will want to help do the selecting for you, but they will be just as fussy – only faster.'
>
> Donald Carroll, *Surprised by France*

Whether food is of better quality or better value in a market than in a supermarket is a moot point, and many market stalls charge up to 50 per cent more than supermarkets for similar produce. There's no doubt, however, that shopping at a market is a more authentic experience, and one where you can practise your French and meet people other than a checkout assistant. Shopping at markets isn't for those in a hurry – queues at stalls often move slowly, as each customer has a chat with the stallholder – but if you shop regularly and get to know stallholders you can make special orders or ask them to keep items for you.

If you see an unfamiliar fruit or vegetable, which is likely in France, don't hesitate to ask fellow shoppers what it is, what it tastes like and how to cook it; they will be only too pleased to give you chapter and verse on the subject.

## FOOD & WINE

The hallmark of French cooking is the use of fresh local produce and, not surprisingly, shopping for food (and preparing it) is a labour of love in France, where the quality and range of fresh food is difficult to beat. Many French housewives shop daily, not only because a freshly cooked lunch is expected in many households, but also out of enjoyment and the opportunity to socialise – and because French bread keeps for only a day.

The French haven't developed a taste for foreign food and wine, and are parochial in their tastes (especially in their choice of wine). This isn't necessarily a problem, as French cuisine is one of the most sophisticated and varied in Europe. However, the growing number of foreign residents has led to the introduction of foreign foods in many parts of France: for example, supermarkets commonly stock British and American products such as bagels and hamburger rolls, Marmite, cream crackers and (proper) tea bags, as well as some oriental, Indian and South American foods and spices.

## Meat & Fish

The French aren't squeamish about meat and will eat virtually every part of any animal. Although most meat is 'prepared' and packaged at the supermarket, butchers will display whole rabbits, chickens and other fowl, pigs' heads and trotters and other 'delicacies' in order to proclaim their freshness. Meat is cut in a particular way (probably differently from the way you're used to), but a butcher will usually prepare it to your requirements, including boning, filleting or mincing. Some butchers sell horse meat (their sign may say *boucherie chevaline*).

| Metric/Imperial Conversion | | | |
|---|---|---|---|
| **Weight** | | | |
| **Imperial** | **Metric** | **Metric** | **Imperial** |
| 1 UK pint | 0.57 litre | 1 litre | 1.75 UK pints |
| 1 US pint | 0.47 litre | 1 litre | 2.13 US pints |
| 1 UK gallon | 4.54 litres | 1 litre | 0.22 UK gallon |
| 1 US gallon | 3.78 litres | 1 litre | 0.26 US gallon |
| **Capacity** | | | |
| **Imperial** | **Metric** | **Metric** | **Imperial** |
| 1 UK pint | 0.57 litre | 1 litre | 1.75 UK pints |
| 1 US pint | 0.47 litre | 1 litre | 2.13 US pints |
| 1 UK gallon | 4.54 litres | 1 litre | 0.22 UK gallon |
| 1 US gallon | 3.78 litres | 1 litre | 0.26 US gallon |
| Note: An American 'cup' = around 250ml or 0.25 litre. | | | |

and it has the advantage of not going off in hot weather, although it keeps for only a few days once opened.

## Fruit & Vegetables

Although the French grow some of the world's finest fruit and vegetables, most of which are abundantly displayed in supermarkets, they don't seem to consume a great deal of either; certainly, when you go out to dinner – whether in a restaurant or at someone's home – vegetables will invariably be used merely for decoration and you won't (except in the most basic restaurants) be offered fruit as an alternative to dessert.

Nevertheless, French shoppers are as passionate about fruit and vegetables as they are about all other food, and will spend several minutes selecting the 'best' melon or bunch of radishes from a display – looking, feeling and sniffing until they find something that meets their exacting standards.

Although the French are generally reluctant to import anything, 'exotic' fruit and vegetables such as dates, kumquats, lychees, passion and star fruit, plantain bananas and sweet potatoes, can be found in many greengrocers and supermarkets.

Fishmongers' (*poissonneries*) are rare in France, as the French generally prefer animal meat; however, most supermarkets have a fresh fish counter offering a wide range of fish (some of which may be unfamiliar) and shellfish, most of which will probably be unfamiliar.

Butchers and fishmongers (including supermarket counter staff) are highly knowledgeable, and will not only tell you how to prepare and cook a particular type of meat or fish, but also suggest recipes to use it in, and wine and vegetables to serve with it.

## Milk

Fresh milk (*lait frais*) is difficult to find and most milk is 'long-life' (UHT) – full cream (*entier*), semi-skimmed (*demi-écrémé*) or skimmed (*écrémé*). You can buy individual cartons or packs of six one-litre or half-litre cartons. If you're used to fresh milk, long-life milk tastes strange to start with, especially in tea. However, you soon get used to it

Most non-packaged fruit and veg must be weighed and priced at the counter – weighing machines may be staffed or self-service, but in either case you're expected to bag produce and knot the bag before weighing – though some items are priced individually (labelled '*la pièce*' as opposed to '*le kilo*'). Always check you've weighed and priced all fruit and vegetables as required before going to the check-out, as you won't be popular with those in the queue behind you if you have to return to the weighing machine before being able to pay.

This system is highly environmentally unfriendly, as bags are invariably plastic and non-biodegradable; market produce is usually put in paper bags or directly into your shopping bag.

## Organic, GM & 'Fair Trade' Food

As in other developed countries, there's an increasing amount of organic agriculture (*agriculture*

*biologique*) in France, where there are now some 10,000 organic farms. Organic products, which are widely available in supermarkets and hypermarkets, are labelled '*bio*'. However, organic food tends to be 30 to 100 per cent more expensive than 'ordinary' food, and a new type of food produced by so-called *agriculture raisonnée* is now available, offering a compromise in both price and production methods.

Free-range (*plein-air*) eggs are widely available – though the French, who are aghast at EU opposition to force-feeding geese for *foie gras*, have few scruples when it comes to the treatment of food-producing animals, being more concerned with the quality of a product than with the ethics of its production. For the same reason, 'fair trade' food (*commerce équitable*), which recently made an appearance in French supermarkets, hasn't caught on.

France imposes strict regulations regarding the production and sale of genetically modified (GM) 'organisms' (*organismes génétiquement modifies/OGM*), which are currently used mainly in animal feed, but can also be added to food such as biscuits, desserts and 'ready meals' without any indication on the label, unless they constitute more than 0.5 per cent of the total content. On the other hand, food containing no GM plants may be labelled '*sans OGM*', and certain French food manufacturers, including Danone, Knorr, Marie Surgelé and Nestlé, claim not to use any GM products.

> French wine snobbery knows no bounds: many French people will drink only certain types of wine, of a certain age and sometimes from a particular producer – often driving hundreds of miles to buy direct from a producer (récoltant) rather than buying from a local shop selling only wine supplied by a wholesaler (négotiant). One Paris teacher claimed to drink nothing but Gevrey-Chambertin.

## Wine

A significant slice of French pride is reserved for its wine, and not only are the products of other countries generally derided, they're often not even recognised. (It comes as a profound shock to most French people that wine is made in England.) As a result, it's difficult to find a good choice of foreign wine outside the 'wine warehouses' of Calais and Boulogne – even most hypermarkets relinquish barely a metre of shelf space (usually behind a pillar) to non-French wines. Most commonly found are Moroccan, Italian and Spanish wines, though the occasional New World wine finds its way onto some shelves.

Fortunately, as any Frenchman will tell you, France has by far the world's greatest variety of wines, so there's no shortage of choice.

Specialist wine shops (*caves*) can be found in most towns, where wine can often be bought by the litre from huge vats; you can also buy wine in general stores, some specialist food shops (e.g. butchers' and fishmongers') and even in service stations (as well as supermarkets). Most of these hold 'wine fairs' once or twice a year, when additional stock is bought in and someone is on hand to advise customers. There are no 'off licences', liquor stores or bottle shops that sell only wines and spirits.

## CLOTHES

Clothes in France vary from cheap and cheerless to chic and costly; as in all countries, you get what you pay for. Cities and large towns have a wide choice of clothes shops, from supermarkets – many of which sell surprisingly good quality clothing at reasonable prices – to boutiques offering limited edition outfits with labels but no prices.

### Sizes

France uses continental sizes for clothes, but these don't always correspond with those in other countries; British women in particular will need to buy a size or two larger in France. Also, as in many countries, manufacturers interpret sizes in different ways, so it's common to find you need one size in one shop but a different one in another. French clothes are generally made for 'smaller' people

and if you're very tall and/or large, it can be difficult to find clothes that fit.

## LAUNDRY & DRY-CLEANING

All large towns have laundries (*blanchisserie*) and dry cleaners' (*nettoyage à sec/pressing*) – there are more dry cleaners' and laundries in Paris than in the whole of many other European countries – most of which also do minor repairs, invisible mending, alterations and dyeing. Dry cleaning is expensive, however, and you must usually pay in advance. Cleaning by the kilo with no pressing is possible in some places, and you can also save money by having your clothes brushed and pressed, rather than cleaned.

Note also that 'express' cleaning may mean a few days rather than hours, even at a dry cleaners where cleaning is done on the premises (nothing is rushed in France). Some shops will collect and deliver items for a small fee. With the exception of Paris, there are few self-service launderettes (*laveries automatiques*), as the French prefer not to wash their dirty linen in public. In some villages, there are still communal *lavoirs*, usually located by a river or near a spring, although these aren't recommended for everyday use.

## INTERNET & MAIL-ORDER SHOPPING

In general, the French aren't keen on buying goods other than in shops, as they take pleasure in shopping rather than regarding it as a waste of time.

### Internet

Online shopping has been slow to take off in France, although buying via the internet is as secure as anywhere else (provided the site is a secure server, with an address beginning https:// rather than http://)

### Continental to UK/US Size Comparison

**Women's Clothes**

| Continental | 34 | 36 | 38 | 40 | 42 | 44 | 46 | 48 | 50 | 52 |
|---|---|---|---|---|---|---|---|---|---|---|
| UK | | 8 | 10 | 12 | 14 | 16 | 18 | 20 | 22 | 24 | 26 |
| US | | 6 | 8 | 10 | 12 | 14 | 16 | 18 | 20 | 22 | 24 |

**Men's Shirts**

| Continental | 36 | 37 | 38 | 39 | 40 | 41 | 42 | 43 | 44 | 46 |
|---|---|---|---|---|---|---|---|---|---|---|
| UK/US | 14 | 14 | 15 | 15 | 16 | 16 | 17 | 17 | 18 | - |

**Shoes (Women's and Men's)**

| Continental | 35 | 36 | 37 | 37 | 38 | 39 | 40 | 41 | 42 | 42 | 43 | 44 |
|---|---|---|---|---|---|---|---|---|---|---|---|---|
| UK | | 2 | 3 | 3 | 4 | 4 | 5 | 6 | 7 | 7 | 8 | 9 | 9 |
| US | | 4 | 5 | 5 | 6 | 6 | 7 | 8 | 9 | 9 | 10 | 10 | 11 |

and most large retailers offer online shopping services. Hypermarkets and some supermarkets offer online shopping but this has yet to catch on, mainly because there's a limited delivery area (e.g. within a 10km radius) and sometimes a minimum amount you must spend, e.g. €80.

## Mail-order

Mail-order shopping (*vente par correspondence* or *vente à domicile*) is popular in France, where the catalogue business is the third-largest in Europe after Germany and the UK. The leading companies include Camif, Neckermann, Quelle, La Redoute, 3Suisses and Vert Baudet. All major companies offer a money-back guarantee, but the returns procedure can be complicated, and is expensive for heavy items.

## Home Deliveries

Most large supermarkets and all hypermarkets offer home delivery,usually free, but there may be a small charge if the bill is under €50.Furniture and domestic appliance stores usually deliver free to your home, and many companies

> When paying by credit card, make sure the assistant enters the right amount before it's rung up; if an error is made, you may be unable to obtain a credit to the card (the French are largely unfamiliar with this procedure) and will be offered a cash refund instead.

include the installation of an appliance (e.g. fridge or washing machine) and the disposal of your old one in the price.

## RETURNING GOODS

Under the French Civil Code, all products sold must be suitable for the use for which they're intended. If they aren't, you're entitled to exchange them or obtain a refund, and it's illegal for traders to use 'small print' (*clauses abusives*) to try to avoid liability, although they will often examine products to check that they haven't been misused. In theory, refunds must be made for faulty or inadequate goods returned within seven days (or if a refund is requested, within ten days in the case of goods installed in the home); after that period, a credit note, replacement or alternative product can be offered. You have the same legal rights whether goods are purchased at the recommended retail price or at a discount during a sale.

Despite all these reassuring regulations, however, obtaining an exchange, let alone a refund, can be a difficult, long-winded and frustrating experience. First, it's essential to keep receipts (*reçu*) and take these when returning a product; secondly it's essential to smile and be apologetic; and thirdly you will need patience, perseverance and little else to do that day.

If you're asked to pay a deposit for an item, check whether this is an *acompte* or *arrhes*. With *arrhes* you have the right to cancel your order, although you will lose your deposit (if the vendor cancels the agreement, he must return twice the amount of the deposit), whereas an *acompte* constitutes the first instalment payment for the item as part of a binding contract to pay the full amount.

## Guarantees

The extent of a guarantee (*garantie*) depends on a variety of factors and you should check the conditions on purchase. Even a new product may not be exchanged or refunded if it's faulty, but sent away for testing or repair – during which time you're left product-less.

## Complaints

Every *département* has a Direction Départementale de la Concurrence, de la Consommation et de la Répression des Fraudes (departmental agency for competition, consumption and fraud repression), whose job is to prevent dishonest vendors from cheating consumers, although it deals only with 'minor' complaints. The Institut National de la Consommation (INC) is the umbrella organisation for all French national consumer associations. Its website (⌨ www. conso.net) provides links to regional consumer organisations, government agencies and other consumer sites, as well as around 100 model letters. For other contact details, look under *Les infos administratives: information des consommateurs* at the front of the yellow pages. However, the mere threat of an official complaint will often have the desired result.

> 'In the US, if you have a problem you get an immediate exchange. If a company consistently sells products that don't work, they're out of business. Not in France. Every sale is accompanied by a long contract in triplicate, explaining that nothing is their responsibility.'
>
> Larry Davis (American businessman)

Mont Saint-Michel, Normandy

# 10.

# ODDS & ENDS

**A**country's culture is influenced by various factors and reflected in myriad ways. Among the principal influences are its climate, geography and religion, which are considered here along with various cultural manifestations, including crime, the flag and anthem, government and international relations, pets, tipping and toilets.

A heat wave in France in August 2003 – when the temperature remained at around 40°C (104°F) or higher for weeks on end – killed almost 15,000 (mostly elderly) people.

## CLIMATE

France has four distinct climates – continental, maritime, Mediterranean and Alpine – and many areas have micro-climates, caused by mountains, forests and other geographical features. The west and north-west (principally Brittany and Normandy) have a maritime climate tempered by the Atlantic and the Gulf Stream, with mild winters and warm summers, and most rainfall in spring and autumn. Many people consider the maritime climate of the west (Atlantic) coast to be France's best, with the heat tempered by cool sea breezes. Central and eastern France have a moderate continental climate with cold winters and hot and stormy summers. The northern Massif Central is prone to huge variations in temperature and it was here that an amazing 41°C (106°F) minimum/maximum temperature difference was recorded **in one day** (on 10th August 1885).

Generally, the Loire river is considered to be the point where the cooler northern European climate begins to change to the warmer southern climate. Spring and autumn are usually fine throughout France, although the length of the seasons varies with the region and altitude.

The Midi, stretching from the Pyrenees to the Alps, is hot and dry except for early spring, when there's usually heavy rainfall; the Cévennes region is the wettest with some 200cm (79in) of rain a year. Languedoc has hot, dry summers and much colder winters than the Côte d'Azur, with snow often remaining until May in the mountainous inland areas. The Côte d'Azur enjoys a Mediterranean climate of mild winters, when daytime temperatures rarely drop below 10°C (50°F), and humid and very hot summers, often over 30°C (86°F). However, it isn't always warm and sunny on the Côte d'Azur and it can get quite cold and wet in some areas in winter.

Most northern French people hanker after the heat and sunshine of the south and don't think it's 'hot' until the mercury is well above 30°C (86°F). As a result, the last decade has seen a pronounced migration away from the north-east towards the south and west, where Languedoc-Roussillon and the Midi-Pyrénées are the fastest-growing regions in France.

### Extreme Weather

France occasionally experiences extreme and unpredictable weather, which has become a favourite topic of conversation in some areas. Violent electric storms, causing flash flooding and power cuts, are almost annual events in the south, and other areas are prone to violent cold and dry winds (*vent violent*), including

the *Mistral* and the *Tramontane*. The *Mistral* is a bitter wind that blows down the southern end of the Rhône valley into the Camargue and Marseille, while the *Tramontane* affects the coastal region from Perpignan, near the Pyrenees, to Narbonne. Corsica is buffeted by these and other winds including the *Mezzogiorno* and *Scirocco*.

## CRIME

France has a similar crime rate to most other European countries and in common with them it has increased considerably in recent years; the number of reported crimes has almost doubled in a decade. Stiffer sentences have failed to stem the spiralling crime rate, and prisons are bursting at the seams with almost 60,000 inmates (around 95 per cent men) – nearly 12,000 more than their official capacity, some housing almost twice as many inmates as they were designed for. There's no death penalty in France, where the maximum prison sentence is 30 years.

Although most crimes are against property, violent crime is increasing, particularly in Paris and the Ile-de-France. Mugging is on the increase throughout France, although it's still relatively rare in most cities. In some towns in southern France, pensioners have been the target of muggers and even truffle hunters have been robbed of their harvest at gunpoint. Sexual harassment (or worse) is common in France, where women should take particular care late at night and never hitchhike alone.

The worst area for crime is the Mediterranean coast (one of the most corrupt and crime-ridden regions in Europe), particularly around Marseille and Nice, where most crime is attributable to the vicious underworld (*Milieu*) of the Côte d'Azur racketeers and drug dealers. Pickpockets (often gypsies, who try to surround and distract you while stealing your purse or wallet) and bag-snatchers are common in Paris (particularly on the *métro*), and in many areas tourists and travellers are the targets of some of France's most enterprising criminals, including highwaymen and train robbers.

> It's a criminal offence not to attempt to help someone who has been a victim of crime or a road accident, at the very least by summoning assistance.

However, crime in rural areas remains relatively low, and it's still common for people in villages and small towns not to lock their cars or houses. You can usually safely walk almost anywhere at any time of day or night.

## FLAG & ANTHEM

Known in France as *le drapeau tricolore* (the three-coloured flag), *le drapeau bleu-blanc-rouge* or simply *le drapeau français*, the familiar blue, white and red flag replaced the *oriflamme* (depicting three golden *fleurs de lys*) in 1794, five years after the Revolution, and is believed to

derive from the colours of Paris' coat of arms. The flag is twice as long as it is wide and is flown with the blue closest to the flagstaff. Originally, the three stripes weren't of equal width, the proportions being 30 (blue), 33 (white) and 37 (red), as it was thought that this would give the impression that they were equal; but Napoleon insisted the stripes be the same width, which they remain today – except in the navy, which in 1853 reverted to the 30:33:37 proportions. A further change came under President Valéry Giscard d'Estaing, who wanted the blue and red lightened. The *tricolore* is one of several tricolour flags, including those of Costa Rica, Ireland, Italy, the Netherlands, Romania and Russia.

France's gruesome national anthem is an 1888 amalgam of the *Chant de Guerre de l'Armée du Rhin* (War Song of the Rhine Army), composed by Claude Joseph Rouget de Lisle in 1792, which became known as the *Marseillaise* when troops from Marseille brought it to Paris, and *L'Internationale*, a poem

**La Marseillaise**

Arise, children of the motherland,
The day of glory has arrived!
Against us, tyranny
Has raised its bloody banner. (repeat)
Do you hear the howling
Of cruel soldiers in the fields?
They are coming into your midst
To slit the throats of your sons and your
wives!

Take up arms, citizens!
Form yourselves into battalions!
Let us march, let us march!
May impure blood
Fill our fields' furrows!

What does this horde of slaves,
Traitors, and scheming kings want?
For whom are these vile chains,
These irons intended? (repeat)
For us, Frenchmen. Ah! What outrage,
What fury they should arouse!
It is us they dare to plan
To return to slavery!

Take up arms, citizens...

What! These foreign cohorts
Would lay down the law in our homes!
What! These mercenary phalanxes
Would cut down our proud warriors!
(repeat)
Good God! With our hands in chains
And our heads bowed under the yoke
We would yield to vile despots
Who would become masters of our
destinies!

To arms, citizens...

numerous popular songs, including The Beatles' 'All You Need is Love' and Marilyn Monroe's 'Diamonds are a Girl's Best Friend', while others, such as Serge Gainsbourg and Yannick Noah, have recorded versions of the anthem.

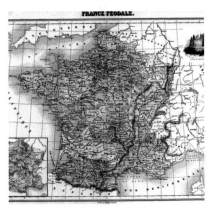

## GEOGRAPHY

France, often referred to as *l'hexagone* on account of its hexagonal shape (the French are also known as *les hexagonaux*), is the largest country in Western Europe. Mainland France (*la métropole*) covers an area of almost 550,000km$^2$ (212,300mi$^2$), stretching 1,050km (650mi) from north to south and almost the same distance from west to east (from the tip of Brittany to Strasbourg). Its land and sea border extends for 4,800km (around 3,000mi) and includes some 3,200km (2,000mi) of coast. France is bordered by Andorra, Belgium, Germany, Italy, Luxembourg, Spain and Switzerland, and the opening of the Channel Tunnel in 1994 connected it with the UK (albeit only by rail). Its borders are largely

written by Eugène Pottier in 1870. Probably the world's longest anthem – it runs to eight verses of eight lines with a four-line refrain, though usually only three are sung (roughly translated below) – it's learned by all French people. It has been quoted in determined by geographical barriers, including the English Channel (*la Manche*) in the north, the Atlantic Ocean in the west, the Pyrenees and the Mediterranean in the south, and the Alps and the Rhine in the east.

Mainland France is divided into 22 regions and 94 departments; the Mediterranean island of Corsica (*Corse*) comprises a further two departments (see map). Corsica is situated 160km (99mi) from France and 80km (50mi) from Italy, covering 8,721km$^2$ (3,367mi$^2$) with a coastline of 1,000km (620mi). There are also six overseas departments (*département d'outre-mer/DOM*) – French Guyana (*Guyane*), Guadeloupe, Martinique, Mayotte, Réunion and Saint-Pierre-et-Miquelon – and three overseas territories (*territoires d'outre-mer/TOM*) – French Polynesia (*Polynésie-française*), New Caledonia (*Nouvelle Calédonie*) and the Wallis and Futuna islands. (Although situated within France, Monaco is an independent principality and isn't governed by France.)

France's geographical and scenic variety and splendour are one of the major reasons the French seldom leave their country, even when holidaying; why go abroad, where people speak indecipherable languages and eat badly, when all this is in your own back yard?

The north and west of France is mostly low-lying; the Paris basin in the northern centre of the country occupies a third of France's land area and is one of Europe's most fertile agricultural regions. The south and south-east of France are mountainous, although despite its many mountain ranges (Ardennes, Alps, Jura, Massif Central, Pyrenees and Vosges), France is largely a lowland country with most land less than 200m (700ft) above sea level. The Massif Central in the southern centre of the country has many peaks rising above 1,500m (5,000ft) and is noted for its extinct volcanoes, hot springs and many rivers. The Alps are by far France's and Europe's highest range, where Mont Blanc is Europe's highest mountain (excluding those of the former USSR), rising to 4,810m (15,781ft).

Almost 90 per cent of France's land is productive, with around one-third cultivated, one-quarter pasture and one-quarter forest. France has a comprehensive network of rivers and canals comprising some 40 per cent of European waterways, including the Garonne, Loire, Rhine, Rhône and Seine. The Loire, 1,020km

(634mi) in length, is France's longest river.

## GOVERNMENT

France has a republican form of government dating from 1792, three years after the Revolution, although it has been much modified and refined since. In fact there have been five Republics (new constitutions) lasting from 3 to 70 years: the First from 1792 to 1795, the Second, after a revival of the monarchy, from 1848 to 1851, the Third from 1870 to 1940, the Fourth from 1946 to 1958 and the Fifth from 1958 to the present. Since 1870, the government has been headed by a President (see below) with a Prime Minister and two houses of parliament.

In many ways, the most important government official in France is the local mayor (*maire*), who not only has considerable power and influence, but can also make or break your endeavour to integrate into the

> **Town Hall**
>
> In a village, the Maire can be found at the Mairie – but only at certain times, which are posted outside; the smaller the village, the less often the Maire will be available but there's no need to make an appointment. In a town or city, you need to go to the Hôtel de Ville, which will be open during normal office hours, but you're unlikely to be able to see the Maire himself (or herself) without an appointment.

community, and is **the** person to keep on the right side of.

### The Constitution

France's rulers are bound by a written constitution detailing the duties and powers of the President, government and parliament, and the conditions of election. The central government is divided into three branches: the executive, legislature and the judiciary (see below). The executive is headed by the President, who's the head of state, while the legislative branch is represented by parliament, comprising the national assembly and the senate. The constitution is protected by a nine-member constitutional council.

### The Judiciary

The French legal system is based entirely on written civil law, originally laid down by Napoleon in 1789 and appropriately called the *code Napoléon* (Napoleonic code). The code governs all branches of French law and includes the *code civil*, the *code fiscal* and the *code pénal*. It's regularly updated and

little of Napoleon's original code survives.

France has two judicial systems: administrative and judiciary. The administrative system deals with disputes between the government and individuals, while the judiciary handles civil and criminal cases.

A public notary (*notaire*, addressed as *maître*) is a public official authorised by the Ministry of Justice and controlled by the Chambre des Notaires. Although they don't deal with criminal cases or offer advice concerning criminal law, *notaires* have a monopoly in the areas of transferring property, and testamentary and matrimonial acts.

Anyone charged with a crime is presumed innocent until proven guilty, and the accused has the right

> France doesn't have a jury system (abolished in 1941) but a mixed tribunal made up of six lay judges and three professional judges, with convictions decided by a two-thirds majority. However, in the cour d'assises (for major cases), nine ordinary citizens make up a jury populaire.

to silence. All suspects are entitled to see a lawyer within three hours of their arrest, a person under judicial investigation must be notified in writing, and an examining magistrate may not remand suspects in custody in a case he's investigating. Under France's inquisitorial system of justice, suspects are questioned by an independent examining magistrate (*juge d'instruction*).

> The French President lives, appropriately, like a king in the Elysée palace in Paris.

## The President

The French President is directly elected by the people and must have an absolute majority. He wields more power than his US counterpart and can assume dictatorial powers in a national emergency. The President 'leads and determines the policy of France' and appoints the Prime Minister and government. He can dissolve the house (once a year) should it pass a vote of no confidence in his Prime Minister and he has considerable powers in the fields of foreign affairs and defence; he cannot, however, block legislation passed by parliament, but can appeal to the people by calling a referendum. This is rarely done – there have been only nine referenda since 1789.

## Parliament

Parliament plays a secondary role in France compared to many other democracies, and it meets in two sessions for a total of just 120 days a year. It has two houses, the National Assembly (*Assemblée Nationale*) and the Senate (*Sénat*). The National Assembly is the senior lower house, to which its 577 deputies (*députés*) are directly elected by the people every five years. Although well paid, many deputies also have other jobs. The Senate (upper house) is indirectly elected by a college of some 130,000 local councillors. It consists of 318 senators (mostly local politicians) with a nine-year mandate, one third of whom are elected every three years. The Senate has limited powers to amend or reject legislation passed by the National Assembly; when an impasse is reached, the National Assembly has the final decision.

## Political Parties

The main political parties in France, in order of popularity, are as follows:

- Union pour un Mouvement Populaire (UMP) – which subsumed the Rassemblement pour la République (RPR), the conservative Gaullist party founded by de Gaulle, the Démocratie Libérale party and the Parti Radical;

- Nouvelle Union pour la Démocratie Française (UDF) – incorporating the Parti Républicain, founded by former President Giscard d'Estaing;

- Parti Socialiste;

- Parti Communiste Français;

- Parti Radical de Gauche – extreme left wing;

- Front National – an extreme right wing party led by the notorious Jean-Marie Le Pen.

Fringe parties include *Les Verts* (Green Party) and *Génération Ecologie*. Most French citizens are apathetic towards politics and abstentionists are the biggest electoral group.

Although the French are happy to discuss politics, they aren't given to broadcasting their political allegiance via T-shirts, 'bumper stickers' and posters.

Only French citizens aged 18 or older are permitted to vote in French elections – sensibly always held on a Sunday. Foreign EU citizens resident in France are eligible to vote in

> The concept of 'left' and 'right' in politics originated in France where, after the 1789 Revolution, monarchists sat to the right and republicans to the left of the President of the National Assembly.

elections to the European Parliament and local municipal elections, provided they've registered at the town hall, and they may also stand as candidates for councillors in municipal elections, but not as mayors or deputy mayors.

## FRANCE & THE EUROPEAN UNION

As a founder member of the European Union (then the European Economic Community), France is not surprisingly a firm supporter of the EU – at least officially – and the EU flag flies outside public buildings next to the French flag. Nevertheless, the French people caused Europe-wide consternation in 2005 when they failed to ratify the proposed European Constitution.

Although the French readily accepted the introduction of the euro in 2002, most of them keep tradition alive by talking in francs (one franc

> 'While the French have devised most of the laws that govern the EU, they also have more court rulings against them for violations of EU law than any other member state.'
>
> Donald Carroll, *Surprised by France*

is worth approximately 15 cents – nostalgically called *centimes* by the French).

Like most of the original six EU members, France is ambivalent about the continued enlargement of the Union, which is seen as diluting the EU's strength; it's strongly opposed to the accession of Turkey.

## INTERNATIONAL RELATIONS

France is a founding member of most major international organisations, including the European Union, NATO, the United Nations and the World Trade Organisation. Despite having had a smaller empire than Britain or Spain (and lost it all by 1945), France has always regarded itself as an international superpower and a leader of the 'free, civilised world' – an attitude that has often antagonised other nations.

In particular, and unlike the UK and Spain, France has remained openly – sometimes defiantly – independent of the US, and strongly opposed its intervention in Iraq. In general, the French regard Americans as uncultured boors. They have a higher regard for the British, but tend to feel sorry for them on account of their supposed dismal weather and

unpalatable food, and their reluctance to adopt the metric system and the euro, and to drive on the 'right' side of the road. Surprisingly, given the fact that France and Germany have been at war three times since 1870 – and France has lost every time, relations with the Germans are geerally good.

Historically, France has close ties with many African countries, particularly Morocco, Algeria and Tunisia, which were all under its 'protection' until the early '60s, but also what are now Chad, the Central African Republic, the Democratic Republic of Congo, Djibouti, Gabon, Mayotte, the Ivory Coast, Senegal and Togo. Former French President Chirac (known as 'Chirac the African') fostered relations with these nations long after they achieved independence, and in early 2007 a total of over 11,500 French troops were still stationed in Africa in an attempt to 'stabilise' local governments.

Politics aside, however, the French would generally be quite happy if the rest of the world didn't exist and they tend to tolerate rather than actively engage with the people of other countries – unless, of course, they live in France.

## PETS

The French aren't a nation of animal lovers. Wild animals are there to be hunted and/or eaten, and pets are generally either fashion accessories or servants – e.g. cats for catching mice and dogs for hunting and guarding premises.

Dogs are by far the most common pet – there are estimated to be over 10m in France, which therefore has the highest dog-to-person ratio in the world (there are reckoned to be more dogs in Paris than children). These tend to fall into two categories: 'toy' dogs that scamper after or (more usually) are carried by their owners; and large or aggressive breeds (German shepherds, Dobermans,

> Paris has a canine *pâtisserie* called Mon Bon Chien (💻 www. mon-bon-chien-paris.com), run by an American pastry chef, where pampered pooches can be kitted out with *haute couture* clothing as well as treated to *haute cuisine* 'cakes'.

Rottweilers, pitbulls, etc.) that bark noisily to ward off intruders.

The former are pampered beyond belief. 'Poodle parlours' (*salons de toilettage*) are common in all but the smallest towns, and toy dogs are commonly seen being carried in bespoke pouch-bags and perched on their mistresses' laps (most owners are women) in cafés, restaurants and even hairdressing salons.

In contrast, guard dogs, many of which double as hunting dogs, are often kept outdoors – in makeshift kennels or, worse, on permanent leads – and it's rare to see them being walked or given any attention. Some 100,000 dogs are abandoned by their owners each year, many at the start of the long summer holiday or the end of the hunting season, and stray dogs are regularly rounded up and taken to the local pound (*fourrière*) to be destroyed. There's no national animal protection service (such as the RSPCA in the UK), and the Société pour la Protection des Animaux (SPA), which is run on a departmental basis, is poorly co-ordinated and severely under-funded.

Sterilisation isn't a common practice in France, where stray dogs and cats are a nuisance in many areas. It's felt to be 'unnatural', although the French have few qualms about killing some or all of a litter if they're unwanted – drowning them and putting them in a freezer are favoured methods.

There's no dog licensing system, but all dogs must be either tattooed or micro-chipped, as well as being vaccinated against rabies. Dogs must be kept on a lead in most public places and there are fines for allowing them to foul the pavement – although you wouldn't think so from the amount of dog mess on most French pavements.

## RELIGION

The French Revolution 'abolished' not only the monarchy and the aristocracy but also religion, and France has been a secular (*laïque*) state for the last 200 years. For several centuries before that, however, it was a predominantly Catholic country and, although many abbeys and monasteries were destroyed after the Revolution, most cathedrals and churches survived, and over 60 per cent of French people are still Catholics.

Since 1905, however, when church and state were officially separated, there has been no direct state funding of the church and many are in poor repair as a result. On the other hand, Catholic private schools (of which there are many) are largely funded by the state. An attempt (by the Socialists in the '80s) to abolish state funding for religious schools generated fierce opposition and was quickly abandoned.

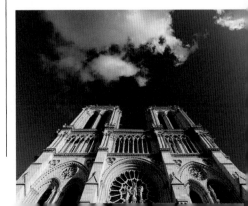

> 'Catholicism has suited them, with its emphasis on sin and exoneration rather than guilt and shame. The notion that it is all right to sin so long as you repent afterwards fits in well with the French insistence that there must be a way round everything.'
>
> Nick Yapp & Michel Syrett,
> *The Xenophobe's Guide to the French*

As in many western countries, church attendance has fallen in recent decades and is now at around 15 per cent (attendance is lowest in Paris and among those aged 18 to 35). Only some 50 per cent of marriages are consecrated in a church and 60 per cent of babies baptised. Parish priests have lost much of their traditional influence and there's a serious shortage of recruits for the priesthood.

Owing to the secularisation of the state, every resident has total freedom of religion, and the majority of the world's religious and philosophical movements have centres or meeting places in Paris and other major cities. The second-largest religious group is Muslims (6 per cent), mostly immigrants from North Africa, a mere 2 per cent are Protestant, while France is also home to some 700,000 Jews.

## TIME DIFFERENCE

Like most of the continent of Europe, France is on Central European Time (CET), which is Greenwich Mean Time (GMT) plus one hour. The French change to summer time (*l'heure d'été*) on the last Sunday in March, when they put their clocks forward one hour. On the last Sunday in October, clocks are put back one hour for winter time (*l'heure d'hiver*). Time changes are announced in local newspapers and on radio and TV, and take place at 02.00 or 03.00. (In 1997, the French tried to abolish the change of time, but were overruled by Brussels!)

Times in France, for example in timetables, are usually written using the 24-hour clock, when 10am is written as 10h or 10.00 and 10pm as 22h or 22.00. Midday (*midi*) is 12.00 and midnight (*minuit*) is 24.00 or 00.00; 7.30am is written as

| Time Difference | | | | | |
|---|---|---|---|---|---|
| **PARIS** | **LONDON** | **JO'BURG** | **SYDNEY** | **AUCKLAND** | **NEW YORK** |
| 1200 | 1100 | 1300 | 2200 | 2400 | 0600 |

7h30 or 07.30. However, the French use the 12- and 24-hour clocks interchangeably in conversation, and you need to make sure that you've understood correctly. In some French towns, clocks strike twice, with a minute's pause in between, just in case you missed it the first time! The time (in winter) in selected major foreign cities, when it's midday in Paris, is shown in the table.

## TIPPING

Tips (*pourboire*, literally 'in order to drink') aren't as freely offered as in the US or even the UK, and have become less common since the introduction of the euro. In some places you may even come across signs forbidding tipping (*pourboire interdit*)! Whether or not you should tip depends largely on whether a service charge has already been included in the price. If service is included, this should be indicated by the words *service compris* (*SC*), *service et taxe compris* (*STC*) or *prix nets/toutes taxes comprises* (*TTC*), which means that prices are inclusive of service and value added tax (*TVA*). If service is extra, *service non compris* (*SNC*) or *service en sus* may be indicated.

Service is now automatically included in all restaurant bills, although you may still leave a tip if you've had exceptional service. In hotels a 15 per cent service charge is usually included in the bill. In bars and cafés, prices usually include service when you sit at a table, but not when you stand at the bar (it should be shown on the menu or bill or the *tarif des consommations*). It's

normal to leave your small change on the bar or in the dish provided.

Those who are usually tipped include porters (€0.80 to €1.60 per bag, which may be a fixed fee), tour guides (€0.80 to €1.60), taxi drivers (10 to 15 per cent) and hairdressers (10 per cent). In first-class hotels it's normal to tip a bellboy, porter, chambermaid or other staff members if you ask them to perform extra services. In public toilets where there's an attendant, there's usually a fixed charge and you aren't required to tip, although when no charge is displayed, it's usual to leave €0.15 to €0.30.

It's usual to tip ushers (*ouvreuse*) in theatres and concert halls and sports stadiums (€0.30 to €0.80), as they may rely on tips for a good part of their income. However, this custom is dying out, and ushers at many cinema chains (e.g. Gaumont, Pathé and UCG) no longer expect tips. In fact, at many modern

Christmas is generally a time of giving tips to all and sundry, including the postman, rubbish collectors (éboueurs) and firemen (sapeurs-pompiers), who will often call in early December or November (sometimes as early as October!) 'offering' you a calendar, for which you're nevertheless expected to pay – unless you don't want your post delivered, your rubbish collected or any house-fires extinguished for the following 12 months!

cinemas, seats aren't numbered and there are no ushers. It's unnecessary to tip a petrol station attendant (*pompiste*) for cleaning your windscreen or checking your oil, although they're poorly paid and are pleased to receive a small gratuity.

The size of a tip depends on how often someone has served you, the quality and friendliness of the service, your financial status and, of course, your generosity. Generally, tips range from €5 to €15, although you may wish to give more to the *gardienne* of your apartment block (it pays to be nice to them). Large tips are, however, considered ostentatious and in bad taste (except by the recipient, who will be your friend for life).

If you're unsure who or how much to tip, ask your neighbours, friends or colleagues for advice (but don't be surprised if they all tell you something different!).

## TOILETS

Although France has a poor reputation for its public toilets (*toilettes publiques*) and even for those in bars and restaurants, standards are improving – slowly. The main difficulty, however, is often finding a toilet at all. Even major supermarkets, for example, often have no toilets, let alone baby changing facilities. The French seem to have an exceptional ability to 'hold themselves' and can spend an entire evening eating and drinking, often until the early hours of the morning, without even 'spending a penny' – hence the lack of toilet provision in public places. If you cannot find a public toilet, you can use one in a bar or cafe, though it's usual to leave a gratuity on your way out.

When you do find a toilet, it will invariably be inadequate for the venue and cramped. It's likely also to lack essential features such as a toilet seat, toilet paper, a towel or (working) hand drier, and to be dirty. (It's worth taking a roll of toilet paper with you.) Thankfully 'Turkish toilets' (i.e. a hole in the floor) are becoming a rarity, although in some ways these were more hygienic than what has replaced them. Some cafes and even restaurants locate their toilets at the rear of the building, with access only from outside – enjoyable when

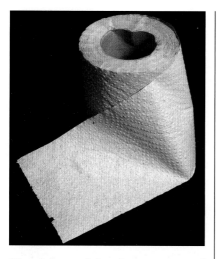

it's raining and there's a queue – and you may even need to ask for a key. Many toilets have an automatic light switch operated by the door lock, while others have a timed switch that plunges you into darkness every minute or two.

Another aspect of French toilets, which will be of particular concern to women, is that men's urinals are often located in a communal hand-washing area – or at least in full view of it, if not in full view of the restaurant or bar itself. To add insult to injury, in some places (e.g. shopping centres and Parisian restaurants) you must pay an attendant for the privilege of using a toilet; the amount may not be specified, in which case you can leave as much or as little as you feel appropriate.

The notorious habit among French men of relieving themselves by the side of the road shows no sign of being abandoned or even modified in the interest of public decency. In fact, not only will Frenchmen stop their cars almost anywhere when nature calls, they will even empty their bladders against buildings in towns and villages, and in other people's gardens when visiting. Oddly, French women never seem to object to their menfolk's atavistic behaviour.

The French have a number of words for the toilet, including *toilettes* (the most commonly used and always in the plural, *la toilette* meaning 'ablutions'), *WC* (oddly pronounced as if spelt *VC* and also in the plural, despite the fact that it stands for 'water closet') and, by analogy, *waters* – the last being somewhat old-fashioned. To ask where the toilet is, say '*Où sont les toilettes/WC/waters, s'il vous plaît ?*'

in some cities and resort areas, there are coin-operated individual public toilets with soap, hot water, towels and air-conditioning (those in Paris are now free).

'France is the only country where the money falls apart and you can't tear the toilet paper.'

Billy Wilder (American film director/producer)

# APPENDICES

## APPENDIX A: EMBASSIES & CONSULATES

### Embassies & Consulates in Paris

Foreign embassies are located in the capital, Paris (those of selected English-speaking countries are listed below), and many countries also have consulates in other cities (British provincial consulates are listed below). Embassies and consulates are listed in the yellow pages under *Ambassades, Consulats et Autres Représentations Diplomatiques.*

**Australia:** 4 rue Jean Rey, 15e (☎ 01 40 59 33 00).

**Canada:** 35 avenue Montaigne, 8e (☎ 01 44 43 29 00).

**Ireland:** 41 rue Rude, 16e (☎ 01 44 17 67 00).

**New Zealand:** 7ter rue Léonard de Vinci, 16e (☎ 01 45 01 43 43).

**South Africa:** 59 quai Orsay, 7e (☎ 01 53 59 23 23).

**United Kingdom:** 35 rue Faubourg St Honoré, 8e (see below) & 18bis rue Anjou, 8e (☎ 01 44 51 31 02).

**United States of America:** 2 rue St Florentin, 1e (☎ 01 43 12 22 20) and 2, avenue Gabriel, 1e (☎ 08 10 26 46 26).

### French Embassies Abroad

Listed below are the contact details for French embassies in the main English-speaking countries. A complete list of French embassies is available from Embassies Abroad (🖥 www.embassiesabroad.com/embassies-of/france).

**Australia:** 6 Perth Avenue, Yarralumla, ACT 2600 Canberra (☎ 02-621 601 00, 🖥 www.ambafrance-au.org).

**Canada:** 42 Promenade Sussex, Ottawa, Ontario K1M 2C9 (☎ 613-789 1795, 🖥 www.ambafrance-ca.org).

**Ireland:** 36 Ailesbury Road, Ballsbridge, Dublin 4 (☎ 01-277 5000, 🖳 www.ambafrance-ie.org).

**New Zealand:** Rural Bank Building, 13th Floor, 34-42 Manners Street (PO Box 11-343), Wellington (☎ 04-384 2555, 🖳 www.ambafrance-nz.org).

**South Africa:** 250 Melk Street, New Muckleneuk, Pretoria 0181 (☎ 12-42 51600, 🖳 www.ambafrance-rsa.org).

**United Kingdom:** 58 Knightsbridge, London SW1X 7JT (☎ 020-7073 1000, 🖳 www.ambafrance-uk.org).

**United States of America:** 4101 Reservoir Road, NW Washington DC 20007 (☎ 202-944 6000, 🖳 http://ambafrance-us.org).

> The business hours of embassies vary and they close on their own country's national holidays as well as on French public holidays. Always telephone to confirm opening hours before visiting.

# APPENDIX B: FURTHER READING

## English-language Newspapers & Magazines

Unless otherwise stated, telephone numbers are French.

**The Connexion** (☎ 04 93 32 16 59, 🖳 www.connexionfrance.com).
Monthly newspaper.

**Everything France Magazine**, Brooklands Magazines Ltd
(UK ☎ 0870-403 0330, 🖳 www.everythingfrancemag.co.uk).
Bi-monthly lifestyle magazine.

**Focus on France**, Outbound Publishing (UK ☎ 01323-726040,
🖳 www.outboundpublishing.com). Quarterly property magazine.

**France Magazine**, Archant Life (UK ☎ 01858-438832,
🖳 www.francemag.co.uk). Monthly lifestyle magazine.

**France-USA Contacts/FUSAC** (☎ 01 56 53 54 54, 🖳 www.fusac.fr).
Free bi-weekly magazine.

**French News**, SARL Brussac (☎ 05 53 06 84 40,
🖳 www.french-news.com). Monthly newspaper.

**French Property News**, Archant Life (UK ☎ 020-8543 3113,
🖳 www.french-property-news.com). Monthly property magazine.

**The Irish Eyes Magazine**, The Eyes (☎ 01 41 74 93 03,
🖳 www.irisheyes.fr). Monthly Paris cultural magazine.

**Living France**, Archant Life (UK ☎ 01858 438832,
🖳 www.livingfrance.com). Monthly lifestyle/property magazine.

**Normandie & South of England Magazine** (☎ 02 33 77 32 70,
🖳 www.normandie-magazine.fr). News and current affairs about
Normandy and parts of southern England, published eight times a year
mainly in French but with some English articles and translations.

**Paris Voice/Paris Free Voice** (☎ 01 47 70 45 05,
🖳 www.parisvoice.com). Free weekly newspaper.

**Property France**, Outbound Publishing Ltd (UK ☎ 01323-726040,
🖳 www.outboundpublishing.com). Bi-monthly magazine.

**The Riviera Reporter** (☎ 04 93 45 77 19, 🖳 www.riviera-reporter.
com). Bi-monthly free magazine covering the Côte d'Azur.

**The Riviera Times** (☎ 04 93 27 60 00, 🖳 www.rivieratimes.com).
Monthly free newspaper covering the Côte d'Azur and Italian Riviera.

## Books

The books listed below are just a selection of the hundreds written about France. The publication title is followed by the author's name and the publisher.

### *Culture*

**The Essence of Style**, Joan Dejean (Free Press)

**France, the Land (Lands, Peoples & Cultures)**, Greg Nickles (Crabtree Publishing).

**French Cinema: From its Beginnings to the Present**, Henri Fournier Lanzoni (Continuum International Publishing Group)

**Paris Jazz: A Guide**, Luke Miner (The Little Bookroom)

**Savoir Flair**, Polly Platt (Distri Books)

**The Alps: A Cultural History**, Andrew Beattie (Signal Books)

**The Complete Merde**, Genevieve (Harper Collins)

### *Food & Drink*

**Best Street Markets in France**, M Anderson & R Fennell (Travellers Temptation Press)

**Bistro**, Laura Washburn (Peters & Small)

**The French Kitchen**, Joanne Harris & Fran Warde (Doubleday)

**The Great Wines of France**, Clive Coates (Mitchell Beazley)

**Love Food Love Paris**, Kate Whiteman (AA Travel Publications)

**The Rubbish on our Plates**, Fabien Perucca & Gérard Pouradier (Prion)

**Truffles and Tarragon**, Anne Gregg (Bantam)

**Vegetarian France**, Alex Bourke & Alan Todd (Vegetarian Guides)

**Vintcents French Food Dictionary**, Charles Vintcent (Harriman House Publishing)

**Why French Women Don't Get Fat**, Mireille Guiliano (Chatto & Windus)

*History*

**Agincourt: A New History**, Anne Curry (Tempus Publishing)

**The French Revolution**, Christopher Hibbert (Penguin)

**The Measure of All Things: the Seven-year Odyssey that Transformed the World**, Ken Alder (Little, Brown)

**Napoleon**, Vincent Cronin (HarperCollins)

**That Sweet Enemy: The British and the French from the Sun King to the Present**, Robert & Isabelle Tombs (Pimlico)

**The Unfree French: Life under the Occupation**, Richard Vinen (Penguin)

**La Vie en Bleu: France and the French since 1900**, Roderick Kedward (Penguin)

**The White Cities**, Joseph Roth (Granta Books)

*Language*

**101 French Idioms**, Jean-Marie Cassagne (Passport Books)

**101 French Proverbs**, Jean-Marie Cassagne (Passport Books)

**Better French**, Monique Jackman (Studymates)

**Colloquial French**, C. Kirk-Greene (Foulsham)

**Conversational French Made Easy**, Monique Jackman (Hadley Pager Info.)

**French Idioms & Expressions**, C. Kirk-Greene (Foulsham)

**French Idioms and Expressions**, C. Kirk-Greene (Foulsham)

**French Language Survival Guide** (Harper Collins)

**Insider's French**, Eleanor & Michel Levieux (The University of Chicago Press)

**Rude French**, Georges Pilard (Harrap)

**Slang & Colloquialisms**, Georgette Marks & Charles Johnson (Harrap)

### Living & Working

**Buying a Home in France**, David Hampshire (Survival Books). All you will ever need to know to successfully buy, rent or sell property in France.

**Find Out About France**, Duncan Crosbie (Barron's Educational)

**Living & Working in France**, David Hampshire (Survival Books). Everything you need to know about life and employment in France.

**Living in Provence**, Dane McDowell & Christian Sarramon (Flammarion)

**Making a Living in France**, Joe Laredo (Survival Books). The ins and outs of self-employment and starting a business in France.

**More France Please** & **More More France Please**, Helena Frith-Powell (Gibson Square)

**Rural Living in France**, Jeremy Hobson (Survival Books). Everything you need to know to create your very own French rural idyll.

### People

**50 Reasons to Hate the French**, Jules Eden & Alex Clarke (Quetzal Publishing UK)

**French or Foe**, Polly Platt (Distri Books)

**How to be French**, Margaret Ambrose (New Holland Publishers)

**Sixty Million Frenchmen Can't Be Wrong**, Jean-Benoit Nadeau (Robson Books)

### Tourist Guides

**AA Explorer France** (AA Publishing)

**Cruising French Waterways**, Hugh McKnight (Adlard Coles Nautical)

**The Food Lover's Guide to France**, Patricia Wells (Workman Publishing)

**France and the Grand Tour**, Jeremy Black (Palgrave Macmillan)

**France (Eyewitness Travel Guides)** (Dorling Kindersley)

**France (Lonely Planet Country Guide)**, Nicola Williams (Lonely Planet)

**France (Rough Guide Travel Guides)** (Rough Guides)

**Provence A-Z**, Peter Mayle (Profile Books)

**Via Ferrata: A Complete Guide to France**, Philippe Poulet (Cordee)

*Travel Literature*

**France in Mind: an Anthology**, Powers Leccese (Vintage Books)

**Next Stop France**, Claire Boast (Heinemann)

**Paris: a Literary Companion**, Ian Littlewood (Franklin Watts)

**Paris & Elsewhere: Selected Writings**, Richard Cobb (New York Review of Books)

**This is Paris**, Miroslav Sasek (Universe Publishing)

**Something to Declare: Essays on France**, Julian Barnes (Alfred A. Knopf)

**Travels with a Donkey in the Cévennes**, Robert Louis Stevenson (Oxford)

**We'll Always Have Paris: American Tourists in France since 1930**, H. Levenstein (University of Chicago Press)

**A Year in Provence**, Peter Mayle (Profile Books)

*Miscellaneous*

**The Changing Face of France**, Virginia Chandler (Raintree)

**France, a Love Story: Women Write About the French Experience** (Seal Press)

**France: Country Insights**, Teresa Fisher (Raintree)

**France: Destination Detectives**, Paul Mason (Raintree)

**French Flea Bites (Mill of the Flea)**, George East (La Puce Publications)

**The French Touch**, Jan de Luz (Gibbs M. Smith)

**My Life in France**, Julia Child & Alex Prud'homme (Random House USA)

**Paris, Shops & More**, Vincent Knapp & Angelika Taschen (Taschen)

# APPENDIX C: USEFUL WEBSITES

The following is a list of websites about France and the French.

## Culture

**French Culture** (💻 www.frenchculture.com). A hip guide to France on the web.

**French Culture** (💻 www.frenchculture.org). The world of French culture in the USA.

**Ministry of Culture & Communications** (💻 www.culture.fr).

## Education

**Alliance Française** (💻 www.alliancefr.org). The famous French language school.

**Ministry of Education** (💻 www.education.gouv.fr).

**Campus France** (💻 www.edufrance.fr/en). A website dedicated to higher education in France.

## Government

**Invest in France Agency** (💻 www.afii.fr). Useful information on living and working in France.

**Ministry of the Economy, Finance and Industry** (💻 www.finances.gouv.fr). Economic and tax information.

**Ministry of Foreign Affairs** (💻 www.diplomatie.gouv.fr/en). Information (in English) about French foreign policy.

**Prime Minister** (💻 www.premier-ministre.gouv.fr/en). Information (in English) about the French Prime Minister's role and function.

**Service-Public** (💻 www.service-public.fr). Official French government portal, with links to all ministry and other sites.

## Living & Working

**Australian Embassy in France** (💻 www.ambafrance-au.org). Plenty of useful information and fact sheets, not just relevant to Australia.

**Electricité de France** (💻 www.edf.fr).

**Gaz de France** (💻 www.gdf.fr).

**French Entrée** (🖳 www.frenchentree.com). Information on every aspect of living in France and a useful forum.

**Legifrance** (🖳 www.legifrance.gouv.fr). Official legal information.

**Living France** (🖳 www.livingfrance.com). Useful information about all aspects of living in France and a lively discussion forum with over 6,000 members.

**Moving to France Made Easy** (🖳 www.moving-to-france-made-easy. com). Plenty of information about life in France.

**Pratique** (🖳 www.pratique.fr). Practical information about life in France (in French).

**This French Life** (🖳 www.thisfrenchlife.com). Articles about setting up a variety of necessary services, from bank accounts to internet connection, as well as some of the more enjoyable things about French life.

## Media

**France Link** (🖳 www.francelink.com). France's radio, press, cinema and television.

**Online Newspapers** (🖳 www.onlinenewspapers.com/france.htm). Links to dozens of French newspaper publishers' sites.

**Radio France** (🖳 www.radiofrance.fr).

## Travel

**Anglo Info** (🖳 www.angloinfo.com). Information, advertisements and forums specific to Aquitaine, French Riviera, Normandy, Brittany, Poitou-Charentes and Provence.

**French Tourist Board** (🖳 www.franceguide.com).

**Just France** (🖳 www.justfrance.org). A website dedicated to travel in France.

**Paris Info** (🖳 www.parisinfo.com). The site of the Paris Convention & Visitors' Bureau.

**Paris Notes** (🖳 www.parisnotes.com). A subscription newsletter about Paris, published ten times a year.

## Miscellaneous

**All About France** (🖳 www.all-about-france.com). General information about France.

**SeniorPlanet** (🖳 www.seniorplanet.com). Information for older people

# APPENDIX D: USEFUL WORDS & PHRASES

The following is a list of useful words and phrases that you may need during your first few days in France. They are, of course, no substitute for learning the language, which you should make one of your priorities. All verbs are provided in the polite *vous* form, which is the correct form to use when addressing a stranger. Where applicable, the feminine form of adjectives has been included (in brackets after the masculine form) – use these if you're a woman.

## Asking for Help

| | |
|---|---|
| Do you speak English? | *Vous parlez anglais ?* |
| I don't speak French. | *Je ne parle pas le français.* |
| Please speak slowly. | *Parlez lentement, s'il vous plaît.* |
| I don't understand. | *Je ne comprends pas.* |
| I need ... | *Il me faut ...* |
| I would like ... | *Je voudrais ...* |

## Communications

### Telephone & Internet

| | |
|---|---|
| landline | *ligne fixe* |
| mobile phone | *téléphone portable* (or simply *portable*) |
| There's no answer. | *Ça ne répond pas.* |
| engaged/busy | *occupée* |
| internet | *internet* |
| email | *email, courriel, mail* or *mél* |
| broadband connection | *haut-débit/ADSL* |
| internet café | *cyber-café* |

### Post

| | |
|---|---|
| post office | *(bureau de) poste* |
| postcard/letter/parcel | *carte postale/lettre/paquet* |
| stamps | *timbres* |
| How much does it cost to send a letter to Europe/North America/ Australia? | *Ça coûte combien d'envoyer une lettre en Europe/aux Etats-Unis/en Australie ?* |

### Media

| | |
|---|---|
| newspaper/magazine | *journal/magazine* or *revue* |
| Do you sell English-language papers/magazines? | *Vous vendez des journaux/revues en anglais ?* |

## Courtesy

| | |
|---|---|
| yes | *oui* |
| no | *non* |
| excuse me/I'm sorry | *excusez-moi* or *pardon* |
| I don't know | *je ne sais pas* |
| I don't mind | *peu importe* |
| please | *s'il vous plaît* |
| thank you | *merci* |
| you're welcome | *je vous en prie* |

## Days & Months

All days and months are written with a small initial letter in French.

| | |
|---|---|
| Monday | *lundi* |
| Tuesday | *mardi* |
| Wednesday | *mercredi* |
| Thursday | *jeudi* |
| Friday | *vendredi* |
| Saturday | *samedi* |
| Sunday | *dimanche* |
| | |
| January | *janvier* |
| February | *février* |
| March | *mars* |
| April | *avril* |
| May | *mai* |
| June | *juin* |
| July | *juillet* |
| August | *août* (pronounced 'oo' or 'oot') |
| September | *septembre* |
| October | *octobre* |
| November | *novembre* |
| December | *décembre* |

## Driving

| | |
|---|---|
| car insurance | *assurance voiture* |
| driving licence | *permis de conduire* |
| hire/rental car | *voiture de location* |
| How far is it to ...? | *... est loin ?* |
| Can I park here? | *Je peux stationner ici ?* |
| unleaded petrol (gas) | *essence sans plomb* |
| diesel | *diesel* (pronounced 'dee-ye-zel') or *gazoil* (pronounced 'gaz-wal') |
| Fill the tank up, please. | *Le plein, s'il vous plaît.* |
| air/water/oil | *air/eau/huile* |
| car wash | *lavage auto* |
| My car has broken down. | *Je suis en panne.* |
| I've run out of petrol (gas). | *Je suis en panne d'essence.* |
| The tyre is flat. | *Je suis crevé.* |
| I need a tow truck. | *Il me faut une dépanneuse.* |

## Accidents, Illness & Crime

### Emergency Phrases

| | |
|---|---|
| accident (car) | *accident (de voiture)* |
| allergic reaction | *réaction allergique* |
| attack (armed) | *attaque (armée)* |
| bleeding (a lot) | *saignant (beaucoup)* |
| broken arm | *bras cassé* |
| broken leg | *jambe cassée* |
| burglary | *cambriolage* |
| chemists/optician | *pharmacie/opticien* |
| doctor/nurse/dentist | *médecin/infirmière/dentiste* |
| fire | *feu* or *incendie* |
| heart attack | *crise cardiaque* |
| hospital/healthcentre/A&E (Emergency Room) | *hôpital/clinique/urgences* |
| I need an ambulance | *j'ai besoin d'une ambulance* |
| I need a doctor | *j'ai besoin d'un médecin* |
| I'm ill. | *Je suis malade.* |
| intruder | *intrus* |
| mugging | *agression* |
| not breathing | *ne respire pas* |
| (I am) on the road to x | *(je suis) sur la route de x* |
| overdose | *surdose* or *overdose* |
| prescription | *ordonnance* |
| surgeon/specialist | *chirurgien/spécialiste* |
| unconscious | *inconscient* |
| wounded | *blessé* |

### Emergencies

| | |
|---|---|
| Emergency! | *Urgence !* |
| Fire! | *Incendie !* |
| Help! | *Au secours !* |
| Police! | *Police !* |
| Stop! | *Arrêtez !* |
| Stop thief! | *Au voleur !* |
| Watch out! | *Attention !* |

## Finding your Way

| | |
|---|---|
| Where is ...? | *Où est ... ?* |
| Where is the nearest ...? | *Où est le/la ... le/la plus proche ?* |
| How do I get to ...? | *Pour aller à ... ?* |
| Can I walk there? | *Je peux y aller à pied ?* |
| How far is ....? | *... est à combien de kilomètres ?* |
| A map, please. | *Un plan, s'il vous plaît.* |
| I'm lost. | *Je suis perdu(e).* |
| left/right/straight ahead | *à gauche/à droite/tout droit* |
| opposite/next to/near | *en face de/à côté de/près de* |
| airport | *aéroport* |
| bus/plane/taxi/train | *bus/avion/taxi/train* |
| bus stop | *arrêt d'autobus* |
| taxi rank | *station de taxi* |
| train/bus station | *gare/gare routière* |
| What does the ... arrive/leave? | *A quelle heure ... arrive/part ?* |
| one-way/return ticket | *aller simple/aller-retour* |
| bank/embassy/consulate | *banque/ambassade/consulat* |

## Greetings

| | |
|---|---|
| Hello. | *Bonjour.* |
| Goodbye. | *Au revoir.* |
| Good morning/afternoon. | *Bonjour.* |
| Good evening. | *Bonsoir.* |
| Good night. | *Bonne nuit.* |

## In a Bar or Restaurant

| | |
|---|---|
| menu | *carte* |
| bill | *addition* |
| well done/medium/rare/very rare (for meat) | *bien cuit/à point/saignant/bleu* |
| vegetarian | *végétarien(ne)* |
| meat/fish | *viande/poisson* |

## Numbers

| | |
|---|---|
| one | *un* |
| two | *deux* |
| three | *trois* |
| four | *quatre* |
| five | *cinq* |
| six | *six* |
| seven | *sept* |
| eight | *huit* |
| nine | *neuf* |
| ten | *dix* |
| eleven | *onze* |
| twelve | *douze* |
| thirteen | *treize* |
| fourteen | *quatorze* |
| fifteen | *quinze* |
| sixteen | *seize* |
| seventeen | *dix-sept* |
| eighteen | *dix-huit* |
| nineteen | *dix-neuf* |
| twenty | *vingt* |
| thirty | *trente* |
| forty | *quarante* |
| fifty | *cinquante* |
| sixty | *soixante* |
| seventy | *soixante-dix* |
| eighty | *quatre-vingts* |
| ninety | *quatre-vingt-dix* |
| 100 | *cent* |
| 200 | *deux cents* |
| 500 | *cinq cents* |
| 1,000 | *mille* |

## Paying

| | |
|---|---|
| How much is it? | *C'est combien ?* |
| The bill, please | *L'addition, s'il vous plaît.* |
| Do you take credit cards? | *Vous acceptez les cartes de crédit ?* |

## Socialising

| | |
|---|---|
| Pleased to meet you. | *Enchanté(e).* |
| My name is ... | *Je m'appelle ...* |
| This is my husband/wife/son/ daughter/colleague/friend | *Je vous présente mon mari/ ma femme/mon fils/ma fille/ma/ mon collègue/mon ami.* |

| How are you? | *Comment allez-vous ?* |
| Very well, thank you. | *Très bien, merci.* |

## Shopping

| What time do you open/close? | *Vous ouvrez/fermez à quelle heure ?* |
| I'm just looking (browsing). | *Je regarde seulement, merci.* |
| I'm looking for ... | *Je cherche ...* |
| Can I try it on? | *Je peux l'essayer ?* |
| I need size ... | *Il me faut une/une ...* |
| | (e.g. *Il me faut un 38.*) |
| bigger/smaller/longer/shorter | *plus grand(e)/plus petit(e)/* |
| | *plus long(ue)/plus court(e)* |
| A bag, please. | *Un sac, s'il vous plaît.* |
| How much is this? | *C'est combien ?* |

---

**Part of a typical chanson populaire:**

> To get to the police station
> Take Road no.3,
> Follow the cars
> And keep straight on, straight on...
> It's a billiard table, it's a runway,
> Not a tree, not a flower,
> How beautiful, how sad.
> You can drive at eighty miles per hour
> But these tarmac roads,
> All these roads
> Depress me.
> If you love me, come, come,
> Sing to me, walk with me,
> And we'll take a short cut:
> This little path...

This is the reason French songs aren't known outside France – they're impossible to translate and would make most non-French people roar with laughter. (Rod McKuen's 'If You Go Away' isn't a translation but a travesty of Jacques Brel's 'Ne Me Quitte Pas'.)

# APPENDIX E: FALSE FRIENDS

The following is a list of some of the most common – and most potentially embarrassing – false friends with examples of the correct use of the French words.

- accommodation: adaptation, use of.

  accommodation (a𝕞commodations): hébergement or logement.

- achever: to finish, e.g. Il a achevé ses travaux. (He has finished his building work.)

  to achieve: accomplir, réaliser or réussir

- actuellement: currently or at the moment, e.g. Actuellement, tout va bien. (Everything's fine at the moment.)

  actually: en fait, e.g. Il n'est pas marié en fait. (Actually, he isn't married.)

- agenda: diary.

  agenda: ordre du jour.

- agréer: to approve, authorise or authenticate, e.g. Un expert agréé. (A licensed professional.)

  to agree: approuver or être d'accord, e.g. Je suis d'accord avec vous. (I agree with you.)

- assister: to attend, go to, e.g. J'ai assisté à un concert. (I went to a concert.)

  to assist: aider.

- attendre: to wait for, e.g. Je les attends depuis une heure. (I've been waiting for them for an hour.)

  to attend: assister à.

- audience: interview, hearing.

  audience: public

- caméra: video camera or camcorder (also caméscope).

  camera: appareil (photo).

- car: coach – also means for, e.g. Je ne l'aime pas, car il est avare. (I don't like him because he's mean.) Car means 'for' or 'because' in this context.

- cave: (wine) cellar.

  cave: grotte.

- commander: to order (e.g. a meal).

  to command: ordonner.

- concerné: affected, e.g. Seuls les étrangers sont concernés par la nouvelle loi. (Only foreigners are affected by the the new law.)

- contrôler: to check, e.g. Les gendarmes m'ont contrôlé les papiers. (The police checked my papers.)

- course: race (appropriately les courses means shopping).

  course: stage.

- demander: to ask.

  to demand: exiger or réclamer.

- déception: disappointment.

  deception: tromperie.

- effectivement: indeed, e.g. Effectivement! (Well, I never!)

  effectively: efficacement.

- entrée (on a menu): starter.

  entrée (or main course): plat (principal).

- éventuellement: if the occasion arises, e.g. J'aurai éventuellement besoin d'un parapluie. (I might need an umbrella.)

  eventually: finalement.

- ignorer: to be ignorant or unaware of, e.g. J'ignore son prénom. (I don't know his first name.)

  to ignore: various expressions depending on the context, although ignorer is sometimes used.

- large: wide.

  large: gros.

- librairie: bookshop.

  library: bibiliothèque (also means bookshelf).

- location: hire or rent.

  location: lieu.

- menu: set menu, e.g. un menu à €10. (A €10 menu.)

  menu: carte.

- monnaie: currency or change.

  money: argent (which also means 'silver').

- normalement: in theory or hopefully, e.g. Normalement, il doit venir. (He should be coming.)

  normally: d'habitude or en général.

- offrir: to give (a present), e.g. Il m'a offert des fleurs. (He gave me some flowers.)

  to offer: proposer.

- particulier: individual or private, e.g. Une maison particulière. (A private house.)

  particular: précis (as in 'a particular colour') or exigeant (as in 'he's very particular').

- passer un test/examen: to take a test/exam.

  to pass a test/exam: réussir à un test/examen.

- photographe: photographer.

  photographe: photo.

- place: seat (e.g. at the cinema) or room, e.g. Il n'y a plus de place. (There's no more room.)

  place: endroit or lieu.

- préservatif: condom.

  preservative: conservateur.

- prétendre: to claim, e.g. Il prétend être riche. (He claims to be rich.)

  to pretend: faire semblant, e.g. Il fait semblant de dormir. (He's pretending to be asleep.)

- raisin: grape (une grappe is a bunch of grapes).

  raisin: raisin sec.

- recette: recipe.

  receipt: reçu.

- regarder: to watch or look at.

  regard: considérer.

- risqué: risky.

  risqué: osé.

- sale: dirty.

  sale: vente (e.g. the sale of a house) or soldes, e.g. Je l'ai acheté en soldes. (I bought it in the sale(s).)

- sensible: sensitive, e.g. Elle est très sensible au froid. (She feels the cold.)

  sensible: sensé or raisonnable, e.g. Sois raisonnable ! (Don't be silly!)

- slip: (under)pants or briefs.

  slip: jupon.

- spécial: peculiar or odd, e.g. Il est vraiment spécial, celui-là. (He's a really odd bloke.)

  special: various words depending on the context.

- supporter: to bear or put up with, e.g. Je supporte mal la chaleur. (I can't stand the heat.)

  to support: soutenir.

Note, however, that supporter can mean to support in a physical sense (e.g. a beam that supports a roof) and that un supporter, pronounced as if it were spelled 'supportère' means a supporter (e.g. of a football team).

- sympathique: nice, friendly, e.g. Les Dupont sont sympathiques. (The Duponts are nice people.)

  sympathetic: compatissant.

- versatile: changeable or unpredictable (person).

  versatile: polyvalent.

# APPENDIX F: REGIONS & DEPARTMENTS

The map opposite shows the 22 regions and 95 departments of France, which are listed below. The departments are (mostly) numbered alphabetically from 01 to 89. Departments 91 to 95 come under the Ile de France region, which also includes Ville de Paris (75), Seine et Marne (77) and Yvelines (78), shown in detail opposite.

| | | |
|---|---|---|
| 01 Ain | 32 Gers | 64 Pyrénées Atlantiques |
| 02 Aisne | 33 Gironde | 65 Hautes Pyrénées |
| 02A Corse-du-Sud | 34 Hérault | 66 Pyrénées Orientales |
| 02B Haute-Corse | 35 Ille et Vilaine | 67 Bas Rhin |
| 03 Allier | 36 Indre | 68 Haut Rhin |
| 04 Alpes de Hte Provence | 37 Indre et Loire | 69 Rhône |
| 05 Hautes Alpes | 38 Isère | 70 Haute Saôn |
| 06 Alpes Maritimes | 39 Jura | 71 Saône et Loire |
| 07 Ardèche | 40 Landes | 72 Sarthe |
| 08 Ardennes | 41 Loir et Cher | 73 Savoie |
| 09 Ariège | 42 Loire | 74 Haute Savoie |
| 10 Aube | 43 Haute Loire | 75 Paris |
| 11 Aude | 4 Loire Atlantique | 76 Seine Maritime |
| 12 Aveyron | 45 Loiret | 77 Seine et Marne |
| 13 Bouches du Rhône | 46 Lot | 78 Yvelines |
| 14 Calvados | 47 Lot et Garonne | 79 Deux Sèvres |
| 15 Cantal | 48 Lozère | 80 Somme |
| 16 Charente | 9 Maine et Loire | 81 Tarn |
| 17 Charente Maritime | 50 Manche | 82 Tarn et Garonne |
| 18 Cher | 51 Marne | 83 Var |
| 19 Corrèze | 52 Haute-Marne | 84 Vaucluse |
| 21 Côte d'Or | 53 Mayenne | 85 Vendée |
| 22 Côtes d'Armor | 54 Meurthe et Moselle | 86 Vienne |
| 23 Creuse | 55 Meuse | 87 Haute Vienne |
| 24 Dordogne | 56 Morbihan | 88 Vosges |
| 25 Doubs | 57 Moselle | 89 Yonne |
| 26 Drôme | 58 Nièvre | 90 Territoire-de-Belfort |
| 27 Eure | 59 Nord | 91 Essonne |
| 28 Eure et Loir | 60 Oise | 92 Hauts de Seine |
| 29 Finistère | 61 Orne | 93 Seine Saint Denis |
| 30 Gard | 62 Pas de Calais | 94 Val de Marne |
| 31 Haute Garonne | 63 Puy de Dôme | 95 Val d'Oise |

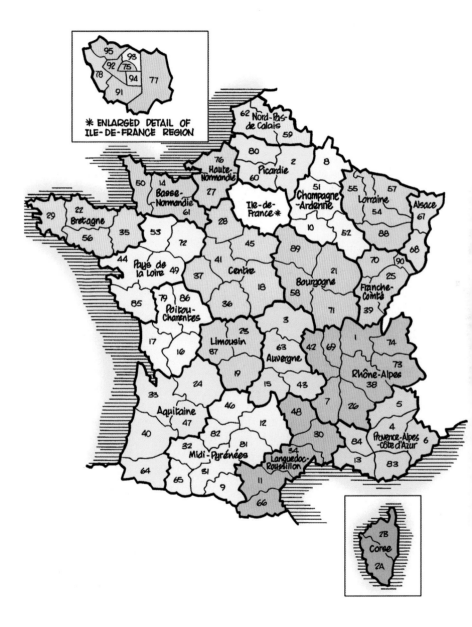

95
93
92
75
78
94
91
77

✳ ENLARGED DETAIL OF
ILE-DE-FRANCE REGION

62 Nord-Pas-
de Calais
59

80
Picardie
60
2
8

76
Haute-
Normandie
27

50 14
Basse-
Normandie
61

51
Champagne
-Ardenne
55 Lorraine 57

Ile-de-
France✳

54

Alsace
67

29 Bretagne
22
35
53

28
45
89
10
52
88
68

56
72

44 Pays de
la Loire 49
37
41
Centre
18
Bourgogne
58
21
70
90
25
Franche-
Comté

85
79 86
Poitou-
Charentes
36
3
71
39

17
16
Limousin
87
23
63
42 69
1
74
73

24
Auvergne
19
15
43
Rhône-Alpes
38
26
5

33
46
7
84
4
Provence-Alpes
-Côte d'Azur
6

Aquitaine
47
12
48
30

40
82
81
34
Languedoc-
Roussillon
13
83

64
32
Midi-Pyrénées
31
11

65
9
66

2B
Corse
2A

Château de Chambord, Loir-et-Cher

# INDEX

# Buying a Home Series

Buying a home abroad is not only a major financial transaction but also a potentially life-changing experience; it's therefore essential to get it right. Our Buying a Home guides are required reading for anyone planning to purchase property abroad and are packed with vital information to guide you through the property jungle and help you avoid disasters that can turn a dream home into a nightmare.

The purpose of our Buying a Home guides is to enable you to choose the most favourable location and the most appropriate property for your requirements, and to reduce your risk of making an expensive mistake by making informed decisions and calculated judgements rather than uneducated and hopeful guesses. Most importantly, they will help you save money and will repay your investment many times over.

Buying a Home guides are the most comprehensive and up-to-date source of information available about buying property abroad – whether you're seeking a detached house or an apartment, a holiday or a permanent home (or an investment property), these books will prove invaluable.

For a full list of our current titles, visit our website at
www.survivalbooks.net

# Living and Working Series

Our Living and Working guides are essential reading for anyone planning to spend a period abroad – whether it's an extended holiday or permanent migration – and are packed with priceless information designed to help you avoid costly mistakes and save both time and money.

Living and Working guides are the most comprehensive and up-to-date source of practical information available about everyday life abroad. They aren't, however, simply a catalogue of dry facts and figures, but are written in a highly readable style – entertaining, practical and occasionally humorous.

Our aim is to provide you with the comprehensive practical information necessary for a trouble-free life. You may have visited a country as a tourist, but living and working there is a different matter altogether; adjusting to a new environment and culture and making a home in any foreign country can be a traumatic and stressful experience. You need to adapt to new customs and traditions, discover the local way of doing things (such as finding a home, paying bills and obtaining insurance) and learn all over again how to overcome the everyday obstacles of life.

All these subjects and many, many more are covered in depth in our Living and Working guides – don't leave home without them.

<u>The</u> Survival Handbooks!

# Culture Wise Series

Our *Culture Wise* series of guides is essential reading for anyone who wants to understand how a country really 'works'. Whether you're planning to stay for a few days or a lifetime, these guides will help you quickly find your feet and settle into your new surroundings.

*Culture Wise* guides:
• Reduce the anxiety factor in adapting to a foreign culture
• Explain how to behave in everyday situations in order to avoid cultural and social gaffes
• Help you get along with your neighbours, make friends and establish lasting business relationships
• Enhance your understanding of a country and its people.

People often underestimate the extent of cultural isolation they can face abroad, particularly in a country with a different language. At first glance, many countries seem an 'easy' option, often with millions of visitors from all corners of the globe and well-established expatriate communities. But, sooner or later, newcomers find that most countries are indeed 'foreign' – and many come unstuck as a result.

*Culture Wise* guides will enable you to quickly adapt to the local way of life and feel at home, and – just as importantly – avoid the worst effects of culture shock.

The essential guides to Culture, Customs & Business Etiquette

# Other Survival Books

**Investing in Property Abroad:** Essential reading for anyone planning to buy property abroad, containing surveys of over 30 countries.

**The Best Places to Buy a Home in France/Spain:** Unique guides to where to buy property in France and Spain, containing detailed regional profiles and market reports.

**Buying, Selling and Letting Property:** The best source of information about buying, selling and letting property in the UK.

**Earning Money From Your Home:** Income from property in France and Spain, including short- and long-term letting.

**Foreigners in France/Spain: Triumphs & Disasters:** Real-life experiences of people who have emigrated to France and Spain, recounted in their own words.

**Making a Living:** Comprehensive guides to self-employment and starting a business in France and Spain.

**Renovating & Maintaining Your French Home:** The ultimate guide to renovating and maintaining your dream home in France.

**Retiring in France/Spain:** Everything a prospective retiree needs to know about the two most popular international retirement destinations.

**Running Gîtes and B&Bs in France:** An essential book for anyone planning to invest in a gîte or bed & breakfast business in France.

**Rural Living in France:** An invaluable book for anyone seeking the 'good life', containing a wealth of practical information about all aspects of French country life.

**Shooting Caterpillars in Spain:** The hilarious and compelling story of two innocents abroad in the depths of Andalusia in the late '80s.

**Wild Thyme in Ibiza:** A fragrant account of how a three-month visit to the enchanted island of Ibiza in the mid-'60s turned into a 20-year sojourn.

For a full list of our current titles, visit our website at
www.survivalbooks.net

# 📷 Photo Credits

# NOTES

# NOTES